THE SOCIAL AND POLITICAL THOUGHT OF HERBERT SPENCER

by

DAVID WILTSHIRE

1978

OXFORD UNIVERSITY PRESS

Oxford University Press, Walton Street, Oxford OX2 6DP

OXFORD LONDON GLASGOW
NEW YORK TORONTO MELBOURNE WELLINGTON
IBADAN NAIROBI DAR ES SALAAM LUSAKA CAPE TOWN
KUALA LUMPUR SINGAPORE JAKARTA HONG KONG TOKYO
DELHI BOMBAY CALCUTTA MADRAS KARACHI

©*David Wiltshire 1978*

British Library Cataloguing in Publication Data

Wiltshire, David
   The social and political thought of Herbert
   Spencer. — (Oxford historical monographs).
   1. Spencer, Herbert, b.1820 2. Sociologists —
   Biography
   I. Title II. Series
   301'.092'4   B1656   77-30202

   ISBN 0-19-821873-7

*Typeset by Hope Services, Wantage
and printed in Great Britain by
Billings & Sons Ltd., Guildford and Worcester*

TO
CARRIE
AND
TAM

PREFACE

This study is a revised version of a Doctoral thesis submitted in the University of Oxford during 1973. In its preparation I drew extensively on Spencer's voluminous writings, his *Autobiography*, and his published and unpublished letters. The following collections of manuscripts were consulted and I would like to thank their curators for their kind co-operation: Ms. Jan Gibbs, of the University of London Library, for permission to read the Spencer Papers, Mr. Derek Clarke of the British Library of Political and Economic Science, for access to the Passfield Papers, and Ms. J. Pingree, of Imperial College, for access to the Huxley Collection. Mr. P.A.C. Jones of the National Library of Wales and Mr. Malcolm Thomas of Friends' House were also very helpful.

I am inestimably indebted to Mr. John Prest, Fellow and Tutor of Balliol, for years of patience, morale-boosting reassurance and imaginative advice in the roles, successively, of undergraduate tutor, graduate supervisor and sub-editor. The merits of this work are largely attributable to him. Dr. W.L. Weinstein helped enormously with close and challenging criticisms of the text, and Dr. Stephen Lukes of Balliol, and Mr. J.D.Y. Peel of Nottingham advised constructively. Whatever faults the work contains are wholly mine.

Thanks are due to Ms. W.J. Cotton, who typed the script of the thesis, and to Madeline, for her encouragement and forbearance during the years it has been in preparation.

CONTENTS

ABBREVIATIONS

Aby	H. Spencer, *An Autobiography* (London, 1904).
D. of E.	H. Spencer, *The Data of Ethics* (Pt. I of *The Principles of Ethics* (London, 1907)).
Education	H. Spencer, *Education: intellectual, moral and spiritual* (London, 1864).
Essays	*H. Spencer, Essays: scientific, political and speculative* (London, 1891).
F.P.	H. Spencer, *First Principles* (London, 1900).
H.S.	Herbert Spencer.
Hux. Coll.	Huxley Collection, Imperial College London.
Justice	H. Spencer, *Justice* (Pt. IV of *The Principles of Ethics* (London, 1907)).
L. L.	D. Duncan, *The Life and Letters of Herbert Spencer* (London, 1908).
M. v. S.	H. Spencer, *The Man versus the State* (London, 1950).
Peel	J.D.Y. Peel, *Herbert Spencer, the evolution of a sociologist* (London, 1971).
P. Eth.	H. Spencer, *The Principles of Ethics* (London, 1881).
Pol. Inst.	H. Spencer, *Political Institutions* (Pt. V of *The Principles of Sociology* (London, 1882)).
'Proper Sphere'	H. Spencer, 'The Proper Sphere of Government', *Nonconformist*, 15 June-14 Dec. 1842.
P. Soc.	H. Spencer, *The Principles of Sociology* (London, 1893).
'S.O.'	H. Spencer, 'The Social Organism', *Essays*, iii.
S. Stat.	H. Spencer, *Social Statics: the conditions essential to human happiness specified, and the first of them developed* (London, 1868).
Stud. Soc.	H. Spencer, *The Study of Sociology* (London, 1880).
'Theory of Population'	H. Spencer, 'A theory of population deduced from the general law of animal fertility', *Westminster Review*, Apr. 1852.
Webb	B. Webb, *My Apprenticeship* (London, 1926).
W.G.S.	William George Spencer.

PART I

BIOGRAPHY AND
INTELLECTUAL DEVELOPMENT

INTRODUCTION

By the late 1960s, Herbert Spencer's reputation had suffered an almost total eclipse. C. Brinton's account of him in *English Political Thought in the Nineteenth Century* (London, 1933) reads like an obituary, and J. Rumney's *Herbert Spencer's Sociology* (New York, 1934) was the last full-length work on him in English for thirty-five years. Even in 1970 there were no indications of imminent resurrection. Since then there has been a remarkable resurgence of interest in Spencer. His major works have been republished, and J.D.Y. Peel's *Herbert Spencer: the evolution of a sociologist* (London, 1971) has dealt admirably with the origins, influence, and content of Spencerian sociology. I have concentrated on Spencer's role as a political theorist, in which his influence was no less pervasive, though perhaps less apparent. Spencer's new lease of life reflects both a recognition of his intellectual importance in the nineteenth century, and the rediscovered relevance of his theories to aspects of our own time. The process of industrialization in 'under-developed' countries and the encroachment of the state upon what has hitherto been regarded as the sphere of private autonomy are two features of the present time upon which Spencer's pronouncements are seen as significant.

The selection of a political approach to Spencer revealed new perspectives and raised new problems. He has hitherto generally been regarded as an evolutionist whose contribution to political thought was a by-product of his scientific theory. I contend that a close survey of his writings reveals a 'primacy of politics'. Spencer was an individualist liberal first and an evolutionist second; individualism is, both genetically and structurally, the core of his thinking. The central problem, then, lies in the relation between individualism and evolution, which Spencer never successfully reconciled.

I have paid more attention than is usual to Spencer himself. Previous writers have tended to agree with George Eliot that his existence 'offers little material for the narrator',[1]

[1] J. Cross, *The Life of George Eliot; as related in her letters and journals* (London, 1885), i. 325.

an excusable omission since Spencer's life is singularly de-
void of landmarks, and he himself saw it as of little interest
to posterity. It is an unhappy story, encompassing a lonely
and joyless childhood, a brief flowering of social intercourse
in early manhood, and a long, bleak descent into despair
and solitude. This depressing cycle is important, however,
for the student of Spencer's political thought, for it corresponds to a parallel development from the optimistic radicalism of youth, through cautious revaluation in middle age,
to bitter, pessimistic conservatism in old age. Spencer is normally regarded as a static thinker; an impression reinforced
by the monolithic consistency of his master-work, the
Synthetic Philosophy. Yet his political opinions underwent
a lifelong and continual transformation, clearly reflected in
his view of the nineteenth century as an era of regression
from individualism to collectivism. Spencer rationalized his
'drift to conservatism' as the outcome of insights afforded
by his study of evolutionary sociology, but the determining
factor was the interventionist fulcrum round which his entire
system pivoted. At the close of life his obsession with this
issue had isolated him, not only from socialists, but from the
mainstream of liberal thinking, and he was beginning to seek
out his supporters among Tory defenders of property against
the menace of 'popular' legislation.

The discussion which follows is divided into two parts. The
first deals with Spencer's life and those aspects of this thought
which required a developmental approach, as being inextricably connected with his personal evolution. The second part
treats the essential structure of Spencerian theory as a static
entity, reflecting the lifelong consistency with which he adhered to its two basic tenets, individualism and evolution.
These concepts, and the broader theories resting on them, are
critically reviewed both in terms of their intrinsic validity and
also historically, with reference to the political, social, and
intellectual environment in which they were promulgated,
and of which they offered a systematic interpretation. The
conclusion to which this investigation comes is that Spencerian evolution, developed to account scientifically for the
postulates of individualism, entails social and ethical conclusions which contradict it, and leads to a vision of society
in which individualism has no place.

1

BOYHOOD AND BACKGROUND, 1820–1836

Herbert Spencer's theory of natural and social evolution emerged out of, and scientifically rationalized, a set of previously formed socio-political principles. These assumptions about society, its competitive ethic and its ideal polity were current in the familial and social circle in which the young Spencer was brought up and educated, and were methodically inculcated by his mentors. His education, therefore, while it introduced him to scientific pursuits and modes of thought, was no less thorough in its political instruction. This chapter examines the intellectual environment of Spencer's boyhood, and helps to establish, at least chronologically, the primacy of politics over science as the crucial determinant of Spencerian theory. It traces his development to the point at which, when sixteen years old, he was capable of putting forward in print a crude but forceful case for social *laissez-faire*, supported not by evolutionary arguments, but by the invocation of biblical texts.

SPENCER'S BOYHOOD, FAMILY, AND INTELLECTUAL ENVIRONMENT

Herbert Spencer was born on 27 April 1820, at 12 Exeter Road, Derby. His father, William George Spencer, a schoolmaster of progressive educational views and inventor of a 'lucid' shorthand, owned thirteen houses in the town and a modest capital. In 1821 he abandoned teaching to seek his fortune in the newly-mechanized and enticingly profitable Nottingham lace industry, at New Radford. The familiar cycle of over-investment, over-production, and contraction ran its course to the financial panic of 1825, and in 1827, his capital exhausted, he returned to Derby. There he offered private tuition and undertook in addition the education of his son, whom he considered too delicate to go to school. Adversity had left its scars. He acknowledged himself, after a nervous breakdown, to be irritable, unstable, and demanding: 'I have at times scarcely any command over my feelings—

they carry me away before I am aware.'[1]

'Irritability and depression', wrote Herbert Spencer later, 'checked that geniality of behaviour which fosters the affections and brings out in children the higher traits of nature.'[2] William George Spencer, invoking his own exemplary childhood, admonished and reproached relentlessly, but temperamental instability denied him the composed, effortless authority necessary to curb his son's obstinate individualism. On the contrary, 'Continual reprobation for disobedience established a certain kind of alienation.'[3] Between the overbearing, censorious father and his grave, meditative little son, however, there grew up a deep sense of solicitous tutelage on the one hand, and a profound, awestruck respect on the other. Herbert's admiration for his father bordered on self-abnegation: 'I consider myself as in many ways falling short of him, both intellectually and emotionally, as well as physically.'[4]

William George Spencer's influence on his son's attitudes and behaviour was naturally considerable. 'My father's conduct', noted Herbert later, was animated by 'the desire to be beneficial to others', a philanthropic urge which 'he wished to make me also recognise . . . as a ruling one.'[5] His non-authoritarian teaching methods strongly influenced his son's educational theories; discipline in his classroom was democratically dispensed by the pupils, while he mitigated their severer sentences. His studied disdain of social conventions was likewise emulated by his son later in life. The elder Spencer never removed his hat, nor addressed anyone by his ceremonial title, and spurned fashion. Artistic and inventive, he bequeathed to his son at least the latter trait. If he had a fault in Herbert's eyes, it was his 'dominant ideality', an obsessive regard for minutiae which Herbert unwittingly shared: 'He never knew when to cease making alterations in details [a tendency which] led to the sacrifice of large ends for small ends.'[6] The 'lucid' shorthand was published posthumously because he never finished revising it.

---

[1] W.G.S. to Thomas Spencer, December 1823, in *Aby.* i. 66.
[2] *Aby* i. 67.   [3] *Aby* i. 82.
[4] *Aby* i. 43.   [5] *Aby* i. 82.
[6] *Aby* i. 54.

Spencer's mother, Harriet, exerted comparatively little influence on his intellectual development. After seven years of courtship William George never forgave her for relinquishing after marriage the enthusiasm for radical politics which had initially attracted him to her, and treated her during Herbert's childhood with peremptory brusqueness. She was sweet-tempered, submissive, dutiful, and selfless, but manifested no vestige of the stout Huguenot nonconformity which she was heir to. In her son's stilted phraseology she was of 'ordinary intelligence and of a high moral nature', but suffered for 'an altruism too little qualified by egoism'. 'Constitutionally averse to change', she viewed his literary aspirations with disquiet: 'My own proceedings and plans she always criticised discouragingly, and urged the adoption of some commonplace career.'[1] After leaving home he wrote seldom to his mother. Even when not cloaked in shorthand, the frequent and weighty correspondence between her husband and son seemed to exclude her, and she abandoned most of Herbert's writings as beyond her comprehension.

Herbert was their only surviving child, and solitude became a way of life for him. His earliest recollections were of loneliness. Having no brothers or sisters, and no schoolfellows until he was ten, he grew introverted and intensely reflective, inhabiting a private world through which he wandered for hours, days, and years in tranquil self-absorption. This penchant for day-dreaming (he called it 'castle-building') he indulged unrestrainedly: 'on going to bed, it was a source of satisfaction to me to think that I should be able to lie for a length of time and dwell on the fancies which at the time occupied me; and frequently next morning, on awakening, I was vexed with myself because I had gone to sleep before I had revelled in my imaginations as much as I had intended.'[2] He frequently talked aloud to himself. His father recorded finding him, aged six, giggling by himself in a corner: 'On saying "Herbert what are you laughing at", he said "I was wondering how it would have been if there had been nothing besides myself."'[3] The foundations of the emotional deprivation and personal isolation of later years were being laid.

[1] *Aby* i. 59.   [2] *Aby* i. 76.
[3] *Aby* i. 68.

'Ever since I was a boy', he afterwards wrote, 'I have been longing to have my affections called out.'[1] His 'characteristic excursiveness of thought' intensified rather than abated with age, and whilst it provided a sound basic training for a synthetic philosopher, it thrived on loneliness, and constituted a childlike retreat from an uncongenial reality.

The tone of the Spencer household was one of austere rectitude and religious fervour. The undiscriminating vigour with which Herbert's canonical education was conducted provoked lifelong alienation: 'Owing to the foolish pertinacity with which, as a child, I was weekly surfeited with religious teachings . . . I cannot hear scriptural expressions without experiencing a certain disagreeable feeling . . . up to seventeen I was constantly in the way of hearing the gospels.'[2] Despite the strong Wesleyan tradition in his family, William George Spencer had seceded from the Derby Wesleyan Church because he resented the secular power of its minister. He chose instead the 'quiet reflection' of Sunday mornings at the Society of Friends' meeting-house, and it was there that Herbert, who began to accompany him at the age of ten, acquired his first experience of religious observance and, apparently, his distaste for it.

From an early age, too, the young Spencer breathed an atmosphere of rarefied intellectualism. His father was secretary of the Derby Philosophical Society, and at the age of eleven Herbert was taken to a lecture on phrenology by Dr. Spurzheim, 'having, however, to overcome a considerable repugnance to contemplating the row of grinning skulls he had in front of him.'[3] His childhood reading consisted largely of medical and Dissenting periodicals, while his boyish taste for adventure fiction had to be 'gratified by stealth', poring over *The Castle of Otranto* and the novels of Mrs. Radcliffe by illicit candlelight. His informal education was completed in the role of eavesdropper to the verbal contests of his father and uncles as they thrashed out the burning political, social, and philosophical issues of the day. Literature, art, and music were foreign to them: 'It was rather the scientific interpretations and moral aspects of things which occupied their

---

[1] *Aby* i. 478–9.
[2] H.S. to Mrs. R. Potter, undated, in *L.L.* i. 104–5.   [3] *Aby* i. 200.

thoughts.'[1] Much of Spencer's childhood, therefore, was spent in sitting inconspicuously alone, absorbing what he could of the bewildering colloquy of his elders.

Solitude and curiosity brought him his first intimate contact with science. He was attracted to quiet, reflective pastimes, such as rambling in the country, fishing, and rudimentary nature-study. His father shrewdly exploited his interest in natural history, encouraging him to 'pass from careless observations to careful and deliberate ones.'[2] Herbert collected everything he could find: larvae, insects, moths, butterflies, and wildflowers, and his father consolidated the incidental knowledge into the basis of a sound, if disconnected, scientific education. Spencer's childlike delight in the artistry of nature never left him, and continued to provide an impulse for his scientific researches in adult life, when he declared that 'those who have never entered upon scientific pursuits are blind to most of the poetry by which they are surrounded.'[3]

For the time being, Herbert Spencer was spared a conventional primary education. His father, who despised 'mechanical' techniques of teaching, gave him elementary instruction in biology, botany, entomology, life-drawing, and mechanics. Alarmed by his ignorance of the ordinary curriculum, however, William George at last dispatched his son, aged ten, to Mr. Mather's day-school. Here the drudgery of rote-learning appalled Herbert ('in repeating lessons I was habitually inefficient') and negated the empirical character of his father's teaching. He evinced a precocious and apparently intuitive reluctance to accept propositions without demonstrable proof: 'The mere authoritative statement that so-and-so is so-and-so, made without evidence or intelligible reason, seems to have been from the outset constitutionally repugnant to me.'[4]

Mr. Mather and Herbert Spencer soon parted company, and Herbert resumed a utilitarian, scientific, and technical education at the school founded by his grandfather and maintained by his Uncle William. He learned the mechanical

[1] *Aby* i. 41–2.   [2] *Aby* i. 71.
[3] *Education*, p. 45.   [4] *Aby* i. 84.

properties of levers and excelled in cartography. His father, meanwhile, taught him some physics with the help of a primitive air-pump, and chemistry from a textbook written by 'an incompetent man named Murray', who distinguished himself at a meeting of the Derby Philosophical Society by blowing up the furniture during an experiment. Herbert gleaned some anatomy and physiology from readings in the *Lancet* and the *Medico-Chirurgical Review*. The gap between this diffuse scientific education and his grasp of the neglected humanities widened inexorably so that at thirteen he knew no Greek, Latin, history, or English grammar: 'Concerning things around, however, . . . and their properties, I knew a good deal more than is known by most boys.' His father's tuition abjured the methodical learning of rules in favour of 'a prompting to intellectual self-help', and encouraged 'a habit of seeking for causes, as well as the tacit belief in the universality of causation.'[1] The empirical cast of mind, the disposition to question and to expect a rationally verifiable answer, was firmly implanted at a very tender age.

The ontological basis and content of Herbert Spencer's education were emphatically those of Dissent. His immediate and extended family circles were deeply imbued with Wesleyan and Unitarian Nonconformity and the political radicalism which sprang from the specific form which these affiliations took. Spencer was weaned on a fierce diet of revealed religion and the Gospel of Work, and although he was formally to repudiate both, their stamp on his personality was ineradicable.

The family into which Spencer was born might almost serve as the embodiment of the Wesleyan ideal, 'diligent in business, fervent in spirit, serving the Lord.' Their diligence may, in some cases, have failed to compensate for a fatal lack of business acumen, and the fervency of some spirits inspired secession from, rather than devotion to, the Methodist orthodoxy, but none the less the Spencers of Derby exhibited most of the characteristics of respectable lower-middle-class Dissent. Spencer's earlier writings resound to the ethical value judgements of an ideology in which right and

---

[1] *Aby* i. 89.

wrong were starkly contrasted, where benefits were strictly related to effort and deserving, where poverty was equated with improvidence, and 'reform' with moralism.

Spencer did not shrink from applying the inheritance of acquired characteristics to his own family tree. His genealogical enquiries revealed him as the heir to heroic traditions of individualism and resistance to religious authority, ranging from Bohemian Hussite and French Huguenot refugees to persecuted followers of Wesley.[1] More immediately, the collective influence of his uncles had a tangible influence on the genesis of his thought, environmental rather than hereditary. His respect for the autonomy of individual judgements, his disdain of authority and his nonconformity were consciously derived from their example: 'Our family was essentially a *dissenting* family; and dissent is an expression of antagonism to arbitrary control.'[2] It was from them that he began to learn his politics. A boy who, at the age of eleven, studied phrenology and browsed for relaxation in the *Medico-Chirurgical Review* was quite capable of assimilating, albeit in half-digested form, the forcibly-expressed dogmas of his elders, whose pronouncements on free trade, disestablishment, electoral reform, and government interference, comprised a political orthodoxy to which he was to adhere, in its essentials, throughout his life.

Recent writers have rightly emphasized the crucial importance of Spencer's formative environment, not least its 'stubborn, narrow, immensely capable provincialism.'[3] It is therefore unnecessary to rehearse at length the components of this background, except to outline those features which demonstrably moulded subsequent thoughts. Spencer, whatever his protestations of originality, was to remain a faithful representative of his family, and of the town in which he was born.

Derby in many ways symbolized the Industrial Revolution. In Thomas Lombe's silk-mill (1718) it boasted the first

---

[1] *Aby* i. 13.   [3] *Aby* i. 89.

[2] D. G. Macrae, ed., introduction to H.S., *The Man versus the State* (London, 1970). See also J.D.Y. Peel, *Herbert Spencer, the evolution of a sociologist* (London, 1971, hereafter cited as 'Peel'), Chap. 1.

authentic factory on English soil, and in Joseph Wright's painting of Arkwright's mill at Cromford, the first artistic romanticization of industrial topography. In 1833 a Derby manufacturer's lock-out brought into being the Grand National Consolidated Trades Union. Municipal power was gradually and reluctantly relinquished by the county families to a prosperous, self-confident bougeoisie, typified by the enlightened radicals of the Derby Philosophical Society.

The Derby Spencer knew was relatively unriven by class conflict, a town of 'social union' rather than of 'social cleavage.'[1] Its ascendant class of silk and hosiery entrepreneurs had slipped unobtrusively into pre-eminence, their political radicalism tempered by a lively sense of civic responsibility. Led by the 'Medici of Derby', the Strutts, they had transformed the town from a 'strange straggling place in a meadow' to 'the flower of provincial capitals', distinguished by 'improvements which blend the two characteristics of perfection—elegance and utility.'[2]

The Strutts of Derby embodied every virtue which Spencer was later to associate with industrial capitalism. They lived lives of conspicuous frugality and were endlessly preoccupied with 'improvement', personal and social. In politics they were idealistic, Utilitarian and democratic; in religion staunchly Unitarian. They supported every liberal-nationalist movement in post-Napoleonic Europe, and constructed an arboretum for the recreation and enlightenment of the masses (entry was free on Sundays, except during service time).[3] On domestic issues their radicalism was distinguished by a measured caution which was first to colour, then to emasculate Spencer's.[4]

The Strutts also shared the Spencers' predilection for a

---

[1] D. Read *The English Provinces, 1760-1960: a study in influence* (London, 1964). The author divides English industrial towns between the categories of class co-operation (e.g. Birmingham, Sheffield) and class antagonism (e.g. Manchester, Leeds).

[2] Descriptions, respectively, by Sylas Neville (1781) in J. Cozens-Handy, ed., *The Diary of Silas Neville* (London, 1950), and S. Glover, *History and Gazetteer of the County of Derby* (1883), cited in R.S. Fitton and A.P. Wadsworth, *The Strutts and the Arkwrights* (Manchester, 1958).

[3] R.S. Fitton and A.P. Wadsworth, op. cit., p. 188.

[4] H.S.'s radicalism is discussed below in Chap. 2, pp. 32-40.

utilitarian, scientific slant to education. William Strutt was among the founder-members of the Derby Philosophical Society in 1781, and a close friend of Erasmus Darwin, founder-member of the still more illustrious Lunar Society of Birmingham and Charles Darwin's grandfather. Spencer consciously and gratefully inherited a strong Unitarian scientific tradition, of which the 'Lunaticks', including Joseph Priestley, Matthew Boulton, James Watt, Benjamin Franklin, and Josiah Wedgwood had been the principal progenitors. Priestley had boasted that while Anglican universities were 'pools of stagnant water', the Dissenting academies of the north were 'rivers, which, taking their natural course, fertilise a whole country.'[1] Spencer echoed this celebration in 1860: 'The vital knowledge—that by which we have grown as a nation to what we are and which now underlies our whole existence, is a knowledge that has got itself taught in nooks and corners: while the ordained agencies for teaching have been mumbling little else than dead formulas.'[2]

Two points are worth emphasizing in this movement. The first is its close correlation of enlightenment and scientific progress with industry and the entrepreneurial class, later to be mirrored in Spencer's identification of industrialization with progress, of which social evolution is so clearly an amplification.[3] The second is the family connection between members of this close-knit provincial circle and the early exponents of the theory of evolution itself. Charles Darwin is linked to it through his grandfather, Erasmus. Another member of the Birmingham circle was Samuel Galton, grandfather of Francis Galton, author of *Hereditary Genius*. The Derby Philosophical Society was thus an offshoot of Erasmus Darwin's scientific lineage, and through it Herbert Spencer may be associated with the Birmingham Lunar Society tradition.

A characteristic enthusiasm of this coterie was phrenology. Spencer, despite his discouraging initiation, became fleetingly fascinated by it, and his writing, even after half a century, remained spattered with its jargon.[4] It served as a stepping-

---

[1] See Peel, p. 47.
[2] *Education*, p. 25.
[3] See below, Chap. 10, esp. pp. 249-50.
[4] For instance, in H.S.'s descriptions of his parents and relatives, *Aby* i, Chap. 3.

stone in the intellectual development of many contemporary rationalists. Of special interest is George Combe, whose writings on the subject contain many evolutionary ideas. Mankind, said Combe, develops through a process of adaptation to an environment so designed (by God) as 'to hold forth every possible inducement to man to cultivate his high powers.'[1] History is the account of his slow, but seemingly predetermined 'improvement' (a moral term here harnessed to an evolutionary scheme),[2] and happiness is defined as 'exercise of the faculties'. Psychological characteristics are seen as being transmitted by inheritance. For Combe, phrenology was the key by which man could adjust himself to a natural law and thus smooth his path to perfection, a conclusion soon jettisoned by Spencer. Combe's proposal that 'the legislature might considerably accelerate improvement by adding the constraining authority of human laws to enactments already proclaimed by the Creator,'[3] was likewise unacceptable. None the less, Spencer's view of evolution is substantially indebted to Combe, of whose writings he could not possibly have remained in ignorance.

The elements of Dissent, radicalism, science and industrialism are inextricably intertwined in Spencer's background. The connection between the 'Protestant Ethic' and the rise of capitalism, although its precise mechanism is contested, is proverbial: 'Capitalism', wrote R.H. Tawney, 'is the social counterpart of Calvinist theology,'[4] echoing Max Weber's assertion that 'the puritan outlook . . . was the most important, and above all, the only consistent influence' in the development of 'the rational bourgeois economic life.'[5] Rather than attempt to disentangle this complex of influences, I will try to identify the points at which it decisively shaped Spencer's thought. Two crucial sectors thus affected are his espousal of political radicalism and his perception of the dynamics and ethics of industrial society.

[1] G. Combe *The Constitution of Man* (Edinburgh, 1835), p. 2.
[2] Ibid., p. 3.
[3] Ibid., p. 65.
[4] R.H. Tawney introduction to M. Weber, *The Protestant Ethic and the Spirit of Capitalism* (London, 1968), p. 2.
[5] R. H. Tawney, op. cit., p. 174.

The term 'Dissent' is convenient, but often misleading. Strictly speaking it should refer not to the Wesleyans (who wished to reinvigorate, rather than to refute, Anglican theology) but to Congregationalists, Baptists, Presbyterians, and Unitarians, each repeatedly subdivided by secessions and revivalist movements. No simple correlation can be assumed, therefore, between Dissent and radicalism, and it is important to differentiate between Nonconformist political affiliations and to isolate those to which Spencer belonged. On issues such as the Ten Hours' Bill, Combination Laws or the Poor Law Amendment Bill, most sects were torn between placating their patrons among the 'millocracy' and retaining their strong working class support. Even the Maynooth Grant, which drove a wedge between Whigs and Dissenters, failed to stimulate a lasting political unity among the latter. The foundation of the Voluntary Movement to oppose the grant was soon followed by the secession from it of a militant wing, composed largely of Unitarians. Their organ was the *Nonconformist*, founded by Edward Miall in 1841; Herbert Spencer's first substantial publication was a series of essays for the paper in 1842, which incorporated disestablishment into a decisively individualistic political theory.[1] Miall himself defined the objective of the *Nonconformist* as 'to show that a national establishment of religion is essentially vicious . . . We ask for nothing more from the state than protection, extending to the life and liberty, the peace and prosperity of the governed.'[2]

This concomitance between Unitarianism and individualism is traceable to Joseph Priestley's *The First Principles of Civil Government* (1786). Priestley prefigured Spencer in three important political pronouncements. He heartily condemned the 'absurd doctrine' of 'the omnicompetence of parliaments': 'they possess no power beyond the limits of the trust for the execution of which they were formed.'[3] He drew the important distinction, heavily emphasized by Spencer, between formal political liberty and actual civil liberty: 'If the power

[1] 'Proper Sphere'.
[2] A.Miall, *The Life of Edward Miall* (London, 1884), pp. 51-2.
[3] J.Priestley, *On the nature of political, civic and religious liberty* (London, 1768), p. 15.

of the government be very extensive, and the subjects of it have, by consequence, little powers over their own actions, that government is tyrannical and oppressive, whether, with respect to its form, it be a monarchy, an aristocracy, or even a republic.'[1] Lastly, he cited the natural rectification of social ills as the basis of his individualism: 'In the excellent constitution of Nature, evils of all kinds . . . find their proper remedy . . . Is it not our wisdom to favour this progress, and allow the remedies of all disorders to operate gradually and easily rather than, by a violent system of perturbation, to retain all disorders till they force a remedy?'[2] Joseph Priestley, more than anyone, united the scientific and political strains of the culture of eighteenth-century provincial nonconformity in which Herbert Spencer was reared.

It is the political and religious creed associated with it which Spencer inherited through his uncles. Its 'uncritical utilitarianism' condoned child labour, upheld social inequalities and rejected all state intervention. Its exemplar, apart from Christ, was the successful businessman: 'How, in serving himself, does the merchant greatly serve society. How wonderful is the scheme of things produced by the desire for gain.'[3] After 1845 the extreme Voluntarist wing became isolated from the main body of Radicalism as from the main body of Dissent, represented by the moderate anti-Maynooth Committee.[4] It took its stand in the Anti-State Church Association (led by Edward Miall) of 1844, which declared that 'all legislation by secular governments in affairs of religion is an encroachment upon the rights of men and an invasion of the prerogatives of God.'[5] It was violently anti-Catholic as well as anti-state. In the general election of 1847 the Association pitted its candidates not against Tories, but against radicals like Richard Cobden and Joseph Hume, who approved the Maynooth Grant from less implacable viewpoints.

[1] J. Priestley, *An essay on the first principle of government* (London, 1768), pp. 50–1.
[2] Ibid., p. 136.
[3] Cited in E.M. Elliott, 'The political economy of English Dissent', in R.M. Hartwell, ed., *The Industrial Revolution* (Oxford, 1970), p. 163.
[4] See G.I.T. Machin, 'The Maynooth Grant, the Dissenters and Disestablishment, 1845–47', *E.H.R.* lxxxii (Jan. 1967).
[5] A.Miall, op. cit., pp. 95–6.

Spencer was educated, therefore, on the extreme wing of Dissent, in an austere Unitarianism indissolubly welded to an iron individualism. From earliest beginnings to the final summation of his philosophy he was never to err from the precepts of the latter.

Unitarian individualism was inseparable from industrialism; indeed the word 'industry' originally denoted a virtue rather than a function.[1] From his experience of Derby Spencer extrapolated a broad concept of 'industrial society'. He saw its virtues enshrined in the entrepreneurial class, the small men who, by dint of thrift, enterprise, and diligence, had established themselves as independent employers. The hosiery industry, organized in small units of production, provided him with his example. Even the Strutts conformed to type, for their wealth was modest by aristocratic standards, and their disposal of it far less profligate. Spencer's error lay in his inability or unwillingness to modify his portrayal of the capitalist in conformity with the tendency towards the separation of ownership from control which characterized capitalist enterprise later in the century.

This limitation of perception also prevented him from acknowledging the existence of class conflict in industrial society. The salient division, as the unitarian-individualist saw it, was between the 'industrious classes' (masters and men) and the 'idle' aristocracy. Religion, rather than income or occupation, was the clearest determinant of social affiliation. Masters administered their factories with Owenite benevolence; artisans read Samuel Smiles and attended the Derby Mechanics' Institute, founded in 1825, whose patrons were the members of the Derby Philosophical Society. Dissent embraced employer and employee alike, and the politically aware 'aristocracy of labour' took their cue from bourgeois radicals. Industrialism had a homogenous culture, its ideal being the 'self-reliant, sober, industrious craftsman.'[2] Spencer's thinking crystallized around this belief in the community of interest between workers and capitalists, and his refusal to accept strife as implicit in the wage-relation, either

---

[1] R.Williams, *Culture and Society* (London, 1964), pp. 13–14.
[2] Peel, p. 54.

theoretically or empirically. His account of social evolution is constructed round this unitarian view of industrial society, derived from the Derby of his youth.

SPENCER'S 'SECONDARY' EDUCATION AND THE INFLUENCE OF THOMAS SPENCER

At the age of thirteen, Herbert Spencer was consigned to the care of his uncle Thomas, rector of Hinton Charterhouse in Somerset. Herbert's journey there was at first disguised as an excursion; he was enthralled by his first experience of long-distance travel, and delighted with his new surroundings, especially 'the new insect-life'. His enthusiasm waned when his uncle began to expound to him the principles of Euclidian geometry, and evaporated when it became clear to him that he was to remain at Hinton. His deep sense of betrayal and rejection was soon deepened by antipathy towards a fellow-student, and by a fruitless and painful introduction to Latin. Homesickness set in, but his response was not to give himself up to self-pity. Instead, in three days, with no money and little food, he walked home to Derby.

This feat, extraordinary for the boldness and stamina it evinced in a boy of his age, and which, Spencer believed, left him permanently debilitated, made no appropriate impression on his elders. His aunt and uncle were outraged by the insult to their hospitality, and declared that 'unless his parents punish him severely, and return him again to us *immediately,* it will not only be *insulting* to us, but *ruinous* to the boy himself.'[1] His mother felt 'ashamed and mortified at Herbert's misconduct'; his father passed 'the whole of the night without sleep, ruminating on the character and prospects of my untoward son.'[2] Allowances were duly made for his age and for the shock produced by his sudden, mysterious displacement, and the anger of his elders subsided, but within the week he was reinstated at the Hinton Charterhouse rectory, there to remain for three years.

He became reconciled to, though never enthusiastic for, his new surroundings, and stayed just long enough to complete

[1] T.S. to W.G.S., Aug. 1833, *L.L.* i. 16.
[2] Ibid i. 17.

his education. He had the companionship of a succession of fellow-pupils, 'who did not raise my conception of the average intelligence.'[1] At thirteen the curriculum comprised Euclid, Latin, and reading; at fourteen were added French, Greek, and trigonometry; and at fifteen mechanics, chemistry, and political economy. This last consisted of readings aloud from Harriet Martineau's *Tales of Political Economy*, with which he was already familiar, but whereas in Derby he had 'read for the stories and skipped the political economy' he now gleaned from Miss Martineau's admonitory novelettes 'something of a solid kind.'[2] Whatever its deficiencies this scheme of study sufficed to equip him for a career in engineering and extended the boundaries of an already wide-ranging scientific knowledge. His first publications, at the age of sixteen, were letters on the formation of crystals and the Poor Law Amendment Act.[3]

Spencer's education, on the debit side, was restricted to functional horizons and conferred an uneven grasp of its component subjects. He had covered Euclid comprehensively and enthusiastically, even challenging the authority of the text on some points, but Greek fell by the wayside, French remained weak and 'as to syntax, not a single rule of any kind was taught to me.'[4] Literature and history were completely neglected, omissions of which the pupil heartily approved: 'The absence of those studies, linguistic and historical, which form so large a part of the ordinary education, left me free from the bias given by the plexus of traditional ideas and sentiments.'[5] Believing that overloading of knowledge stifles originality, Spencer rejoiced that the gaps in his education had stimulated his intellectual development. His blank literary and historical ignorance, however, were to prove a weakness later on.

His uncle's regime was as austere as his father's, and was upheld by a more formidable authority. The same asceticism and obsession with 'duty' prevented Thomas Spencer from

[1] *Aby* i. 111.
[2] *Aby* i. 110-11.
[3] Published in The *Bath and West of England Magazine,* Feb. and Mar. 1836.
[4] *Aby* i. 108.
[5] H.S., 'The Filiation of Ideas', *L.L.* ii. 307.

'adequately recognising the need for positive amusement', an attitude exemplified by the memorable injunction: 'No Spencer ever dances.'[1] Herbert was allowed to skate, and was proud of his early-acquired proficiency, but his permitted recreations were predominantly 'useful', and included the detested pursuit of gardening. More seriously, his uncle's hectoring and his own intense self-consciousness combined to generate new pressures. He became obsessed by a compulsive and insatiable urge for self-improvement, and developed an exaggerated sense of his own shortcomings, which gave rise to a disproportionate phobia of wasted time and forgetfulness: 'I do not seem to have strength of mind enough to overcome my idle inclinations, and I begin to be fearful that I shall forget a great part of what I have learned.'[2] This internalization of the exacting expectations of his mentors set up permanent tensions. He assumed full responsibility for their inconsiderate perfectionism, signing his letters 'Your intended obedient son' and 'Your affectionate and improving son', and he was to remain throughout life haunted by self-criticism and imagined inadequacy.

The exercise of avuncular discipline entailed a confrontation of two strong wills. Thomas Spencer was able to report that 'My authority over him is great, and I am quite satisfied with his obedience to me, but I fear that he would not submit himself in like manner to any other person.'[3] Spencer later acknowledged that his adolescent character was marked by 'an individuality too stiff to be easily moulded', but concluded that 'It was better to be under a control which I no doubt resented, but to which I had to conform, than to be under a control which prompted resistance because resistance was frequently successful.'[4] By the spring of 1836, however, he was ready to reassert himself, and relations became strained. Spencer's retrospective rationalization was that his physical growth-rate of more than three inches per annum had deprived the moral faculties of the brain of an adequate blood supply, but more probably he had come to resent the persistent autocracy exercised over him. He galloped through

[1] *Aby* i. 28.   [2] H.S. to W.G.S. 1836, *L.L.* i. 21.
[3] T.S. to W.G.S. 1833, *L.L.* i. 21.   [4] *Aby* i. 116.

the last six books of Euclid in a week and a half, and returned to Derby.

Thomas Spencer, though an Anglican by religion, was a redoubtable radical, and accordingly subjected his nephew to a vigorous course of political instruction. Herbert Spencer's conscious commitment to individualism, free trade, and Dissent date from this period. The underlying social values, improvidence identified as the cause of poverty, capital as the observable sign of worthiness, disdain of aristocratic mores and the cult of fashion, were deliberately reinforced. Childless himself, Thomas Spencer had a semi-paternal regard for his nephew, and they continued to correspond after Herbert's departure. When, in 1847, Thomas relinquished his living and moved to London to devote himself wholeheartedly to radical causes, he was able to furnish Herbert with some useful political and literary contacts.

Thomas Spencer had been an assiduous and prominent campaigner for temperance and the abolition of slavery. He was the only Anglican clergyman in the anti-Corn Law League, saying Grace at its first and last banquets and touring throughout the country. Herbert was inordinately proud of this: 'Out of some ten thousand *ex officio* friends of the poor and needy, there was but one . . . who took an active part in abolishing this tax on the people's bread for the maintenance of landlords' rents.'[1] Thomas was present, too, at the inaugural meeting of the Complete Suffrage Movement, and instrumental in involving Herbert in its campaign for electoral reform. He wrote and published twenty-three pamphlets and tracts, on such varied topics as liturgical reform, disestablishment, education, Poor Laws, Corn Laws, and state intervention. Circulation reached 23 000 each, and he addressed a wider public in the course of ceaseless lecture-tours, including a visit to America, where he carried his disregard of normative conventions so far as to denounce slavery to southern audiences.

His Poor Law doctrines found the deepest echoes in Herbert Spencer's thought. Thomas had opposed the Old Poor Law on humanitarian grounds, and provided Hinton with a

---

[1] 'Parliamentary Reform; its dangers and safeguards', *Essays*, iii. 361.

school, a clothing-club, allotments, and meat dinners on Sundays for selected labourers and their families. These philanthropic enterprises were abruptly checked by the Poor Law Amendment Bill of 1834: 'Previously, my uncle had always been a paupers' friend . . . but the debates during the passage of the Bill through Parliament had opened his eyes.'[1] In the capacity of Chairman of the Vestry he rigorously applied the new law to his flock, cutting the village rate from £700 p.a. to £200 p.a., an achievement which was recognized in his election to the chair of the Board of Guardians of the Bath Union. His brisk, unsentimental approach to poverty hardened during his tenure of office: 'In the course of years . . . he became conscious of the mischiefs done by aid inadequately restrained,'[2] a view consolidated by his 'intimate knowledge of pauperism' into the 'crude notion that merit and demerit always bring their normal results.'[3]

Herbert, a resident of Hinton throughout this conversion, completely assimilated his uncle's new-found enlightenment. The *Bath and West of England Magazine* for March 1836 contained 'a very ignorant letter' on the Poor Laws, and Spencer wrote a reply which reproduced his uncle's sentiments with a forbidding asperity which belies the author's sixteen years:

The whole of your argument implies . . . that a person is not to be allowed to raise himself by his exertions. What?: is not a man to be benefitted by his superior industry? . . . is there no reward to be held out to perseverance, no punishment for idleness? . . . as to the complaint of want of work, everybody knows, who has bothered to inquire into the subject, that it is generally a mere pretence, and that it has been used by labourers as a plea for relief when there has been abundance of employment.

Idleness, 'the parent of mischief', lies at the root of rural distress. Its ideal antidote is the workhouse, that 'great safeguard against imposition'; 'This is the true test of success . . . if a man is starving he will gladly accept the offer of the workhouse; if he is not starving, he is not a proper object of relief.' This simple formula is hammered home with a stern injunction to virtuous labour:

[1] *Aby* i. 116.
[2] *Aby* i. 28.
[3] *Aby* i. 324.

Do you then deny, or have you forgotten, those declarations: 'In the sweat of thy brow shalt thou eat bread', 'Six days shalt thou labour,' 'If any will not work, neither let him eat'? The whole system of man's responsibility and of his future reward or punishment, depending upon his being diligent in business, fervent in spirit, serving the Lord, seems completely set aside by your reasoning.[1]

It is tempting to dismiss this letter as the striking of youthful postures, yet Herbert Spencer's fundamental conviction that poverty and hardship are the outward manifestations of vice was never abrogated: indeed, it gained strength from the subsequent addition of evolutionary theory. The vindication of social evolution rests finally on the assumption that it culminates in 'a proportioning of rewards to merits.'

Nemesis caught up with Thomas Spencer in fine poetic style. In 1849 he invested half of his capital in Isambard Kingdom Brunel's South Wales Railway Company, which went bankrupt. Henceforth, chastened by experience, he 'made large allowances for the unfavourable circumstances of those who fell into degraded habits of life.'[2] His style of preaching forthwith shifted from 'stern enunciations of rectitude' to the expression of fellow feeling. Unfortunately this object lesson was lost on Herbert, who, whilst admitting that 'his was one of the natures that are improved by misfortune', never related his uncle's hubris to the discredit of the principle.

Thomas Spencer was instrumental in the composition and publication of Herbert Spencer's first anti-interventionist essays. Edward Miall had been a close friend and fellow-campaigner of his on several reformist platforms. The first of Herbert's letters on 'The Proper Sphere of Government', sent for publication in the *Nonconformist*, was accompanied by an introductory letter from Thomas, and the content of all twelve missives, later republished in a commercially disastrous pamphlet, was the outcome of conversation with him on a specified aspect of state interference. It was thus under Thomas Spencer's guidance that Herbert Spencer first formulated his individualistic version of liberalism, which he later acknowledged to have been his family's creed:

[1] H.S., 'Reply to T.W.S', *Bath and West of England Magazine*, Apr. 1836.
[2] *Aby* i. 34.

The mental attitude of the Spencers was unlike that now (1879) displayed by those who call themselves Liberals—an attitude of subordination to the decisions of Mr. Gladstone . . . With the absence of that party 'loyalty' which consists in suspending private judgement to men who are in office . . . there naturally went a tendency to carry individual freedom as far as possible; and by implication, to restrict governmental action.[1]

'The Proper Sphere of Government' was the studied application of this principle to selected governmental activities.

Herbert Spencer was not oblivious to his uncle's faults, and noted his excessive reserve, querulousness and lack of humour. These shortcomings, and Thomas Spencer's premature death in January 1853, convinced Herbert that the single-minded pursuit of duty could be a distortion of the real purpose of life: 'Due participation in the miscellaneous pleasures of life, would have made his existence of greater value, alike to himself and to others.'[2] Herbert's subsequent repudiation of the 'Gospel of Work', in theory if not in practice, was a conscious rejection of one aspect of his familial training. The great majority of its doctrines, however, remained with him, to become firmly incorporated into his philosophy.

The negative theory of state competence and the identification of poverty with improvidence were seminal thoughts from which there grew up a whole system. The belief that distress constituted the just deserts of the vicious, and its corollary that the vicious could thereby be identified, slanted the ethical basis of Spencerian evolution in such a way that starvation and suffering could be accepted as the lot of the constitutionally inferior without a qualm. Meanwhile, the negative conception of state duty, elaborated under Thomas Spencer's direction in 1842, survived the intellectual upheaval caused by the development of Spencer's theory of evolution, to reappear with unattenuated force in *The Man versus the State*, written in 1884. The socio-political outlook of all the Spencers, and of the 'advanced Dissenters' of whom they were so representative, was condensed in Thomas Spencer's indoctrination of his nephew, and passed in refined and intensified form into the canons of Spencerian theory. The

[1] *Aby* i. 208.
[2] *Aby* i. 415.

concept of social evolution can be interpreted as an exposition, in scientific terms, of Thomas Spencer's 'radical' moralism, in all its Malthusian rigour.

RAILWAY ENGINEERING AND RADICAL POLITICS,
1837–1846

The years 1837–46, spanning Herbert Spencer's late ado-
lescence and early manhood, encompass his career as a railway
engineer, the vocation for which his technical and utilitarian
education had prepared him. This period is mainly significant, however, for an interlude in 1841–2 in which he engaged
in radical politics, and during which he produced the first and
almost definitive formulation of his concept of political individualism. There followed an equally instructive but less
comforting insight into the workings of contemporary capitalism, when Spencer returned to the railways in a more adventurous role. His first-hand experience of business speculation is important, since it cast over his recent triumphant
assertion of *laissez-faire* a doubt which could never completely
be dispelled. In 1846 Spencer was on the threshold of his
intellectual career. His political convictions, however, were
already substantially formed, and were to harden as his
scientific speculations broadened.

Spencer's career as a railway engineer was preceded, at his
father's prompting, by an exploratory period of teaching.
William George Spencer looked to his son to follow the
family vocation and to continue the Spencer tradition of enlightened educational practice. In the slim volume entitled
Education: intellectual, moral and physical (1860) Herbert
Spencer later recognized 'more than anywhere else, the direct
influence of my father.'[1] The opportunity which fell to him,
however, offered little scope for the application of advanced
techniques, for it occurred in Mr. Mather's day-school, whose
'mechanical' regime had proved so inimical to him as a pupil.
Herbert considered himself a good teacher: 'a certain facility
of exposition being natural to me, my lessons were at once
effective and pleasure-giving.' Being himself 'by nature prone

[1] *Aby* i. 438.

to resist coercion' he made sparing use of magisterial authority.[1] He soon realized that his days with Mr. Mather were
numbered, for, having 'a great intolerance of monotony' he
detested the treadmill routine of teaching by rote, yet feared
parental hostility to anything more sophisticated. The unexpected offer of an engineering position was therefore gratefully accepted; it was, after all, 'just the kind of thing for
which my past studies have fitted me.'[2]

Charles Fox, an erstwhile employee of Robert Stephenson
and now chief engineer of the London–Birmingham line, was
an old friend of uncle William, and it was through this family
connection that Herbert's appointment was contrived. He
arrived in London on 8 November 1837 to take up his duties
at a salary of £80 per annum ('not amiss for a youth of
seventeen'). His contract stipulated six months' surveying for
the extension of the London–Birmingham line from its Chalk
Farm terminus to Euston. The work was conducted in all
weathers ('it was especially annoying when, in pelting rain,
the blackened water from one's hat dripped onto the note-
book') but he quickly learned to enjoy it, and to feel at home
in the expanding, adventurous world of the pioneer railway-
men. Life in the metropolis, however, he found less enthralling.
During eleven months spent in London 'I never went to a
place of entertainment; nor ever read a novel.'[3] Totally un-
used to leisure, he spent much of his spare time grappling
with mathematical problems, or walking alone through the
gas-lit streets. The austerity of his upbringing was riveted
upon his personality, and on his return to Derby 'my old
schoolmaster expressed his satisfaction that I had not come
back to the paternal roof injured by dissipation, as many
young men do.'[4]

Charles Fox thought highly of his young employee, and at
the expiration of his contract he was retained at a salary of
£120 to work on the Birmingham–Gloucester Railway. He
left London for Worcester on 4 September 1838, ambitious
and confident, assuring his father that 'the more I see of

[1] *Aby* i. 122.
[2] H.S. to W.G.S., 1836, *L.L.* i. 27.
[3] *Aby* i. 132.
[4] *Aby* i. 189.

engineering the more I like it; no other profession would have suited me so well.'[1] His new appointment meant a cessation of outdoor work and confinement to a drawing-office. There his conscientiousness struck an odd note among his new companions, the junior members of the staff who, in his classification, 'belonged largely to the ruling class, and had corresponding notions and habits.' Their casual levity and occasional lewdness constituted a mode of behaviour to which he was unacclimatized, and they, in turn, regarded Spencer as 'an oddity', and according to one account, 'a little bumptious.'[2] He made scant efforts to win their approbation, and, fortified by the support of a new-found friend, G.B.W. Jackson ('a Moravian, and very steady') he flaunted his individuality by wearing an unfashionable brown frock-coat and by openly criticizing his superiors. Although his carefree young associates eventually discovered that 'within the prickly husk, the kernel was not quite so harsh as was supposed,'[3] his emerging propensity for antagonizing senior personnel did not enhance his prospects, not least because, in technical arguments he was usually in the right, 'because of my better mathematical culture.' This critical and self-asserting tendency, however, served only to disguise a continuing sense of insecurity. Letters home reveal him persistently harassed by the demands of self-discipline: 'I know that I might have made better use of my time in the way of study and that there have been many opportunities of improvement or of gaining information that I have let slip. It is a great pity that a just estimate of the value of knowledge is only made after the means of gaining it are lost.'[4]

Meanwhile, he continued to combine skill and keenness in his job. In May 1839 he published his first full-length article, on 'Skew Arches' in the *Civil Engineers' and Architects' Journal*. He travelled widely in the course of engineering projects, and became enthusiastically absorbed in the development of railway technology, devising, among other things, a 'velocimeter' to measure the speed of trains, and a contrivance for snatching up mailbags at speed. In 1840 his plan for

[1] H.S. to W.G.S., Sept. 1838, *L.L.* i. 29.   [2] *L.L.* i. 30.
[3] *L.L.* i. 145.   [4] H.S. to W.G.S., 15 Apr. 1840, *L.L.* i. 35.

widening the Severn Bridge at Worcester was preferred to that of his head of department, Captain Moorsom, who was sufficiently impressed to appoint Spencer as his private secretary. He was duly installed at Moorsom's house at Powick in April 1840.

Here he began to experience a more relaxed social existence, and to gain in confidence as a result. It was at this time that he overcame his 'dread of correspondence' and began to enjoy writing: 'instead of as heretofore having to urge my pen along with difficulty, it now seems as though it were inclined to run away from me.'[1] This information elicited from his father a rare, reluctant token of approbation: 'I am glad indeed that your eyes are beginning to open, and to see what a great attainment it is to be able to write freely and well.'[2] Although his daydreams were firmly focused on making a fortune by one of his inventions, Spencer toyed fleetingly with the idea of authorship: 'I should like to make public some of my ideas upon the state of the world and religion, together with a few remarks on education. I think, however, that I may employ my time better at present.'[3]

During the summer of 1840 Spencer seems, for the first and only time, to have fallen in love. The object of his affection was Captain Moorsom's niece, who took to passing her time, unaccountably unchaperoned, in his drawing-office at Powick. Spencer brought to the relationship a disarming combination of good looks and innocence; this was his 'first experience of more than mere formal meetings.' He later insisted that the arrival of the young lady's fiancé, an undergraduate of Oxford, occurred before 'any entanglement of feeling', and that 'no harm of any kind happened, notwithstanding the length of time which we daily passed together.' However, she must have made a profound emotional impact, for he declared to her that 'I shall always continue to look back upon the time I have spent in your society with a mixture of pleasure and regret,'[4] and no less than fifty years later, in a fit of nostalgia, he was to write to her requesting

[1] H.S. to W.G.S., 31 Mar. 1840, *Aby* i. 156.
[2] W.G.S. to H.S., 26 Apr. 1840, *Aby* i. 160.
[3] H.S. to W.G.S., 15 Apr. 1840, *Aby* i. 58.
[4] *L.L.* i. 39.

that she send him a photograph. There is no trace of any other romantic attachment in Spencer's life.

Whether this tentative affair precipitated the termination of his contract with Moorsom, Spencer does not say. Stronger motives pointed to a breach, and engineering gradually began to feel too constricting for his excursive intellect. In 1839 a Committee of the Privy Council for Education was set up by Lord John Russell's administration to administer an Education Grant of £30 000. This reawoke his attention to the undesirability of state intervention, and politics began to pre-occupy him, to the detriment of his work. Office-hours were consumed in political altercation, and Captain Moorsom (in consultation with Spencer's father) attempted to 'take some of the philosophy out of him' by setting him the most complex problems available. Accordingly, when Herbert's contract expired early in 1841, he rather impetuously refused a renewal without waiting to hear terms, and returned to Derby on 20 April 'with a considerable sum laid by.'

During the hiatus in Spencer's engineering career the political involvement which had estranged him from Captain Moorsom took a practical turn. The fervour with which he threw himself into the cause of electoral reform was characteristic of his youthful whole-heartedness; he adopted extreme radical views, denouncing the sacraments, baptism, and ordination in the Church, monarchy and aristocratic hegemony in the State. His more moderate friends, including G.B.W. Jackson, were surprised and alienated; one gravely counselled him against 'committing yourself to the current which may over-whelm you.'[1] This indiscriminate radicalism was short-lived, but a more durable facet of the Spencerian theory took shape at this time. In consultation with his uncle Thomas he prepared the twelve letters defining 'The Proper Sphere of Government' (the *Nonconformist*, June–September 1842) containing a model of administrative *laissez-faire* to which, in most essentials, he still adhered in 1903. The limits of the state's legitimate role are delineated, its ethical basis explained, and tentative references are made to natural selection as one argument against state interference. Spencer's major

[1] *Aby* i. 221.

contribution to political thought was thus substantially formed at the age of twenty-two, and was to undergo little subsequent modification.

In the months following his resignation from the Birmingham–Gloucester Railway, Spencer lacked a coherent purpose. He toyed with inventions, sketched, studied mathematics, botany, and phrenology, but all his experiments and speculations ended without tangible result. His political commitment followed the pattern of these heterogenous and transitory enthusiasms.

The Complete Suffrage Movement was founded to bridge the gulf between Chartism and the anti-Corn Law League. Its moving spirit was Joseph Sturge, a celebrated veteran of the anti-slavery agitation and a prominent Quaker. Sturge 'had watched with deepest sorrow and anxiety' the rising turbulence and class antagonism entailed by the depression of 1838–40, and 'thought it would be doing good service to both classes if, by weaning the one from the dangerous theories which inspired so much distrust and dislike of their cause, he could induce the other to listen in a more generous temper to the claim of so large a body of their fellow-countrymen.'[1] The movement came into existence in November 1841, and Herbert Spencer was among its earliest recruits.

The outlook for such a scheme was more propitious than might be supposed from Chartist distrust of the anti-Corn Law 'millocrats.' The failure of the Chartist petition of 1839 had irrevocably split the movement into 'moral-force' and 'physical-force' factions, and it was to the former, rallying strongly and embracing most of Chartism's charismatic leaders, that the C.S.M. directed its appeal. It was based in Birmingham, a stronghold of class co-operation in the pursuit of reform. Thomas Attwood's 'currency movement' had thrived there, and his Birmingham Political Union had made the city a focus of the successful agitation of 1832. By 1833, however, the B.P.U. was already denouncing the Whigs for betraying the people's trust. In 1837 Attwood revived the B.P.U., only to see his cause pre-empted by the Chartists. Class feeling began to run high, and a Chartist meeting of 1839

[1] A. Peckover, *The Life and Death of Joseph Sturge* (London, 1890), p. 66.

was broken up by magistrates who had once been B.P.U.
members.

Reconciliation, then, was Sturge's first priority. In Edward
Miall's *Nonconformist* the movement had a ready-made
platform for its programme of class compromise. Miall considered that England 'was to all appearances on the brink of
revolution', and accordingly 'conceived it to be his duty as
the exponent of the principles of civil and religious equality
to aim at a reconciliation of the lower and middle classes.'[1]
The idea began to take root. The attitude of the anti-Corn
Law League itself, if ambivalent, was not overtly hostile.
Richard Cobden, although determined that the League
should not commit itself, regarded Joseph Sturge's efforts as
'something in our rear to frighten the aristocracy,'[2] while
John Bright openly supported it.[3] Some middle-class radicals
were ready to turn in the direction of parliamentary reform
following recent checks to the Corn Law agitation; as Cobden
put it, 'Something *new* is wanting to give novelty to our
proceedings. The League has grown somewhat stale.'[4] The
C.S.M. soon boasted sixty branches, and when Sturge visited
Derby on his promotional tour he lodged with the Spencers,
as a result of which Herbert was appointed secretary of the
Derby branch.

In April 1842 the C.S.M. convened its first joint con-
ference with Chartist representatives. It was a moderate
success, a degree of *rapprochement* being effected between
the two movements, although the retention of the word
'charter' in any forthcoming statements remained proble-
matical. Otherwise their objectives were identical: universal
male suffrage, no property qualifications, secret ballot, equal
electoral districts, remuneration for M.P.s. A group of
O'Connorites from Bradford who attempted to disrupt the
harmony of the proceedings was 'discountenanced' by the
moderate majority.

---

[1] A. Miall, op.cit., p. 74.
[2] D.Read, *Cobden and Bright: a Victorian political partnership* (London, 1967),
p. 30.
[3] L.M. Macaulay, *The Life of John Bright* (London, 1913), pp. 66–7.
[4] Cobden to Bright, 9 Oct. 1841 in G.M. Trevelyan, *The Life of John Bright*
(London, 1913), p. 65.

Herbert Spencer, who did not attend, experienced a minor crisis of his own in September 1842. One of the C.S.M.'s most accomplished speakers was Henry Vincent, a 'Temperance Chartist' of the moderate persuasion, who was invited to speak in Derby on 1 September on 'The present state of the country and the necessity and safety of extending political power to all classes of people.' The Tory gentlemen of the local Bench, unduly alarmed by the orator's supposed role in the Newport Rising of 1839, determined to prevent the meeting. They had notices torn down, forced the owner of the premises to close them, and finally broke up the meeting by 'the sheer intimidation' of 'a posse of constables.' Vincent was arrested; Spencer sat up till 3.00 a.m. drafting 'An address to the magistrates of Derby on the imprisonment of Henry Vincent,' which appeared in the national press.[1] He accused them of jeopardizing public safety and suppressing free speech, but his tone signified the cautious and respectable tenor of the movement. Reform is clearly viewed as a preventive remedy for public disorder, a level-headed solution to the problem of mass power. 'The Tory press', it declares, 'has openly exposed its dread of the Movement in consequence of its peaceful character . . . let it be remembered that the placard earnestly entreated the attendance of the middle class, and this fact alone was ample guarantee for the peaceful intentions of the assembly.'

The reconciliation which Joseph Sturge was working towards was to prove elusive, although he had since won a by-election at Nottingham on a platform of purity of election and class-collaboration. On 27 December 1842 a second joint meeting was held at Birmingham Mechanics' Institute, at which most of the 374 delegates present were Chartists.[2] The gulf between the two organizations widened irreparably. If Spencer's attitude to Chartism was typical, then there was at best a slim chance of success: 'The Chartists', he declaimed, 'would listen to no compromise. Fanatics soon acquire passionate attachments to their shibboleths.'[3]

The Chartist ranks were stiffened, numerically and ideo-

[1] *Morning Chronicle*, 6 Sept. 1842; *Sun*, 7 Sept. 1842.
[2] J. Maccoby, *English Radicalism, 1832–52* (London, 1935), p. 242.
[3] *Aby* i. 219.

logically, by the presence of Feargus O'Connor and his supporters, and this time the division over the word 'charter' proved decisive. The C.S.M. had produced a body of no fewer than ninety-nine demands, but were determined to call it a 'Bill of Rights'. Outvoted by two to one, their contingent, which included John Bright, Thomas and Herbert Spencer, withdrew to another hall where they passed a resolution signed, by Herbert, 'in a state of great excitement'. For all practical purposes, however, the C.S.M. was dead, and mourned by scarcely anyone. Joseph Sturge was effectively isolated among the Quaker fraternity in his conviction that to withhold the franchise from the working class was 'un-Christian'. Most of the brethren distrusted politics as 'detracting from inner piety,'[1] and Sturge's biographer noted that his associates 'felt thankful that this result left him at liberty honourably to withdraw from such uncongenial friendship.'[2]

Spencer's interest persisted, with decreasing intensity, for two years. In 1843 he wrote pamphlets on *Pledging Electors* and *Electoral Bribery*, and in August 1844 was offered an editorial assistantship with the *Pilot*, a radical newspaper which Sturge was launching in Birmingham. Its editor was James Wilson, General Secretary of the C.S.M., and it first appeared on 28 September 1844. Its first six editions carried leading articles from Spencer's pen, but his zeal for electoral reform was now almost extinct, and only one of them even referred to it. When, in the course of an argument with Wilson, he admitted to being an agnostic, he was politely asked to leave, and so concluded Spencer's period of political activism.

SPENCER'S POLITICAL RADICALISM

Herbert Spencer's political radicalism had shallow roots and flowered only briefly. This can be explained by the fact that his enthusiasm, though genuine, was consolidated by no long-term temperamental or intellectual commitment. His championship of the cause was not long sustained by his rationalist

---

[1] S. Hobhouse, *Joseph Sturge: his life and work*, (London, 1919), p. 29.
[2] H. Richard, *Memoirs of Joseph Sturge* (London, 1864), p. 318.

optimism, and the logic of his theories was against it. Its only lasting legacy was the political moralism on which it was partly based. This moralism, derived from his Calvinist upbringing, traced a thin but unbroken line throughout his literary career, and powerfully motivated him in his search for universal principles of conduct.

During his active participation in politics Spencer associated with many of the prominent radicals of his time: Richard Cobden, John Bright, Joseph Sturge, Henry Vincent, William Lovett, James Bronterre O'Brien, Edward Miall, and of course the ubiquitous Thomas Spencer. His brief advocacy of electoral reform was vigorous and cogent, borrowing ideas from Chartist and moderate sources. Occasionally he gave vent to unequivocal affirmations in favour of democracy:

> The buoyant spirit of democracy can never more be repressed, and we defy all the legislators that ever are or have been in the world, with all their cunning and sagacity, their wily statesmanship and subtle policy, their regulations and enactments, their soldiers and police, and their multitudinous appliances of state manoeuvering, to subdue its rising power; to re-fetter it with the shackles of aristocracy; or to crush it beneath the stern heel of despotism.[1]

Writing with unqualified assurance and zeal, Spencer chided the scaremongers who attempted to blacken reform by associating it with the excesses of the French Revolution: 'confusion, bloodshed, spoliation of property, national bankruptcy, universal ruin . . . these are the stark prophecies with which statesmen and their disciples meet requests to allow due scope to the representative principle.'[2] He even denounced the 'betrayal' of the 1832 Reform Act: 'Elated with their success, the reformers settled down, and having secured themselves, cared but little for those who helped them to power.'[3]

Yet for all his rhetoric, Spencer was never far from Joseph Sturge's preventive viewpoint. Sturge's motivation in preaching reform was compounded of a hatred of 'aristocracy' (the traditional bourgeois indictment of 'Old Corruption') and the

---

[1] H.S., 'Effervescence: Rebecca and her daughters', *Nonconformist*, 28 June 1843.
[2] H.S., 'The Political Smashers', *Standard of Freedom*, 14 Oct. 1840.
[3] *Pilot*, 9 Nov. 1844.

desire to purchase social stability with 'the cheerful concession to the working class of the electoral franchise.'[1] Reform is a means of forestalling revolution by fostering the political enlightenment of the masses. The degradation of the working class reflects its political powerlessness; elevate the working man to social responsibility and he will respond with self-improvement, the political by-products of which are stability and order. Repress him, and uncontrollable anger will be the response:

Raise the tone of his self-respect by raising his position, and you will awaken in his bosom an honourable intention to act his part with becoming dignity. The extension to the people of complete suffrage, so far from exciting insubordination . . . would give a mighty impulse to popular intelligence and morality . . . Revolution: Spoliation: Yes, if we compel the excluded millions to wrestle with us for their own, the very heat of passion generated by this conflict may inflame them with the spirit of retaliation, in the frenzy of which nothing would be safe.[2]

Here is seen that strange mixture of sentiments which characterized the middle-class radicalism of the period: a fear of the revolutionary potential latent in the working class, a seemingly paradoxical faith in the peculiar political quiescence of the English race, and an optimistic confidence in the ability of the middle class to contain and assimilate the radical aspirations of the lower orders. Joseph Sturge's *Reconciliation between the middle and labouring classes* encapsulates it completely:

They are too numerous a body to be deprived with impunity . . . the suffrage they will have—the only question that remains is the course of time. Which, then, is the wisest course? To withhold their rights until compelled to give them up or, of our own free will and sense of justice to proffer immediately our assistance and cooperation? If we do the first we allow time and afford occasion for revolutionary designs to lay fast hold of the hearts of working men . . . if the last they would gladly join us in hunting out of society every unjust and every mischievous interest.[3]

This combination of generosity and discretion underlay

[1] J. Sturge *Reconciliation between the middle and labouring classes* (Birmingham, 1842), p. 5.
[2] Ibid., p. 19.
[3] J. Sturge, op.cit., p. 32.

Spencer's early political tirades. After ranting against the 'stern heel of despotism' he enunciated the formula which alone would assuage the 'reeking, roaring heap of discord'. It is 'to allow the popular spirit to re-absorb that full equivalent of natural rights with which it was primitively combined . . . and in place of its now hot and caustic condition, it will become cool and innocuous'. Justice for the people, accordingly, affords 'a sure mode, and the only mode, of warding off impending social dissolution,'[1] an objective unquestionably dear to the hearts of readers of the Nonconformist. Sturge reassured them that reform would be followed not by revolution, but by a period of comfortable apathy: 'the more probable it is that, after the first exercise of their newly-acquired power, they would sink for a period into a state of listlessness in reference to public affairs.'[2]

The same note of pre-emptive caution pervades most contemporary English radicalism. George Eliot, for example, contrasted the political sophistication of the volatile French with the staid gradualism of the English: 'there is nothing in our Constitution to obstruct the slow process of political reform. This is all we are fit for at present. The social reform which may prepare us for great changes is more and more the object of effort both in Parliament and out of it. But we English are slow crawlers.'[3] Raymond Williams traces this fear of political violence through her works, and through those of Mrs. Gaskell.[4] It is tempered with self-congratulation; extreme continental solutions were deemed, by consensus, to be inappropriate to English forward development, a judgement with which Spencer concurred. As a result his conception of reform underwent a gradual evolution, from democracy as a natural right, through utilitarian rationalization, disquiet, and modification, to outright rejection. By 1860, though still committed to reform in principle, he had already begun to veer in the direction of conservatism.

Spencer began by asserting democracy as a 'natural right'.

---

[1] H.S., 'Effervescence: Rebecca and her daughters', Nonconformist, 28 June 1843.
[2] J.Sturge, op.cit., p. 31.
[3] In R. Williams, op.cit., p. 113.
[4] Ibid., pp. 99–103.

'Our main motive to action', he wrote in 1844, 'takes its rise in the consciousness that we once held possession of right, and we were deprived of it, and deprived unrighteously.'[1] The pre-existence of this right is explicit in Spencer's Burkean conception of the English Constitution as consisting of three 'estates', crown, lords, and commons, in an equilibrium of power guaranteed by a system of checks and balances. Pernicious aristocracy, however, by infiltrating the third estate, has upset the constitutional equilibrium. The House of Commons is 'not a commons house at all . . . but a thing made up of Lords, Right Honourables, baronets, admirals, generals, younger sons of the nobility, nominees of dukes, in short, a supplementary House of Peers.'[2] Only universal suffrage can wrest the institution from their clutches.

During the 1840s Spencer came to adopt a more cautious, defensive posture. In 1848 we find him rebutting the allegation that the masses are too ignorant and immoral to be trusted with the vote, and advancing the thesis that society enjoys a uniform level of morality transcending all classes; 'it devolves upon those who raise the objection for the enfranchisement of the working man to discover a class that is *not* immoral, a class that cannot be charged with venality . . . is there a caste in society amidst whose daily acts the slimy trails of vice are not discernible?' The answer is embodied in an exhaustive catalogue of iniquity, implicating shopkeepers, lawyers, clergymen, farmers, politicians, aristocrats, and statesmen, leading to the uncomfortable conclusion that 'vice, venality and dishonesty pervade all ranks.'[3]

This argument is conceptually reinforced in *Social Statics* (1851), where the upper classes are shown to share not only the workers' moral turpitude, but also their ignorance. The currency among them of protectionist fallacies, including 'the ridiculous idea that corn-speculation is harmful' invalidates their claim to 'great superiority over the non-electors.'[4] The organic analogy is introduced: 'Whilst the virus of depravity exists in one part of the body politic, no other part

---

[1] *Pilot,* 9 Nov. 1844.
[2] H.S., 'The Political Smashers', *Standard of Freedom* 14 Oct. 1840.
[3] H.S., 'Tu Quoque', *Standard of Freedom,* 11 Nov. 1848.
[4] *S. Stat.,* p. 261.

can remain healthy.'[1] Spencer sympathetically acknowledges the greater temptation to crime implicit in lowly circumstances, from which there results a rare moment of compassionate eloquence:

Surely the lot of the hard-handed labourer is pitiable enough without having harsh judgements passed upon him . . . Think of him now with his caged-up desires doomed to a daily, weekly, yearly round of painful toil, with scarcely any remission but for food and sleep. Observe how he is tantalised by the pleasures he sees his richer brethren partaking of, but from which he must be forever debarred. Note the humiliation he suffers from being looked down on as of no account among men. And then remember that he has nothing to look forward to but a monstrous continuance of this till death. Is this a salutary state of things to live under?[2]

Spencer's sympathy, it must be noted, was firmly based in his acceptance of the working-class predicament as natural and, for the foreseeable future, unalterable. A recital of injustice, however heart-rending, is no substitute for its alleviation. None the less, the popular spirit behind the utterance cannot be impugned.

Social Statics, in so far as it concerns itself with the question of reform, is mainly directed at meeting objections to it, such as Lord Macaulay's contention that it would 'consummate the revolution'. Conservatives feared the enfranchisement of the urban proletariat, on the grounds that it would facilitate 'class-legislation'. Spencer countered that sectional power is best neutralized by the broadest possible representation: 'The interests of the *whole* society can be secured only by giving power into the hands of the whole people.'[3] The alternative is that 'the few must continue to trespass against the many, lest the many should trespass against the few.'[4] Should this offer cold comfort to the few, Spencer reassured them that the urban mass 'is too great, too incongruous, too scattered for effective combination.'[5] It is noteworthy that in *Social Statics* (1851), despite its preventive view of reform, Spencer went so far as to acknowledge the right of female

---

[1] Ibid., p. 256.
[2] Ibid., p. 250-1.
[3] S. Stat., p. 243.
[4] S. Stat., p. 244.
[5] S. Stat., p. 245.

suffrage, deducing from his 'law of equal freedom' that 'the rights of women must stand or fall with those of men.'[1] Male domination, in his view, demonstrates the persistence of barbaric sentiments in a semi-evolved social state; it is 'an evanescent form of the theory that women have no souls.'[2] Spencer jettisoned this visionary deduction long before he repudiated the generalized principle of universal suffrage, and for specific reasons.[3]

The strong vein of political moralism running through Spencerian theory also had its source at this time. The preoccupation of governments with 'expediency' at the expense of right principle is admonished in a distinctly sermonic tone; 'Justice and government have been all the world over looked upon as things totally incompatible,'[4] so that world history provides 'one continuous evidence of the impolicy of deviating from right principles.'[5] Spencer postulated an inflexible moral law regulating the conduct of society, disobedience of which is not only wrong but ultimately self-defeating. His demand for public propriety, therefore, is an injunction to accept the inevitable.

Herbert Spencer in the early 1840s, entertained the millenarian conviction of rationalists everywhere that society contained an irresistibly growing moral force: 'The day is fast coming when men will no longer blunder on in the darkness . . . and will one day learn that submission to the law of Justice is as essential to our safety in the moral world as obedience to the law of gravity is to our security in the material one.'[6] He deplored political violence, not because he lacked sympathy with its objectives, but because it dissipated moral energies generated by the consciousness of injustice: 'The strong emotions which have been wrongfully allowed to expend themselves in a torrent of angry passions should have been treasured up as a resevoir of fervent energy wherewith to work out great moral purposes.'[7]

[1] S. Stat., p. 190.
[2] S. Stat., p. 179.
[3] H.S.'s repudiation of female suffrage is related below, Chap. 5, pp. 114–15.
[4] Pilot, 16 Nov. 1844.
[5] Pilot, 7 Nov. 1844.
[6] Pilot, 23. Nov. 1844.
   H.S., 'The non-intrusion riots', Nonconformist, Oct. 1848.

Spencer's career can be interpreted as a quest for the formulation of transcendental rules of conduct, and a crusade
for their acceptance. *Social Statics* opens with a plea for
'scientific morality', and though it contains the last invocations of the Deity to appear under Spencer's name, it is
basically an attempt to construct for ethics an alternative
secular basis in nature; to replace both discredited Christianity
and the Utilitarian scheme of public morality based on the
reconciliation of interests. It is in every sense a work of moral
emphasis, and one in which Spencer paid his dues to the provincial tradition from which he sprang.

Spencer, like most rationalists, found it easier to discard
Christian theology than to divest himself of its moral assumptions. W.E. Houghton points out a paradox in intellectual
radicalism, namely that 'it produced a frightened clinging to
conservative morals, especially at a time when agnosticism
was under attack for its supposed tendency to destroy the
moral life.'[1] The 'cult of Earnestness' represented the response of Victorian intellectuals to the challenge of a
morality shorn of its religious basis. Like George Eliot,
Spencer found that 'the rejection of the doctrine of atone-
ment did not relieve one from the obligation to one's neighbour or a duty to oneself . . . religion could be cut off without abandoning reverence or morality.'[2] The search for a
soundly-based secular morality was also motivated by the
notion of religion as an agent of social cohesion and therefore of political stability. Its obsolescence seemed to betoken
the disintegration of the social fabric; it was not only re-
actionaries who equated atheism with revolution.

Another vestige of the Calvinist theology clung to Spencer
and his contemporaries long after the substance had been discarded; its philosophic necessitarianism.[3] Since secular
morality was necessitated by loss of faith, it is not surprising
that this quasi-predestinarian element crept in; morality is
vindicated by the ultimate triumph of the 'moral sense'.
Much later, Spencer is found describing the 'fittest' as the

---

[1] W.E. Houghton, *The Victorian Frame of Mind* (New Haven, Conn., 1957),
p. 238.
[2] J.M. Prest, *The Industrial Revolution in Coventry*, (Oxford, 1960), p. 6.
[3] See Peel, Chap. 4.

'evolutionary elect'. The danger in this certitude is the 'enervating fatalism' which Spencer, according to George Eliot, was so anxious to avoid, and which could rob human betterment of its motive force. This debilitating influence of necessitarianism was felt by John Stuart Mill, who recorded feeling 'as if I was scientifically proved to be the helpless slave of antecedent circumstances.'[1] Charles Bray, author of *The Philosophy of Necessity*, fended it off by the ingenious temporal device whereby the past could not have been otherwise but the future is malleable by free will.[2] This confusion between the 'necessitarian optimism' and the moral duty of man as a free agent which was based upon it recurs throughout Spencer's writings.[3]

His optimism was soon dissipated, not least because a cheek-by-jowl confrontation with contemporary business ethics destroyed for him the myth of an emergent morality: 'Examine into trade practices; read over business correspondence; or get a solicitor to detail his conversations with clients; you will find that in most cases conduct depends, not upon what is right, but upon what is legal.'[4] Spencer never ceased to campaign for rectitude, nor to emphasize the urgency of discovering and observing the 'laws of life', for 'if they really exist, then only by submission to them can anything permanently succeed.'[5] His youthful embroilment in politics thus laid the foundations of his political thinking for life, and his subsequent tergiversation on electoral reform should not be allowed to conceal the paramount importance of 'The Proper Sphere of Government' as the decisive, almost conclusive statement of his negative theory of state competence, and the inception of his search for a scientifically-couched, universally operative law governing all conduct, of which social evolution was the outcome, even though he very rarely afterwards made a personal appearance in the political arena.

---

[1] J.S. Mill, *An Autobiography* (London, 1879), pp. 168–9.
[2] J.M. Prest, op.cit., p. 8.
[3] C.F. H.S.'s treatment of the individual and the 'social organism' in Chap. 9, pp. 235–42.
[4] *S. Stat.*, p. 465.
[5] *S. Stat.*, p. 56.

RAILWAY ENGINEERING AND THE 'MORALS OF TRADE'

Having exhausted his enthusiasm for politics Spencer launched his first abortive but determined campaign to establish himself as a freelance journalist. Elated by the publication of 'The Proper Sphere of Government' in serial form, he decided to publish it as a pamphlet. This fiasco cost him £10 in printer's bills, of which he recouped, in sales, 14s. 3d. Undeterred, he resolved to seek his fortune in London, and settled himself there in May 1843.

He found the city lonely and inhospitable, and led a 'rather solitary life, frequently not speaking a score of words in a day for nearly a week together.'[1] The market was unreceptive; he sold three small pieces on phrenology in the Zoist, an esoteric magazine of minuscule circulation, and one on organic chemistry in the Philosophical Magazine, but by August 1844 he could not afford to stamp the letter requesting his father for a subsidy. He persevered, none the less: 'I have made up my mind . . . to make my way in the literary world, and it will be nothing but real necessity which will induce me to make another change.'[2] Real necessity it was which forced him to 'raise the siege' soon afterwards. Unlike many disgruntled literary aspirants he blamed himself: 'Evidently I took nothing like adequately decisive steps, but was very much in the mood of Mr. Micawber—waiting for something to turn up, and waiting in vain.'[3] Fortunately his entry into a competition to design an extension to London Docks brought him to the notice of W.B. Pritchard, with whom, after a further interlude of experiments and inventions, he resumed engineering.

The railway boom was now in full swing, and Spencer was brought into intimate contact with the burgeoning capitalism which he was later to glorify as a sociological 'type.'[4] First impressions, however, were far from favourable. 1844 had been a bumper year for railway construction, enriching shareholders, contractors, landowners and, indirectly, not a few M.P.s. There resulted a confluence of these interests 'uniting

---

[1] H.S. to E. Lott, 10 May, 1843, Aby i. 226.
[2] H.S. to W.G.S., Aug. 1843, L.L. i. 57.
[3] Aby i. 238.
[4] For H.S.'s notion of 'industrial society', see below, Chap. 10, pp. 249-50.

to urge on railway enterprise'. So securely profitable did railway investment appear that indiscriminate speculation ensued; as Spencer observed, 'It needed but to take a map of
Great Britain, and look out for a comparatively blank space
where there were towns of some size; run a pencil-line
through a string of them; gather together some known local
names, headed, if possible, by one with a title; issue flaring
advertisements; and people rushed in to take shares.'[1] W.B.
Pritchard's first pencil-line ran through Northampton, Warwick, and Worcester, and Spencer was agreeably occupied
during the autumn of 1845 surveying its course.

His constructive imagination was soon recognized, and he
was installed at Wilmington Square in London at the enormous salary of £4 a day, with the task of superintending his
employer's later, more fabulous ventures, including such unlikely starters as the 'Erewash Valley Extension' and the
'Warwick–Birmingham Canal-Railway Conversion', and of
convincing aristocratic figureheads and rich speculators of
their technical and commercial soundness. The overt rapacity
of these gentlemen disturbed him: 'Neither intellectually nor
morally did they commend themselves to me. In some, the
eager grasping at pecuniary advantage was very conspicuous.'[2]
He advised his father, who had joined the throng of small
investors, to withdraw while there was still time: 'I do not
speak without good grounds, for I have come in contact
with many of the directors and promoters of them, and I
know most certainly from their conversations that their
great, and I may say only, object, is to get their shares to a
good premium and then sell out.'[3]

Spencer was no less critical of his new employer, whose
career evoked for him the fable of the monkey 'which,
putting its hand into the jar of fruit, grasped so large a quantity that it could not get it out again.'[4] Deficient alike in
engineering skill and 'general culture', Pritchard 'furnished
an illustration of the success which may be achieved by audacity in pushing.'[5]   By March 1846, however, Pritchard's

[1] *Aby* i. 284.
[2] *Aby* i. 285.
[3] H.S. to W.G.S., Oct. 1845, *Aby* i.289.
[4] *Aby* i. 293.   [5] *Aby* i. 236.

'decoy-ducks' were losing confidence, and when plans for a further extension of the London–Birmingham line failed to pass Parliament, owing to defective drafting, the bubble burst. Pritchard spent the next four years suing the printers, and Spencer was pursued by subpoenas wherever he went. His last emolument as an engineer was an award of £80 under the winding-up act.

This concluding phase of Spencer's brief engineering career gave him his first and only view of capitalism at close quarters, and he recoiled. The antics of some railway proprietors even raised doubts as to the inappropriateness of state supervision of commerce. He certainly had no illusions about the self-regulating stability and probity of the stock-market, refusing shares in his own enterprises. Henceforth, although he remained a firm advocate of capitalism, Spencer never invested in shares.

Disillusionment prompted his decision to expose in print the venality of railway entrepreneurs and beneficiaries. The publication of his essay 'Railway morals and railway policy' in the *Edinburgh Review* (Oct. 1854) caused 'a greater stir than anything I ever wrote', and provoked threats of libel action.[1] It highlighted 'the genesis of that elaborate system of tactics by which companies are betrayed into ruinous undertakings which benefit the few at the cost of the many';[2] directors were accused of ballot-rigging, uttering threats, passing bribes and assuming a tone of offended dignity to stave off enquiries at shareholders' meetings. Although the worst frauds were perpetrated by cunning directorial oligarchies, ultimate responsibility was widely diffused. Shareholders acquiesced out of deference to power, wealth, and respectability, and thus incurred some blame. Landowners, at first stoutly opposing the encroachment of the railway on their properties, had become greedy for compensation. M.P.s, responsible for the final endorsement of ventures, had succumbed to corruption; no fewer than 157 of them appeared on the registers of new railway companies during 1845. Lawyers, scenting the enormous fees to be scavenged from contractual battles, employed 'vigorous

[1] *Aby* i. 451–52.
[2] H.S., 'Railway morals and railway policy', *Essays*, iii. 55.

efforts and sagacious devices' to promote fresh companies and widen the market. Railway engineers and contractors, 'insatiate as millionaires in general', and needing constant employment of plant, combined to create artificial confidence and attract investors. Railway directors, fattening on 'the belief in the identity of directorial and proprietorial interests', completed the cycle of self-perpetuating avarice. The greatest delinquencies concerned the appropriation of share-capital for investment in schemes not originally stipulated, so that investors were often ruined by the failure of enterprises they had never even heard of.

The chief significance of the article, however, lies in its conclusions of wider application concerning the justifiability of state interference in joint-stock enterprises and the ethics of big business. Nagging doubts about the desirability of state intervention as a result of his engineering experiences raised a discordant note in Spencer's anthem in praise of private enterprise. It is interesting to note that his denunciation of railway chicanery was based on a clear understanding of the separation of ownership from control in this sector of capitalism, which was ignored in all subsequent statements on the model of possessive individualism and perfect competition which he later constructed. The full implications of a prevalent and explicit immorality in the world of free enterprise were likewise never explored. Thus in 1854 Spencer contended that the context of a corporate enterprise induced 'laxity of principle', since the collective conscience was less compulsive than the individual. Yet in 'Representative government: what is it good for?' (1860) he was to argue strongly for the moral properties of private enterprise as part of his case against state interference.[1]

Spencer was never again to become personally involved in the world of business. He seemed, by the end of 1846 to have come seriously adrift, a young man of wide-ranging and undoubted talents but little sense of a purpose to which to apply them. Engineering was behind him, politics had disillusioned him and journalism offered him little prospect of security or independence. He did not, at the age of twenty-

---

[1] See below, Chap. 6, pp. 150-1.

six, show much indication of his future eminence, but his mind seethed with a ceaseless ferment of ideas, out of which was gradually maturing the project which would give direction to his life and a lasting achievement to his name.

3

INTELLECTUAL UNIFICATION, 1846–1860

Between his departure from the railway industry in 1846 and the launching of the *Synthetic Philosophy* in 1860, Spencer moved from a position of relative insecurity and indecision to one in which his whole life appeared to be dedicated to the missionary dissemination of a single idea. To his already fixed political dogma he was to add an equally comprehensive and inflexible metaphysical theory (or scientific synthesis as he preferred to regard it), the product of a gradual, uninterrupted unification of his speculative thought, described in theoretical detail at the end of this chapter.

The bulk of this chapter is concerned with the changes in his personal situation and environment which helped him to attain this new clarity of thought. In 1860 he was forty years old, resigned to bachelorhood, and intellectually committed. He had moved to London, initially to join the staff of the *Economist*, where the influence of Thomas Hodgskin helped to confirm and strengthen him in his political beliefs. In the capital he found a new, lively, and intellectually formidable circle of friends, and won their acceptance, and that of a restricted but not insignificant circle of readers, as a thinker of considerable ability and originality. On a grimmer note, he had by 1860 suffered a serious breakdown of his nervous system, the first in a long series of such disorders which were to mar the remainder of his life.

For Spencer the literary landmark of these years was the publication, in 1851, of *Social Statics: the conditions essential to human happiness specified, and the first of them developed*, a sophisticated treatise on political ethics, which made his reputation and contained, side by side with the perfected formulation of his political individualism, significant traces of his developing interest in the theory of social evolution. The ensuing decade was spent in pursuing and refining this concept until, in 1860, Spencer was sufficiently confident of it to renounce all other commitments and consign the rest of his life to expounding it and to demonstrating its universality.

After leaving the railway industry Spencer continued for a time to indulge his inventive urge. His projects ranged from a flying machine, 'combining terrestrial traction with aerial suspension' to a binding-pin, which he succeeded in having manufactured. Later contributions to technological advance included a planing-machine, a levelling-stave, a system for raising water, a 'revolutionary' method of boot-making, an excruciating adjustable bed for invalids, and a machine which effected euthanasia by centrifugal force, which was never tested 'owing to lack of space'. By the end of 1847 he had abandoned hope of 'making a fortune by inventions'.

Spencer's life during this period had no pattern: merely a succession of ephemeral enthusiasms. The year 1846, however, saw the inception of a scheme that was to lead much further, the writing of *Social Statics*: 'at what time was formed the resolution to set forth my views on political ethics is uncertain, but during these early months of 1846 I commenced a course of reading in furtherance of my project.'[1] He had, as yet, no intention of making authorship his career, but the manifest shortcomings of 'The Proper Sphere of Government' prompted him, in the first instance, to seek a 'common principle' on which its doctrines could be based; a dissatisfaction 'not so much with the conclusions set forth, as with the foundations on which they stood.'[2] By April 1847 the large mass of material which he had collected was beginning to 'ferment violently' and during the summer he commenced to write.

With autobiographical hindsight Spencer saw the watershed between his aimless phase and the ensuing dynamic period as his appointment to the sub-editorship of *The Economist*, whose editor-proprietor, James Wilson,[3] sought to turn it into 'the organ of the mercantile world'. Thomas Spencer had been a friend of Wilson since their days in the anti-Corn Law League, and when the sub-editorship fell

[1] *Aby* i. 304.
[2] *Aby* i. 305.
[3] Not the James Wilson for whom H.S. worked on the *Pilot*.

vacant he recommended his nephew. Two interviews were arranged, and 'The Proper Sphere of Government' submitted for consideration. Spencer was selected from seventy applicants and offered a salary of £100 per annum, cheap accommodation above the editorial office in the Strand, and bonus payments for leading articles. It met his needs precisely: security, financial independence, and spare time. In December 1848 Spencer left Derby for London 'to commence the journalistic studies which, in course of years, led, step by step, to my special business in life.'[1]

It was in the offices of *The Economist* that Spencer's individualism hardened to an adamantine consistency. His colleagues included James Wilson, who elevated the principle of *laissez-faire* almost to the status of a religion, Nassau Senior, after David Ricardo its premier economist, and Thomas Hodgskin, arguably the greatest single influence on Spencer's thought. *The Economist* not only widely propagated *laissez-faire* but helped to formulate and elucidate it.[2] The identity of 'self-love and social' was insisted upon almost obsessively in its pages: 'if the pursuit of self-interest, left equally for all, does not lead to the general welfare, no system of government can accomplish it.'[3] The school of thought from which it drew its inspiration stretched back via Jeremy Bentham to Adam Smith. Bentham, although his *Constitutional Code* carried a prototype of modern interventionist government, was nevertheless suspicious of the state: 'The general rule is that nothing ought to be done or attempted by government. The motto or watchword of government . . . ought to be—"Be Quiet".'[4] Adam Smith, in *An Enquiry into the Nature and Causes of the Wealth of Nations* not only preached free trade, but associated the negative role of government with the natural upward development of civilization:

---

[1] *Aby* 1. 337.
[2] See G.Gordon, 'The London *Economist* and the high-tide of *laissez-faire*', *Journal of Political Economy*, lxiii. 1955.
[3] The *Economist*, 2 Nov. 1846.
[4] Cited in R.B. McCallum, *The Liberal Party from Grey to Asquith* (London, 1963), p. 45.

Little else is requisite to carry a state to the highest degree of opulence from the lowest barbarism but peace, easy taxes and a tolerable administration of justice; all the rest being brought out by the natural order of things. All governments which thwart its natural course, or which endeavour to arrest the progress of society at a particular point are unnatural, and to support themselves are obliged to be oppressive and tyrannical.[1]

Spencer was continually being reminded of this in the course of his duties, which consisted mainly of abstracting from newspapers material pertaining to 'matters of contemporary policy', on which *The Economist* then passed judgement from a *laissez-faire* viewpoint. During Spencer's period of employment this technique was applied, *inter alia*, to Trades Unionism, Socialism, sanitary regulations and state education. All figure prominently in *Social Statics* as transgressions against 'natural law'.

The strongest personal link between this individualistic tradition and Spencer was Thomas Hodgskin. Hodgskin was an anti-Benthamite radical whose proletarian sympathies alarmed fellow-radicals, but who worked assiduously to extend the principle of *laissez-faire* from economics to society at large. He joined *The Economist* in 1846, and contributed regularly until 1857. His association with Spencer as subeditor must have been close during the years (1848–51) in which *Social Statics* was undergoing the final stages of preparation. The broad concurrence of its views with those of Hodgskin is hardly coincidental.

Thomas Hodgskin, following William Godwin, believed in natural rights and natural law, on which he based his repudiation of utilitarianism. He viewed nature, like Spencer after him, as an enlightened despot, 'absolute in the moral as in the physical world, governing and regulating every part with her thorough mastery, but kindly compassionate to the infancy of her children.'[2] She had, however, a sterner side, which the activities of 'meddling philanthropists and factitious demagogues' succeed only in making more implacable:

---

[1] Loc. cit.
[2] T. Hodgskin, *Natural and artificial rights in land contrasted* (London, 1832), p. 59.

'Suffering and evil are nature's admonitions; they cannot be got rid of, and the impatient attempts to banish them from the world by legislation, before benevolence has learned their object and their end, have always been more productive of evil than of good.'[1] Hodgskin's anti-interventionism, then, was based on a notion of beneficent social evolution, through which nature works to purge the world of misery. Hodgskin presaged Spencer's disdain of man-made laws, believing that 'all evils are due to man's interference with the universe'. He predicted the evanescence of government, and described a crude, episodic, and deterministic scheme of historical development, proceeding from 'nomadic' to 'scientific' modes of social organization. His influence is also clearly discernible in Spencer's early treatment of the 'land question'. He based property-rights on labour as the source of wealth, maintaining that 'All the effects usually attributed to the accumulation of circulating capital are derived from the accumulation or storing up of skilled labour.'[2] His *The Natural and Artificial Rights in Land Contrasted* (1832) distinguished between the valid rights of the people to the land, based on their labour, and the inequitable claims of the aristocracy, based on conquest.

Almost the whole of *Social Statics* could be interpreted as an elaboration of the theories of Thomas Hodgskin, whose contribution nevertheless goes unacknowledged (Spencer's *Autobiography* awards him one incidental mention). This is partly because of Spencer's normal reticence on the subject of intellectual obligation, and partly because of Hodgskin's later reputation as a socialist luminary. *Labour Defended against the Claims of Capital* remained his best-known work; Karl Marx acknowledged his influence and trade unionists drew strength from his advocacy of free combination. When the political cohorts of the late nineteenth century formed up, Spencer and Hodgskin were on different sides. Yet the difference was occasioned by the selection of priorities drawn from near-identical premises. Thus, where Spencer denounced the Corn Laws, Hodgskin wrote of them: 'Execrable

[1] G. Gordon, op.cit., p. 475.
[2] T. Hodgskin, *Labour defended against the claims of capital* (London, 1922), p. 49.

as they are in principle, and mischievous to the whole community, they do not impose anything like so heavy a tax on the labourer as capital.'[1]

Herbert Spencer's five-year sojourn with *The Economist* constituted, in retrospect at least, a sort of golden age. His daily existence was comfortable, leisurely, and pleasurable, and although he became more deeply absorbed in his literary enterprise, for the first time in his life he felt no pressure. He saw James Wilson about once a month, and contributed no leaders, considering his private work to be of greater importance than the extra remuneration. None the less he gave satisfaction: 'I have been complimented . . . upon the improvement the paper has undergone, more particularly in the news department, under my administration.'[2] He spent his working day, which ended at 1.00 p.m., scrutinizing the daily papers for controversial material, and farming out books to reviewers (the latter a task which kept his finger firmly on the pulse of contemporary intellectual life). He passed his afternoons aimlessly, browsing in books and periodicals, but devoted most evenings, when not taking advantage of the complimentary theatre or opera tickets that flowed into his office, to serious writing and research. He remained brightly optimistic about his literary project, regarding it as 'popular in its aspirations . . . well fitted to the time, and written in a style that is likely to commend it to the general reader.'[3] His father's critical verdict was guarded; he approved of the chapters on sanitation and education, but noted in others 'an unnecessary amount of bitterness'. *Social Statics* was completed during the summer of 1850.

It ran into difficulties immediately. Its rationalism and weightiness told against it as a commercial proposition, and Spencer secured its publication only by borrowing money to offset production costs. Its publisher was John Chapman, editor of the nonconformist journal the *Leader* (to which Spencer, because of its 'socialistic' reputation, contributed anonymously), and at that time 'the only respectable publisher

---

[1] Ibid., p. 77.
[2] H.S. to his mother, Dec. 1848, *L.L.* i. 74.
[3] H.S. to W.G.S., 1 Apr. 1849, *L.L.* i. 74–5.

through whom could be issued books which were tacitly or avowedly rationalistic.'[1] The necessary introduction was made, inevitably, by Thomas Spencer. Chapman gave the work the benefit of three lengthy and eulogistic reviews in the *Leader*, and *Social Statics* was more widely and favourably received than most subsequent offerings. *The Economist*, in particular, was predictably enthusiastic: 'though the high praise is qualified with some blame, there is not more of this than is needful to prevent the suspicion that I had written the review myself.'[2] The first cherished suggestions of fame began to filter through to him; three written requests for his autograph arrived, and a 'working stonemason' offered to restore the Chapman family monument in return for a copy of *Social Statics*.

Spencer's social life during this period is of central importance, for he cultivated a new, brilliant vintage of friends, while some of the more featureless of his former acquaintances dropped away. G.B.W. Jackson emigrated to New Zealand, where he drowned shortly afterwards: 'Though the world did not lose in him a bright intellect', wrote Spencer, a trifle guardedly, 'yet it lost a fine nature.'[3] Family influence, however, persisted as strongly as ever. He kept up a voluminous correspondence with his father, and Thomas Spencer, his nature suitably 'improved by misfortune', moved to Notting Hill in 1849. Herbert unfailingly spent his Sunday evenings there until his uncle's death in 1853.

Spencer's most fruitful and exciting social engagements, however, were the regular soirées given by John Chapman, who brought him into contact with the most eminent writers and thinkers of his day, including Charles Kingsley, Frances Newman, Francis Galton, Robert Browning, James Froude, Frederick Harrison, and John Tyndall. Spencer seems to have blended happily into this bright, vigorous circle, and swiftly acquired a reputation for his conversational stamina and irrepressible enthusiasm for his evolutionary mission. Of Chapman's circle John Morley afterwards wrote: 'I have never

[1] *Aby* ii. 53.
[2] H.S. to W.G.S., 8 Feb. 1851, *L.L.* i. 76.
[3] *Aby* i. 371.

known such a high perfection of social intercourse.'[1] The one discordant note was struck by Spencer's meeting with Thomas Carlyle, his *bête noire* of irrationalism, who 'displayed an inability to think discreditable to an ordinary cultivated intelligence, much more to one ranked as a thinker.'[2] His thoughtless vehemence, and his 'daily secretion of curses which he had to vent on somebody or something' greatly offended Spencer's rational sensibilities. They shared an instant and inveterate detestation.

At this stage Spencer began to display the characteristic of which he was most proud, his 'constitutional' disdain of authority and convention. He regarded nonconformity of dress and manners as integral to his political rejection of a society framed in error, a gesture of calculated defiance towards the sinister 'authority' enslaving the perceptions of those around him. His unorthodoxies were frequently petty; he amused himself on Sunday mornings by walking in the opposite direction to the stream of churchgoers, and in old age boasted of having 'intentionally refrained' from University Boat Races and cricket matches at Lords. In 'Manners and Fashions' (1854), however, he expounded the role of the 'revolutionary of custom' in more heroic terms.

The phenomena of fashion, which he found to be remotely descended forms of obeisance to autocratic rulers, shared their authoritarian character: 'All regulations, formal or virtual, have a common character; they are all limitations of man's freedom.'[3] Evolved out of forgotten forms of hierarchical deference we have 'a reign of mere whim, of unreason, of change for the sake of change' regulated by 'spendthrifts and idlers, dandies and silly women.'[4] This castigation of 'society' echoes the contempt of respectable Dissent for the frivolous, parasitic existence of the leisured class, and the determination of members of the radical intelligentsia to 'distinguish, in conduct as well as concept, the sham from the genuine, appearance from reality'. Spencer viewed himself as a martyr to conformity: 'To the true reformer no institution

[1] J. Morley, *Recollections* (London, 1917), i. 371.
[2] *Aby* i. 381.
[3] H.S., 'Manners and Fashions', *Essays,* iii. 4.
[4] Ibid., iii. 30.

is sacred, no belief above criticism . . . Manifestly, the fire of sneers and angry glances which he has to bear is poured down upon him because he will not bow down to the idol which society has set up.'[1] His commitment to the martyr's crown, however, was strictly limited. When, in later life, he was invited to attend a Foreign Office reception for Tsar Alexander III of Russia he declined because of his 'insuperable objection' to wearing a levee dress. The invitation was then repeated, on the understanding that he could come as he liked, but he again refused, this time on the grounds that he would look too conspicuous.[2] His rebellion against the prevailing social mores never went beyond the wearing of 'primly neat but quaintly unconventional garments.'[3]

At the personal level close and enduring friendships were forged at this time. In 1850 Spencer met George Lewes, author of *Problems of Life and Mind* and *A Biographical History of Philosophy*, and later composer of the splendid epigram: 'With Spencer, everything is continually evolving except his own theories.' Spencer found it 'impossible to be dull in his company', and accompanied him on long, discursive country rambles, sharpening his concepts of evolution against Lewes's scepticism. At about the same time he met Marian Evans who, as yet uncommitted to novel-writing, edited the *Westminster Review* (owned by Chapman) in the office next door to Spencer's own. Throughout 1852 they met every day, frequently visited the opera or theatre, and became the subject of gossip. Marian's correspondence speaks of their 'delightful camaraderie', but an oblique reference by Spencer suggests that only his perfectionism prevented the consummation of their spiritual alliance in marriage: 'Physical beauty is a *sine qua non* with me; as was once unhappily proved where the intellectual traits and emotional traits were of the highest.'[4] He found Marian distressingly ugly, and was anxious to minimize the depth of their relationship: 'There were reports that I was in love with her, and that we were about to be married. But neither of these reports was

[1] Ibid., iii. 33-4.
[2] F. Galton, 'Personal reminiscences of Herbert Spencer', *L.L.* ii. 262.
[3] Webb, p. 25.
[4] *Aby* ii. 445.

true.'[1] For her part, Marian found more than camaraderie in the arms of George Lewes, to whom Spencer himself introduced her in 1851. The three remained friends throughout the duration of the 'domestic association' which ensued.

Other important friendships date from this period. In 1850 Spencer met Octavius Smith, a dissenter and individualist, whose intellectual support and warm companionship were to be indispensable during the lonely years to come. 'In later years', wrote Spencer, 'I owed him the larger part of my chief pleasures in life.'[2] In 1852, while planning a book on population, Spencer came across a paper on Hydrozoa, whose thesis accorded with the pre-Darwinian 'development theory'. Its author was Thomas Huxley, whom Spencer approached for advice and information, and there ensued a lifelong friendship. Huxley campaigned indefatigably in the evolutionary cause, and his collaboration was priceless to a self-educated synthetic philosopher. All Spencer's biological proofs were submitted to Huxley, on whom he depended heavily for factual accuracy, 'There is no-one', he wrote much later, 'whose judgement on all subjects I so much respect, or whose friendship I so highly value.'[3] Their lives were nearly coterminous, and apart from one quarrel in the 1880s they remained firm friends.

At Christmas 1844 Spencer had first met Richard Potter, and from 1846 was a regular visitor to the Potters' house at Standish in Gloucestershire. Potter, an ex-rentier turned successful businessman (he was later Chairman of the Great Western Railway) was, for Spencer, 'the most lovable being I have yet seen.'[4] He remained totally indifferent to Spencerian philosophy, dismissing it, with the successful businessman's brutal logic, as 'mere words', but this established no tension between them. Spencer's affection for Mrs. Potter was equally warm. A disciple of David Ricardo and Rev. Thomas Malthus, she argued with him late into the night, long after her husband had given up and gone to bed. Probably their greatest gift to Spencer, apart from the tranquillity of their

[1] *Aby* i. 399.
[2] *Aby* i. 375–6.
[3] H.S. to T.H. Huxley, 1 June 1872, Hux. Coll., vol. vii.
[4] H.S. to E. Lott, 1 Feb. 1844, *Aby* i. 260–1.

country residence, was the affection and understanding, later in life, of their youngest daughter, afterwards Beatrice Webb.

Spencer spent a fretful, anticlimactic year after the publication of *Social Statics*, revising his maiden work for a second edition and wrestling indecisively with the theoretical problems it had raised. Restless and dissatisfied, he considered emigrating to New Zealand, believing for some reason that his matrimonial prospects would thereby be enhanced, but decided that his parents were too old for the journey. He eventually resolved to leave *The Economist* and to concentrate on coming to terms with 'the overwhelming accumulation of thoughts which now bother me'. He hoped to support himself by freelance journalism: 'I find', he confided to his father, 'that five and six hundred a year are common incomes obtained by the pens of men of no great original talent.'[1] When, in 1853, the death of his uncle Thomas brought him a legacy of £500, assuring him of at least a respite of financial security, he gave in his notice.

The market for serious periodical literature was probably at its peak at this time, enabling Spencer to place several important essays. These included 'Over-legislation',[2] 'Manners and Fashions',[3] and 'Railway Morals and Railway Policy.'[4] These literary exertions, however, inflicted on Spencer a serious degree of nervous strain. He had already taken to the fretful meandering from lodging to lodging which characterized the remainder of his life, and had first experienced insomnia during the writing of *Social Statics*. In the autumn of 1853 he suffered 'cardiac disturbances', underwent hydropathic treatment and convalesced in France. Early in 1854 he returned, to begin writing a long-projected study of evolutionary psychology ('my private opinion is that it will stand beside Newton's *Principia*').[5] The struggle to complete it brought on his first nervous breakdown. From the outset he travelled constantly in search of a restful environment, from Treport, which he found monotonous, to Paris, where he

[1] H.S. to W.G.S., 3 Sept. 1851, *Aby.* i. 385.
[2] *Westminster Review*, July 1853.
[3] *Westminister Review*, Apr. 1854.
[4] *Edinburgh Review*, Oct. 1854.
[5] *L.L.* i. 98.

found no friends, to Brighton, where he squabbled with those he had, to London, where he was lonely again. He finished the book in Derby, writing a few lines at a time, interspersed with hours of pottering in the garden, 'a persistence in physiological wrongdoing which brought on further serious symptoms.'[1] The bizarre remedies which he devised at this time, which included sleeping with his head swathed in a wet salt rag 'to keep up the cerebral circulation', did little to alleviate his distress.

The final blow to his tottering nervous stability was dealt by the excitement of a public dinner, attended by Edwin Chadwick, Frederick Ward, and Robert Owen, where 'I had the audacity to make an attack on all these sanitary leaders—charging them with garbling evidence, misleading the public etc.' The ensuing altercation, he claimed, was ruinous; 'Health, in the full sense of the word, was never again to be overtaken.'[2] His breakdown clearly resulted from a combination of overwork and financial insecurity. The *Psychology*, furthermore, raised more questions than it resolved, intensifying his search for unifying evolutionary principles. Having finally formulated these, in 1860, he committed himself to a massive effort of exposition. Work had become compulsive, and recovery from his nervous disorders was indefinitely postponed, so that his narrative of the ensuing years becomes increasingly preoccupied with physical and neurological deterioration and hypochondria.

The *Psychology* was an ill-fated venture. Arduous negotiations with publishers foundered upon its implied agnosticism, and Spencer was forced once again to make himself liable for any losses incurred. It was badly received. The *Nonconformist*, stamping-ground of Spencerian radicalism, attacked it as 'materialistic and atheistic', while Richard Hutton, in the *National Review* dealt scathingly with it under the title 'Modern Atheism'. Only 200 copies had been sold by April 1856. 'The days', reflected Spencer ruefully, 'were days when the special-creation doctrine passed almost unquestioned.'[3]

---

[1] *Aby* i. 467.   [2] *Aby* i. 468.
[3] *Aby* 1. 472.

Having completed the *Psychology* Spencer resumed his quest for health. At Treport an overdose of quinine brought on 'a state of hot head that lasted several days'. The supposedly therapeutic properties of the open air then took him to Devonshire, where he threw himself enthusiastically into grubbing up tree stumps: 'It is not simply exhausting exercise, but it is interesting, and fully occupies the attention.'[1] At Standish, he put his rationality on trial by sleeping in a reputedly haunted room, 'a rather sharp test for one labouring under a nervous disorder.'[2] It took his first of many visits to Ardtornish, the Octavius Smiths' house on Loch Aline, to restore him: 'I am enjoying myself much here—so much so that I think scarcely at all about myself or my ailments . . . I do not remember to have had any sensations in the head for a week or more.'[3] The odyssey was completed with another trip to Paris, where he made the brief acquaintance of Auguste Comte. The two synthetic philosophers, more alike than either cared to admit, were mutually disenchanted, and their conversation was in any case stunted by Spencer's hesitant French. Having at last exhausted the compulsion to travel, he returned to Derby in November 1856.

The year 1857 was devoted largely to the compilation and revision of his first volume of essays. The first days of 1858, however, saw 'the inception of the undertaking to which the rest of my life was to be devoted'. The correction of his essays for republication had prompted Spencer to seek out principles common to them all, and there resulted a sudden, blinding revelation of the universality of their underlying assumptions: 'Within the last ten days my ideas on various matters have suddenly crystallised into a complete whole. Many things which were before lying separate have fallen into their places as harmonious parts of a system that admits of logical development from the simplest general principles.'[4]

This sudden systematization created practical problems. A multi-volume scientific synthesis was commercially unpromising, and with seriously impaired health the prospect of

---

[1] H.S. to his mother, 7 Feb. 1856; *L.L.* i. 103–4.
[2] *Aby* i. 480.
[3] H.S. to W.G.S., 16 Aug. 1856, *Aby* i. 490–1.
[4] H.S. to W.G.S., 9 Jan. 1858, *Aby* ii. 17.

combining an undertaking of this magnitude with the journalistic endeavours necessary to finance it seemed bleak. He therefore began to cast about for an alternative source of income, deciding, with bland disregard of ethical consistency, to join the 'swarms of officials'. In July he approached John Stuart Mill with a request to find him a sinecure in the Indian Administration 'which would give me an income sufficient for my modest bachelor needs, while it would allow adequate leisure for the prosecution of these aims.'[1] Mill's reply was 'sympathetic, but disappointing'. Spencer subsequently applied for a prison governorship, a distributorship of stamps, a consular post, and even a seat on the Educational Commission. By the end of 1858 his financial position was desperate, his capital swallowed up in convalescent peregrinations, and his earning capacity reduced by illness. Dreams of £600 a year had long since evaporated: 'it was not easy for me, though practising every economy, to meet my expenses.'[2] The prospect of a decisive start to *The System of Philosophy* seemed to recede, yet Spencer refused to give up hope.

In the autumn of 1859 he finally hit upon subscription as the means of establishing an independent financial basis from which to launch his project. His subscribers would each pay 10s. yearly, and receive four quarterly instalments of six sheets (80–90 pages) until the series was complete. On 29 March 1860, after a winter spent in canvassing support, he issued a comprehensive programme of *The Synthetic Philosophy*, with an impressive list of endorsements by eminent scientists, writers, and public figures enrolled through the good offices of John Stuart Mill, Thomas Huxley, and John Tyndall. The total of subscribers reached 440. Their contribution, less the cost of binding and printing, left Spencer a marginal income of £120 per annum, but this was augmented by the timely conversion to the evolutionary cause of Edward L. Youmans, 'a popular and intelligent lecturer on scientific subjects' in America. In the capacities of missionary and fiscal provider he rapidly proved himself indispensable. He mustered 200 transatlantic subscriptions, and 'from that

[1] H.S. to J.S. Mill, 29 July 1858, *Aby* ii. 23.
[2] *Aby* ii. 12.

time . . . devoted his life mainly to spreading throughout the United States the doctrine of Evolution.'[1] In April 1860 Spencer published 'Parliamentary Reform; its dangers and safeguards' in the *Westminster Review*. Thereafter 'years passed before I interrupted my chief work to do anything more in the way of essay-writing.'[2]

THE DEVELOPMENT OF THE THEORY OF EVOLUTION

The unification of Spencer's evolutionary theory in 1860 was the culmination of a long period of speculation and the integration of a series of initially unrelated ideas. Two motives inspired him: a consuming love of nature and a compulsive tendency to synthesize. Spencer denied that he was a materialist, arguing that for him, science retained a transcendental element, since phenomenological knowledge 'always leaves us in presence of the inscrutable'. A geometrical theorem could stimulate in him 'feelings of wonder and awe;'[3] 'there appears to be in me', he declared, 'a dash of the artist, which has all along made the achievement of beauty a stimulus; not of course beauty as commonly conceived, but such beauty as may exist in a philosophical structure.'[4] At the same time, he was enslaved by his 'analytical tendency' to reduce everything to a state of ordered simplicity; 'I have a great horror of confusion, and never could bear anything that was not straightforward.'[5] For this reason he relentlessly pursued the theory of evolution back to its last logical reduction, and was to spend the rest of his life trying to organize the sum total of human knowledge into conformity with it.

The perfected theory of evolution as expounded in *First Principles* synthesized a variety of scientific and philosophical lines of thought, some picked up at random from books, others instilled during his education, some seemingly (to Spencer at least) intuitive. The process by which he achieved it throws light on certain of its difficulties of interpretation, which may be ascribed to the eclectic manner of its formulation. By tracing the theory from its source, furthermore,

[1] *Aby* ii. 53.   [2] *Aby* ii. 55.
[3] *Aby* i. 165.   [4] *Aby* ii. 451.
[5] H.S. to W.G.S., 23 Aug. 1840, *Aby* i. 173.

it is possible to isolate the important contributions of other thinkers to it.

The starting-point of Spencer's quest was his repudiation of Christianity. His early writings refer to the 'Divine Law', the 'Almighty', and the 'Creator', but rarely to 'God', and his last monotheistic references occur in the 1851 edition of *Social Statics*, though he may have discarded his family's faith long before. Of the year 1840, he wrote: 'My father's letters written during this period from time to time called my attention to religious questions and appealed to religious feelings—seeking for some response. So far as I can remember, they met with none.'[1]

He found Christianity both intellectually and emotionally inimical at an early age. His cultivated empiricism was affronted by a belief which required the suspension of rationality; his independence of spirit and strong sense of self by the implications of worship: 'the expression of adoration of a personal being, the utterance of laudations, and the humble professions of obedience, never found in me any echoes.'[2] When, in 1847, his father charged him with succumbing to the influence of Ralph Waldo Emerson, he replied that his 'rationalistic convictions . . . had been slowly and insensibly growing for years; being, as already intimated, caused by perception of the radical incongruity between the Bible and the order of nature. Such writings as those of Emerson and Carlyle simply served to present to me my own convictions under other aspects.'[3] He had arrived at a militant agnosticism, declaring himself 'content to leave the question as the "insoluble mystery" ', and in *First Principles* the 'insoluble mystery' became formulated as the Unknowable. This repudiation of Christianity was an essential prelude to the development of a naturalistic philosophy of evolution. William George Spencer, however, refused to give up hope: 'From what I see of my son's mind', he wrote in 1860, 'it appears to me that the laws of nature are to him what revealed religion is to us . . . and so long as he makes a holy use of his present knowledge, it is my privilege to believe that he will be led into all truth.'[4]

[1] *Aby* i. 150.   [2] *Aby* i. 151.
[3] *Aby* i. 312.   [4] W.G.S. to Mrs. White-Cooper, Jan. 1860, *Aby* i. 556.

Scepticism had begun to overtake Spencer as early as 1840, when he read Charles Lyell's *The Principles of Geology*, one chapter of which was devoted to a refutation of Jean Baptiste Lamarck's view of the origin of species. Characteristically, Spencer's inclination was to accept Lamarck's version 'due to its harmony with that general idea of the order of nature towards which I have, throughout life, been growing.'[1] He regarded such sources as a means of confirming pre-existing thoughts; of his acceptance of Lamarckianism he wrote 'It seems as though I knew by intuition the necessity of equivalence between cause and effect.'[2] It was a decisive breakthrough, almost, in Spencer's eyes, a revelation: 'inadequate as was the evidence, and great as were the difficulties in the way . . . my belief in [the development theory] never afterwards wavered, much as I was, in after years, ridiculed for entertaining it.'[3] His published writings after this date reveal the progress of Spencer's evolutionary ideas towards coherence and universality.

'The Proper Sphere of Government' (1842) contains evidence of the growth of embryonic evolutionary convictions. Lamarck has taken root, but the soil was already fertilized by longer-held assumptions, the most important being 'an unhesitating belief that the phenomena of both individual life and social life conform to law.'[4] 'Society', he writes, 'has as certainly its governing principles as man . . . their action may be more complicated, and it may be more difficult to obey them, but nevertheless analogy shows that they must exist.'[5] Lamarck finds echoes in Spencer's insistence on the progressive adaptation of constitution to conditions, which confirms an already strong leaning towards a materialistic and evolutionary interpretation of nature: 'Instincts and organs are preserved only so long as they are required. Place a tribe of animals in a situation where one of their attributes is unnecessary, take away its natural exercise—diminish its ability and you will gradually destroy its power.'[6] In the years immediately following, the crudeness of this rudimentary exposition prompted Spencer 'to enter on new fields

---

[1] *Aby* i. 176.   [2] *Aby* i. 152.
[3] *Aby* ii. 177.   [4] *Aby* ii. 7.
[5] 'Proper Sphere', 15 June 1842.   [6] Ibid., 14 Dec. 1842.

of thought and enquiry.'[1] The period was one of ceaseless intellectual prospecting, embracing journalism, invention, and scientific experiment: 'New ideas of some kind daily occupied me.'[2]

The outcome of these investigations was *Social Statics*, which, though primarily a study in ethics, evinces a more highly-developed stage of several aspects of the development theory. 'Sympathy' and 'benevolence' are seen as faculties which grow as the scope for their exercise increases, a Lamarckian deduction of 'the inheritance of functionally-produced changes of structure'. The survival of the fittest makes an appearance as Spencer writes of the 'beneficence of the process by which, among animals and men, the inferior disappear and leave the superior to continue the race.'[3] The organic analogy with society is introduced, the most primitive societies being likened to the lowest animals, in what they are both shown to possess simple units exhibiting uniformity of function. The development theory itself was continually evolving:

In *Social Statics* there is everywhere manifested the belief in the evolution of man and of society. There is also manifested the belief that this evolution is in both cases determined by the incidental conditions —the actions of circumstances. And there is further . . . a recognition of the fact that organic and social evolution conform to the same law.[4]

At this stage, however, these components of evolutionary theory remained disorganized. Spencer's awareness of it in 1851 was little more sophisticated than a generalized conviction in the continuity of upward development decorated with various unrelated and hypothetical by-processes. The process of theoretical integration was haphazardly intuitive rather than strictly 'synthetic'. Contributory insights occurred at random. During a country ramble in 1850 George Lewes surprised Spencer by 'asserting the view that functional adaptation is the sole cause of development', while on another occasion scrutiny of a stray leaf suggested to Spencer a

[1] *Aby* ii. 273.
[2] H.S., 'The Filiation of Ideas', *L.L.* ii. 311.
[3] *L.L.* ii. 314.
[4] H.S., 'Reasons for Dissenting from the Philosophy of M. Comte', *Essays,* ii. 137-8.

symmetrical pattern to natural development. His reading of Milne Edwards's *The Physiological Division of Labour* 'gave greater distinction to pre-existing thoughts', but the catalyst which fused these scattered intuitions into a coherent theory was Spencer's chance discovery, in 1851, of Karl von Baer's principle of universal transformation, from homogeneity to heterogeneity. This new insight provided the inspiration for his next essay, 'The Development Hypothesis,'[1] in which 'there took a definite shape the germ out of which originated the general system of thought elaborated in subsequent years.'[2]

In 'A theory of population deduced from the general law of animal fertility' (1852), the demographic application of the evolutionary thesis thus far clarified, Spencer came within an ace of anticipating Charles Darwin's *Origin of Species*:

> All mankind in turn subject themselves more or less to the discipline described; they may or may not advance under it, but in the nature of things, only those who do advance under it eventually survive . . . for as those prematurely carried off must, in the average of cases, be those in whom the power of self-preservation is least, it unavoidably follows that those left behind to continue the race are those in whom the power of self-preservation is greatest—are the select of their generation.[3]

This passage was written seven years before the publication of Darwin's masterpiece. By an uncharacteristic failure to follow his reasoning through to a definite conclusion Spencer just missed the point: 'if so, this must be in all cases a cause of modification. Yet I completely overlooked this obvious corollary—was blind to the fact that here was a universally-operative factor in the development of species.'[4] Spencer, still adhering to Jean Lamarck's doctrine, neglected natural selection, saw the inheritance of functionally-produced modifications as the sole cause of evolution and failed to extrapolate from this social process a universal law. With a keen sense of *esprit de l'escalier* he wrote:

[1] *Leader,* Mar. 1852.
[2] *Aby* i. 388.
[3] 'Theory of population', pp. 499–500.
[4] *Aby* i. 390.

That which I failed to recognize was the cooperation of these actions in the struggle for existence and the survival of the fittest with the tendency to variation which organisms exhibit. The result being that I perceived only the power of these processes in producing a higher form of the same type, and did not perceive their power in producing divergencies, and consequent differentiations of species, and eventually of orders, genera and classes.[1]

To perfect his evolutionary hypothesis Spencer delved deeper in search of an ultimate cause. The observable manifestations of evolution assumed for him the character of the exposed tip of an iceberg; his interest now lay in exposing the dynamic properties of the submerged nine-tenths. In 1862 he had pursued the motive-force of evolution to its source.

During the writing of the *Psychology* the question arose of whether the trend from homogeneity to heterogeneity observable in psychological evolution was in fact universal: 'the question needed only to be asked to be answered affirmatively.'[2] At the same time he hit upon the idea of the 'multiplication of effects' (every cause produces more than one effect), and in January 1856 started work on the essay 'Progress, its law and cause',[3] which contained 'the inception of the general doctrine of evolution.'[4] Still the search continued for the ultimate *dénouement*. In 'Transcendental Physiology' (1857)[5] the plot thickened with the discovery of the 'instability of the homogenous', seemingly the prime mover of evolution (the term 'evolution' had here replaced 'development' for the first time). But the consummation of the theory eluded him. At Christmas 1857, watching ripples on a pond, he conceived of the universality of rhythm in natural forces, and deduced from it the 'persistence of force', a primitive forerunner of the conservation of energy theory. If this were to prove a universal trait of natural dynamics, then all phenomena must be related in terms of it.

The re-reading of his own essays on varied topics, which intensified this search for a common principle, had a more practical but no less momentous effect. On 6 January 1858

[1] Spencer Papers, University of London Library.
[2] H.S., 'The Filiation of Ideas', *L.L.* ii. 323.
[3] *Westminster Review*, Apr. 1857.
[4] *Aby* i. 402.
[5] *National Review*, Oct. 1857.

Spencer drew up his first *Sketch-Plan of the Synthetic Philosophy*. The urge to unify knowledge under the aegis of a single natural law suddenly materialized into the resolution to undertake an enormously ambitious, encyclopaedic synthesis of all the sciences, hence of all knowledge. His thoughts suddenly crystallized in this daunting project. He would formulate the rules of all transformation, all evolution, and subject each division of observable phenomena to them. The close resemblance between the scheme as thus suddenly conceived in, and the final layout of the *Synthetic Philosophy*, completed in 1896, surprised even Spencer. The comprehensive integration of the evolutionary hypothesis followed almost automatically upon realization of the need for it. *First Principles* (1862), the first instalment of the system, expressed 'not a stage in the development of the doctrine, but the developed doctrine itself.'[1]

SPENCER, DARWIN, AND COMTE

As a postcript to this rapid survey of the growth of the Spencerian theory of evolution, we may note its author's insistence that it constituted, appropriately enough, an evolutionary process. All his conclusions, he claimed, 'have been arrived at unawares, each as the ultimate outcome of a body of thoughts which grew slowly from a germ', and thus 'little by little, in unobtrusive ways, without conscious intention or appreciable effort, there would grow up a coherent and organised theory.'[2] It emerged involuntarily, almost organically, as though from some innate seed. Spencer was convinced that intellectual effort was self-defeating, and that one flash of intuition is worth a lifetime of stolid, *a posteriori* reasoning: 'a solution reached in the way described is more likely to be true than one reached in the pursuance of a determined effort [which] causes perversion of thought.'[3] This helps to confirm the contention that Spencer's evolution was allowed to develop out of his already finalized political convictions, even though he was later to describe *laissez-faire*

---

[1] *Aby* ii. 74. The fundamental laws of evolution as set forth in *First Principles* are recounted below, Chap. 8, pp. 192–7.
[2] *Aby* i. 400–1.
[3] *Aby* i. 401.

as a 'deduction' from evolutionary 'laws'. The use of evolution to bolster individualism thus involved Spencer in a circular re-validation of his own beliefs.

Spencer's willingness to convert intuitions into universal precepts suggests a high degree of intellectual self-confidence. This is reflected in a disdainful attitude to sources: 'All my life I have been a thinker and not a reader, being able to say with Hobbes that "if I had read as much as other men I would have known as little." '[1] He visualized a stream of autonomously-developing theory with few tributary sources, and was constitutionally averse to reading 'ideas and sentiments of alien kinds'. Immanuel Kant's *Critique of Pure Reason* and Plato's *Dialogues* were among the works which he discarded after the first few irritating pages, and when a friend asked his opinion of Thomas Henry Buckle's *History of Civilisation*, 'his reply was that on looking into the book he saw that its fundamental assumption was erroneous, and therefore did not care to read it.'[2] John Fiske drew attention to his 'incomprehensible way of absorbing knowledge through the pores of his skin . . . he never seemed to read books.'[3] This lack of systematic reading, whether prompted by concern for originality, or by arrogance, left Spencer, as he grew older, dangerously isolated from the mainstream of intellectual life, and vulnerable to hasty impressions usually gleaned from conversation, of what was going on there.

It also makes his theoretical sources a matter for conjecture. Jean Baptiste Lamarck's *Philosophie Sociologique* (1809), for example, had argued the mutability of species via the inheritance of acquired characteristics. This concept passed into English thought in Robert Chambers's seminal work *Vestiges of the Natural History of Creation* (1844). Spencer, if he never read Chambers, knew of the book's contents; he recalled 'surprising Mr. Lewes by rejecting the interpretations set forth in it',[4] yet elsewhere he admits to having read only 'books which promised to furnish illustrative material'. On rare occasions he notes that a particular item

---

[1] *L.L.* i. 247.
[2] A.R. Wallace, *My Life: a record of events and opinions* (London, 1905), ii. 31.
[3] J. Fiske, *Essays: literary and historical* (New York, 1902), ii. 205–6.
[4] *Aby* i. 348.

confirmed an intuition of his own, and, in the cases of Charles Lyell, Karl von Baer, and Samuel Taylor Coleridge's *Idea of Life*, that new concepts were suggested to him. Otherwise, there are no indications of intellectual obligation; indeed Spencer's pride in the originality of his system made him acutely sensitive to suggestions of derivitiveness. This preoccupation is most clearly illustrated by his determination to free himself from the shades of Charles Darwin and Auguste Comte, the two thinkers most often cited as having had a formative influence on him.

The phrase 'social Darwinism', frequently misapplied to Spencerian social theory, suggests a false perception of the relation between Charles Darwin and Herbert Spencer. Spencer would probably have relished Beatrice Webb's description of himself as Darwin's John the Baptist.[1] It was Spencer who coined the terms 'evolution' and 'survival of the fittest', but he candidly acknowledged the necessity of incorporating 'natural selection' into the body of his thought, an unusual admission of indebtedness: 'I have arrived at a point of view from which Darwin's doctrine of "Natural Selection" is seen to be absorbed into the general theory of evolution as I am interpreting it.'[2] He stoutly maintained, however, that his view of evolution in 1859 had been independently formulated, though in the *Autobiography* he was a little fastidious about proving it. In 1858 he sent Darwin a copy of his essays. Darwin's reply would have demonstrated his [Spencer's] originality, but 'I decided to omit it . . . I leave the error to be otherwise corrected.'[3] The correction was effected posthumously (as Spencer took good care that it would be)[4] by David Duncan, who quotes the letter in full: 'Your remarks on the general argument of the so-called "development theory" seem to me admirable . . . your argument could not have been improved on, and might have been quoted by me with great advantage.'[5]

---

[1] B. Webb, B.B.C. radio broadcast, 27 Feb. 1928, from transcript in the Passfield Collection, British Library of Political and Economic Science, vi. 79.
[2] H.S. to W.G.S., 9 June 1864, *Aby* ii. 99–100.
[3] *Aby* ii. 28.
[4] In the Spencer Papers the letter is marked 'very important' in Spencer's hand.
[5] Darwin to H.S., 25 Nov. 1858, *L.L.* i. 113.

Spencer and Darwin shared common sources and confronted a common problem, that of 'struggling towards a synthesis of struggle and progress.'[1] Both owed a substantial debt to Charles Lyell, who had demonstrated that 'processes observable in the present' could be held to account for the metamorphoses of the past; Darwin wrote 'I always feel as though half of my books came out of Lyell's brain.'[2] In their attitudes to Lyell, however, lies the clue to important distinctions between their visions of evolution. Lyell himself could not reconcile struggle with progress; he rejected Lamarck because he could not envisage an 'unfit' species surviving long enough to hand down its modifications through heredity. Spencer, following Lamarck, retained progress as a feature of evolutionary transformation. Darwin explained how species became transformed, but accepted that variations occurred spontaneously, and at random. Spencer's view of evolution was necessitarian, and therefore predictive; Darwin's was descriptive. The difference is neatly summarized by J.D.Y. Peel: 'Darwin's theory accounted for the secular transformation of each species by the mechanism of natural selection, while Spencer's attempted to explain the total configuration of nature, physical, organic and social, as well as its necessary process.'[3] This distinction becomes crucial where evolution is applied to society. Lamarck's inheritance of acquired characteristics is a plausible explanation of sociocultural growth, yet since Spencer maintained that nature and society obeyed the same laws, this involved the reconciliation of Lamarck with Darwin's theory of organic evolution based in the necessity of struggle. No other evolutionist besides Spencer was prepared to undertake this transposition; for Darwin especially, nature and society remained distinct.[4]

This emerges most clearly from their respective treatments of the Revd. Thomas Malthus, whose *Essay on the Principle of Population* probably did more to create the atmosphere in which 'social Darwinism' flourished than did any other work. Darwin once referred to natural selection as 'the doctrine of

[1] M. Harris, *The Rise of Anthropological Theory* (London, 1969), p. 113.
[2] Ibid., p. 112.
[3] Peel, p. 142.
[4] For a fuller discussion, see below, Chap. 9, pp. 225-9.

Malthus, applied to the whole animal and vegetable kingdom.'[1] Spencer based his own theory of population on a
critique of Malthus, but borrowed significantly nevertheless.
Where Darwin abstracted the stark element of struggle,
Spencer compounded from Malthus a synthesis of natural
competition with the Enlightenment view of the indefinite
perfectibility of men through Reason; struggle brings progress. From their selective approach to their sources, therefore, transpires the essential difference between Spencerian
and Darwinian evolution.

The two evolutionists, who had much else in common, including neurasthenic tendencies, corresponded amicably. Darwin once acclaimed Spencer as 'by far the greatest living
philosopher in England, perhaps equal to any that have lived',
but his respect was qualified by distrust of Spencer's *a priori*
strengths and *a posteriori* weaknesses: 'If he had trained himself to observe more, even at the expense of . . . some loss of
thinking power, he would have been a wonderful man.'[2]
Darwin's reputation has long and deservedly outlasted Spencer's, but to identify him as the father of evolutionary social
theory, relative merits notwithstanding, does less than justice
to Spencer.[3]

In 1854 was published Harriet Martineau's abridged trans-
lation of Auguste Comte's *Philosophie Posivitique*. Spencer
was surrounded at this time by positivists, including George
Lewes, George Eliot and Frederick Harrison, and he was to
expend much energy throughout his life denying that he was
a 'Comtist'. In 'Reasons for dissenting from the philosophy
of M. Comte',[4] Spencer saluted the *Philosophie Posivitique* as
a 'vast achievement', and its author as a man of 'remarkable
breadth of view, great originality, immense fertility of
thought, unusual power of generalisation.'[5] He even acknowledged certain points of concurrence between Comte's
attempt to systematize and extend the scope of scientific

---

[1] See R.M. Young, 'Malthus and the evolutionists', *Past and Present,* xliii, 1969.
[2] F. Darwin, *The Life and Letters of Charles Darwin* (London, 1887), iii. 120.
[3] See H.E. Barnes and H.Becker, *Social Thought from Lore to Science* (Washington, 1952), ii. 32.
[4] *Westminster Review,* Feb. 1864.
[5] H.S., 'Reasons for dissenting from the philosophy of M. Comte', *Essays,* ii. 211.

inquiry and his own, and between their underlying epistemo-
logical assumptions. These concurrences, however, related to
premises common to every scientific thinker: 'All men of
science have been more or less consistently positivists; and
the applicability of M. Comte's title to them no more makes
them his disciples, than does its applicability to men of
science who lived and died before M. Comte wrote, makes
them his disciples.'[1] Spencer declared that his perception of
the empirical basis of scientific inquiry, and of the currency
of universal natural laws, was no clearer for having read
Comte's affirmation of it, than it was before.

The differences between the principles distinctive of
Comte's system and Spencer's own, meanwhile, were fundamental. Spencer's repudiated Comte's pivotal 'law of the
three stages'; his own view of the development of philosophic
method was of evolution to the point at which philosophy
attains consciousness of a 'universal causal agency', but 'without any change in the nature of the process.'[2] Believing,
furthermore, that feelings were the crucial determinant of
both actions and ideas, he rejected Comte's view that ideas
governed the world. He also rejected Comte's triadic explanation of the development of the sciences, averring that each of
the three 'orders' of science, abstract, abstract-concrete, and
concrete, evolve simultaneously and in continuous interaction. Thus did Spencer dissociate himself from the organizing principles of Comte's system.

He found some of its secondary implications equally
repugnant. Comte held species to be immutable, in obvious
contradiction of evolutionary doctrine, and identified the
highest social state as that most intensively regulated by state
agencies and hierarchical in structure, a concept outrageous
to Spencer's individualism. The 'Religion of Humanity',
which Comte advocated as the necessary 'legitimising myth'
of secular society, was repudiated by Spencer, to whom all
religion was atavistic and self-abnegatory. Spencer archly conceded to Comtean thought 'the benefit of an antagonism
which cleared and developed my own views', his attempts to
refute it having contributed to the clarification of his

[1] H.S., op. cit., ii. 120.   [2] Ibid., ii. 126.

thoughts. Notwithstanding, the Comtean tag, like the Darwinian, was to pursue him into the twentieth century.

April 1860 constitutes a turning-point in Spencer's life and career. The first forty years had seen the development of his theories, political, social, and scientific, to a maturity from which, in their essentials, they were neither to progress nor to recede. The next forty years were a period of consolidation, exposition, and the trimming away from the evolutionary and individualist core of his thought the dispensable paraphernalia of unconsidered radicalism. He had set himself a monumental task, fourteen volumes, demanding enormous efforts of theoretical integrity and consistency, and a massive corpus of accurate factual evidence. For its completion he set himself the target of twenty years: 'a sanguine anticipation for one well in body and brain; and for one in my state . . . an absurd anticipation.'[1]

By 1860, then, Spencer had virtually ceased to function as a speculative thinker. The evolution subsequently undergone took the form of a gradual withdrawal from overt radicalism into apparent conservatism, a process rationalized by the application of the precepts of individualism and evolution.[2] Of these the former, chronologically first and more firmly rooted, was the more satisfying concept in terms of its logical consistency. Spencerian evolution, a composite theory made up of random intuitions and derivations, some contradictory, was further weakened by its author's stubborn refusal to endanger his hypothesis by wider reading. Spencer's political preconceptions demanded a theory which encompassed progress and struggle; Lamarck combined uneasily with Darwin, and the ensuing synthesis produced a 'scientific' strain of Spencerism at odds with its political premises. Hence arose the fundamental schism of Spencerian thought.

[1] *Aby* ii. 56.
[2] This process is described and analysed in Chap. 5, pp. 105–10.

4

WRITING THE *SYNTHETIC PHILOSOPHY*, 1860–1896

The second half of Spencer's life was devoted almost exclusively to writing the *Synthetic Philosophy*, a singleness of purpose amounting to self-enslavement. His momentous decision to launch his project was followed by thirty six years of unremitting and exhausting labour. The first two decades were not without their consolations; having surmounted his financial difficulties he was able to settle to a comfortable existence which combined stimulating companionship, an orderly working life and frequent recuperative holidays. However, the encroachment of nervous disorder, and a deepening loneliness underlay the superficial serenity, and in 1882 Spencer suffered a severe nervous breakdown. Thereafter the completion of his task was a bitter struggle against physical and psychological deterioration.

This chapter reviews the significant events of the period for Spencer, and examines his style of life, friendships, and the creative environment in which his *magnum opus* took shape. It contrasts Spencer as he saw himself with glimpses of Spencer as others saw him, at a time when his imagined idiosyncrasies, no less than his literary prowess, were making him a public figure. Finally, it relates the effort of completing the *Synthetic Philosophy* to his premature decline into neurotic senility.

Work commenced on 7 May 1860, but success must have seemed remote in the light of initial setbacks. His delicate neurological balance faltered before the abstractions of *First Principles*, and before the first chapter was complete he embarked upon a typical rambling itinerary in search of peace, quiet, and mental regeneration. Financial pressures, intensified by the expense of constant travel, began to be felt. His income from subscriptions, adequate on paper, shrivelled away in reality, prompting Spencer to remark of his subscribers, many of them prominent academics and writers, that he 'was not, and never have been, under the delusion that intellectual culture produces moral elevation.'[1] Crisis was averted by the death of his uncle William who, in the pursuance of a family feud made Herbert his principal beneficiary, but his bequest of £300 was more reprieve than release.

Nervous exhaustion and insomnia posed constant threats, and Spencer's life became a continual evasive action. Since 1858 he had performed all literary tasks through the medium of dictation, but found the strain of composition, though lessened, still very great, and restricted his efforts to a cautious three hours per day. He thought, according to James Collier, his first amanuensis, 'in platoons', the difficulty being less that of summoning his thoughts than of marshalling them:

Smoking half a cigar to promote the mental flow (the cigar carefully cut in two to prevent excess), his voice never rising or falling, the eyes faintly lit up with the thinker's faraway look . . . without changes of physiognomy or a single gesture, he passionlessly unrolled the panorama of his thought.[2]

He could sustain even spasmodic intellectual activity only for a limited period, and migrated northwards every autumn to recoup with the Octavius Smiths. His favourite relaxation, here as elsewhere, was fishing: 'Nothing else served so well to rest my brain and fit it for resumption of work.'[3] Ardtornish came rapidly to assume a crucial importance in Spencer's life as a reliable source of regeneration and refuge from his enervating toil.

In 1862, despite all tribulations, *First Principles* was belatedly finished. Completion of this, the pivotal and most mentally tasking stage of the theory, was a great satisfaction: 'the doctrine is now safely set forth, whatever happens to me.'[4] He derived considerably less gratification from its reception in the press, where it was generally ignored or mentioned in passing, and what attention it did receive was focused on its agnosticism. Throughout his career Spencer

---

[1] *Aby* ii. 64.
[2] J. Collier, 'Reminiscences of Herbert Spencer', in J. Royce, ed., *Herbert Spencer, an estimate and review* (New York, 1904), p. 219.
[3] *Aby* ii. 213.
[4] *Aby* ii. 77.

considered himself persecuted by reviewers, professing astonishment at a favourable notice and resignation in the face of hostility or dismissiveness. This sense of grievance broadened in later life into a thoroughgoing antipathy for the press, which intensified as the 'misrepresentations' of which he complained in intellectual discourse were extended into his private life. Certainly agnosticism formed the basis of his wider reputation. Once, while staying at a Scottish hotel, he was denounced as anti-Christ by a Free Church minister, who 'straightway covened a prayer-meeting in the billiard-room as a fumigatory measure.'[1]

Undeterred by critical indifference, Spencer embarked upon the *Biology*, but his nervous symptoms, aggravated by frequent recourse to morphia, delayed the first volume until the autumn of 1863. It received less notice than *First Principles*, with the result that when Volume II appeared in October 1865, no review copies were sent out, Spencer having decided that the reviewers were discouraging potential readers. In February 1866 mounting pressure on his resources brought a fresh and alarming financial crisis. An extensive vacation had exhausted the legacy, the number of paying subscribers had dwindled to 350, and his father, too old and infirm to teach, required financial assistance. Since 1850 Spencer calculated irretrievable losses of £1 100 on his publications and accordingly, with Number 15 of the serial, he issued notice of cessation.

The response was immediate, gratifying, and totally unexpected. John Stuart Mill offered to cover all losses on the third volume of the *Biology*, an act of generosity which Spencer rightly called 'a manifestation of feeling between authors that has rarely been paralleled',[2] but could not bring himself to accept. Mill then recruited John Lubbock, John Tyndall, and Thomas Huxley, who between them canvassed 'a number of persons interested, chiefly wealthy' to take out 250 new subscriptions 'for distribution'. Spencer was uneasy about the arrangement, expressing 'satisfaction, that so much sympathy should be shown me by distinguished friends . . . and dissatisfaction, that such measures should be needful.'[3]

[1] *Aby* ii. 75–6.   [2] *Aby* ii. 136.
[3] *Aby* ii. 137.

At the end of 1866 Spencer's father died, followed swiftly by his mother. The inheritance of his father's estate was supplemented by the unstinting efforts of Edward L. Youmans, who was circulating Spencer's writings in the United States as extensively as possible, and 'in such a manner that you might share the pecuniary results.'[1] Spencer's wealthier transatlantic admirers were underwriting his costs, an 'extreme self-sacrifice' which clashed with his personal code of self-help. Youmans threatened that unless he accept, the money would revert to his publishers and Spencer, who detested publishers more than he disliked charity, could not refuse. During 1866, furthermore, Youmans collected 7 000 dollars from among the American readers of the *Synthetic Philosophy*, and this sum was invested on Spencer's behalf. Only thus, at the expense of his deeply-felt principles, was Spencer able to continue.

The loss of both parents within six months was devastating. In his father Spencer lost a *confidant* to whom he had been able to unburden himself without reserve, a critic whose judgement he had relied on, and a confessor before whom he could unburden himself of his anxieties. Since the age of thirteen he had submitted every scheme, speculation, and decision for his father's consideration. Now, suddenly alone, he reproached himself with filial neglect, despite having effectively supported his parents for some time. His concern for their welfare, though never floridly expressed, was typically practical—his letters to them are full of amateur diagnoses and quackish remedies for their ailments, suggesting a real, if uninformed solicitude. Their deaths constituted an emotional watershed in Spencer's life, confronting him with the bleak reality of isolation and homelessness. Significantly, the lodgings at Lancaster Gate to which he now moved were to be his home until 1887.

Bereavement, the executorship of his parents' estate, and nervous disorder combined to delay the completion of the *Biology* until his return from Derby in 1867, whereupon he began revising *First Principles* for a new edition. He was slowly beginning to be aware of a growing influence. The

[1] *L.L.* i. 143.

Chairs of Mental Philosophy and Logic at London University, and Moral Philosophy at Edinburgh University were offered to him. The first tentative Russian translations of his work fell foul of the Tsarist censorship ('Manners and Fashions', with its materialist dissection of the origins of monarchical authority, touched a tender nerve). Its translator was indicted for high treason, but the charge was subsequently withdrawn as being disproportionately severe.

With *The Principles of Biology* complete, and *The Principles of Psychology* in preparation, Spencer looked ahead to the time, three or four years distant, when he would confront sociology, and was alarmed by an enormous gap in information. To close it he initiated *The Descriptive Sociology*, a vast compendium of sociological facts culled from historical and anthropological sources, illustrating social evolution with an unashamed selectivity much criticized by later, more empirically-minded sociologists. He enlisted David Duncan and set about instructing him in the sociological method, which consisted of reading together through travelogues, pausing for the annotation of relevant (or it must be suspected, convenient) facts. The consequent monotony brought on a relapse, and in February 1868, leaving Duncan to his own devices, he fled to Italy for the winter. The tour did nothing to relieve his ailments, and he was profoundly unimpressed by 'a land of beautiful distances and ugly foregrounds.'[1]

In May 1868, defying 'an attack of greater nervousness than usual', Spencer began to dictate *The Principles of Psychology*, adopting bizarre procedures for the conservation of nervous energy. He dictated on the banks of the Serpentine between bouts of rowing, or in sheds adjoining his favourite athletics club in Pentonville between chaotic games of racquets. Visitors were amazed by the incongruity between the imposing orderliness of the finished product and the haphazard manner of its creation. Volume I of the *Psychology* was published in December 1870, delayed again by the length and scope of his convalescent vacations.

If insomnia and neurasthenia remained obstacles, by 1869

[1] *Aby* ii. 197.

he could joke about his financial tribulations: 'You will see how the sales of my books are increasing. If things go on thus, I shall make a fortune by philosophy.'[1] He received a dwindling income from subscriptions, but was principally indebted to Edward L. Youmans, who kept up an ample flow of transatlantic royalties at a time when piracy was the norm in international publishing. 'From this time forth', he wrote, 'the remainder of my life-voyage was through smooth waters.'[2] He was surprised (and perhaps a little mortified) to find that his work was becoming respectable. In 1870 he visited Oxford and discovered that *The Principles of Biology* was prescribed as a university text-book. He was amused, however, by the refusal of the University of London to accept it as required reading, even after repeated representations by the students. He took a quiet pride in notoriety. His reputation received a further boost with the publication, in 1873, of *The Study of Sociology*. This work, which broke the tedious rhythm of the *Synthetic Philosophy*, served Spencer as an introduction to *The Principles of Sociology* proper, and taught him a great deal about sociological method and objectivity. It also demonstrated a lucrative means of publication, appearing chapter by chapter in successive issues of the *Contemporary Review* and the American *Popular Science Monthly*, and grossing £1 500, a remarkable figure for a serious work on an as yet obscure subject. In 1876 he finally abandoned his few remaining subscribers to the original serialized *Synthetic Philosophy*, and adopted this new format, each instalment appearing simultaneously in six countries during the later stages.

Early in 1874, after a refreshing bout of polemics with critics, Spencer commenced work on *The Principles of Sociology*. The effort imposed a still more restricted way of life. Publication was hampered by progressively severe and prolonged cycles of relapse and convalescence; his health was so delicate by this time that he had begun in May 1873 to dictate a rough draft of his *Autobiography*, partly for relaxation, partly in order to forestall would-be biographers. The

[1] *L.L.* i. 211.   [2] *Aby* ii. 207.

Autobiography, recently unkindly referred to as 'a master-piece of unconscious humour,'[1] is certainly a disconcerting book; its tone, apart from a few exceptional passages, is as dispassionately analytical as is the bulk of the *Synthetic Philosophy*. Its purpose was 'to demonstrate how large a part emotional nature plays in determining the intellectual activi-ties',[2] but this self-analysis reveals only a barren catalogue of quasi-phrenological stereotypes, 'an unusual capacity for the intuition of cause', a 'synthetic tendency' and so on, behind which the personality remains concealed.

In 1876, with Volume I of the *Sociology* substantially complete, he again deviated from his original scheme. His customary insomnia was by this time wretchedly complicated by bouts of sciatica, fended off with heavy doses of quinine and chloric ether. Alarmed by this apparently serious decline in health he resolved to turn to *The Principles of Ethics*: 'Since the whole system was at the outset, and has ever con-tinued to be a basis for the right rule of life, individual and social, it would be a great misfortune if this, which is the out-come of it all, should remain undone.'[3] An energetic round of 'social distractions', including visits to the Gaiety Theatre, and even a fancy-dress ball effected an improvement, and in June 1878 he commenced to dictate *The Data of Ethics*. Wintering on the Riviera proved therapeutic and the work proceeded smoothly, as it seemed to whenever he departed from his prearranged schedule. *The Data of Ethics* was pub-lished in June 1879 and was accorded, by Spencer's grudging admission, 'a more favourable reception than I had been accustomed to.'[4]

By way of celebration he decided to visit Egypt. Taking as travelling companions Margaret and Kate Potter (having first ascertained whether or not this would cause malicious gossip) he sailed up the Nile in September, having joined a party of sightseers which included Canon and Mrs. Barnett, whose account of the expedition affords a rare, fascinating

---

[1] J.W. Burrow, *Evolution and Society: a study in Victorian social theory* (Cam-bridge, 1966), p. 182.
[2] *Aby* i. 435.
[3] H.S. to E.L. Youmans, 16 Feb. 1878, *Aby* ii. 314.
[4] *Aby* ii. 324.

view of Spencer as others saw him. Canon Barnett found him intellectually blinkered by his theories, and ignorant in most other fields: 'There are few matters which he knows enough of, or is interested enough in, to discuss. He likes gossip or chaff.'[1] Nor was he 'the companion with whom to see places'. Mrs. Barnett describes their first view of the Nile:

At last we stood on the bank of the Old Nile. A hundred thoughts and pictures of the lives, joys, pains of the multitudes who had lived by it, in it, for it, chased each other through our minds. We stood silenced by its historic beauty till Mr. Spencer broke the pause with 'The colour of the water barely vouches for its hygienic properties.'[2]

Spencer's diffidence and fear of contention were misconstrued by his travelling companions as rudeness and arrogance. A typical confrontation occurred when an inoffensive admirer, a 'professor of world-wide renown', approached him for conversation: 'The gaunt philosopher received him standing, did not ask him to sit down, and after an awful pause—for Mr. Spencer had the power of shrivelling people up—he said "Monsieur, je n'aime pas les introductions qui ne viennent à rien. Bon jour." '[3] In other ways, however, he enlivened the proceedings considerably. His sententious evolutionary dissertations on trivial subjects caused much suppressed mirth, whilst his stranger exploits included losing himself in the desert during a solitary walk, and spending a whole day heaving huge boulders from a cliff-top into the Nile, while a line of bemused *fellaheen* clung to his coat-tails lest he overbalance.

In late December 'fancies, afterwards seen to be morbid' forced him to leave the party. The Barnetts 'felt pity for the lonely, unloved, unloving old man', but were not sorry to see him go, and rather put out when twelve days later he returned. This time he made greater efforts at coexistence, even participating in communal poetry-readings, where he 'read Shelley with much gentleness and feeling.'[4] He was not, however, to be reconciled to Egypt, 'the land of decay and death,

[1] Mrs. Barnett, *Canon Barnett: his life, work and friends* (London, 1918), i. 230–1.
[2] Ibid., i. 232.
[3] Ibid., i. 231.
[4] Mrs. Barnett, op.cit., i. 239.

dead men, dead races, dead creeds.'[1] His distrust of the people bordered on fear: 'He learned only a few words of Arabic, and these were words of refusal, banishment or contempt, which he frequently used with provocative brandishments of his sturdy umbrella.'[2] His return to London in February 1880 gave him 'more pleasure than anything else that occcurred during my tour', and found him in better health. He declared that he could 'drink beer with impunity' and boasted that on his sixtieth birthday he could run up the steps of the Athenaeum three at a time.

The next two years were busy and vigorous. Spencer issued *Political Institutions*, and in April 1882 Part II of *The Principles of Sociology* was 'delivered to the inattention of the reviewers'. *The Descriptive Sociology*, however, was reluctantly abandoned in October 1881. It had grown into a scheme of enormous (and typically Spencerian) ambition; a massive factual catalogue so arranged as to make incontrovertible the evolutionary interpretation of social development. By 1881 it had cost Spencer £4 425 to produce, of which only £1 054 was recouped in sales. He was bitterly disappointed:

Should the day ever come when the love for the personalities of history is less and the desire for its instructive facts greater, those who occupy themselves in picking out the gold from the dross will perhaps be able to publish their results without inflicting on themselves losses too grievous to be borne—nay, may possibly receive some thanks for their pains.[3]

This disaster notwithstanding, the spring of 1882 found Spencer with two-thirds of the *Synthetic Philosophy* behind him and a smooth path to completion apparently before him, provided he carefully husbanded his resources of nervous energy. This condition, however, was not fulfilled, and he succumbed to a breakdown of unexampled severity, caused by an uncharacteristically precipitous decision to involve himself in politics, and by an exhausting expedition to America. By the end of the year he was, in his own words, 'a wreck, fit for nothing and for no society', and the completion of his life's work was to be delayed by ten years of

[1] *Aby* ii. 341.
[2] Mrs. Barnett, op.cit., 1. 240.
[3] *Aby* ii. 352.

misery and endurance. Throughout the preceding two decades, however, his life had not been unrelievedly unpleasant.
The *Autobiography*, largely preoccupied with declining
health, conjures the misleading image of Spencer as an ageing
recluse, yet only after 1872 did there commence a gradual
withdrawal from 'social excitements', and despite chronic
insomnia he remained reasonably active.

Spencer's social circle was intellectually formidable, and
collectively exercised an enormous influence over the world
of science and ideas. Thomas Huxley, John Tyndall, John
Lubbock, Joseph Hooker, John Stuart Mill, George Lewes,
and George Eliot were all close friends. He knew William
Ewart Gladstone, William Makepiece Thackerary, Cardinal
Manning, Thomas Carlyle, and Alfred Tennyson, indeed
practically anyone with a 'name' in literary or political life.
He distinguished sharply between friendship and acquaintance, and it was from the wider circle, the 'social treadmill',
that he gradually dissociated himself during the 1870s.
Having no family of his own, friendship acquired for him a
desperate importance: 'If I can have the constant feeling',
he wrote to Thomas Huxley, 'that I have friends at hand . . .
it will serve to keep my spirits up, and I will do very well.
Otherwise I am at my wits' end to know what to do.'[1] Unfortunately, his deliberate retreat from 'society' in the
broader sense coincided with a shrinking of his more intimate
circle by the ravages of time. His loneliness in old age
stemmed from longevity; he simply outlived his friends.

In the 1860s his social life was strenuous, as recent recognition brought invitations, and the controversial nature of his
views invited dissension. Prolonged wrangling over theoretical
abstractions left him mentally taut and unable to sleep. By
1862 the pressure had begun to tell, and he observed that
'Dining out three days running is more than I can stand with
impunity.'[2] He continued, however, to spend most weekends
with the Lubbocks and fellow-guests, and to go out 'a good
deal, and indeed rather too much.'[3] He regularly attended

[1] H.S. to T.H. Huxley, 20 Sept. 1888, Hux.Coll. vii.
[2] H.S. to W.G.S., 13 Apr. 1862, *Aby* ii. 73.
[3] H.S. to W.G.S., 9 June 1863, *L.L.* i. 142.

John Stuart Mill's dinner-parties at Blackheath, and on one such occasion he accepted John Morley's challenge to expound his philosophy, completing a breathtaking synopsis in twenty minutes, to the astonished admiration of some guests and the utter confusion of others.[1]

In the early sixties he associated with a clearly defined group of radical intellectuals, united in the commitment to Darwinism and identified by their participation in the movement to prosecute Governor Eyre of Jamaica, whose 'pacification' of the island after an inconsiderable rebellion entailed indiscriminate executions, floggings, and burning of homes. Denounced by the humanitarians of 'Exeter Hall', Eyre was defended by the patriotic 'right' on the grounds that, in Carlyle's quaint phraseology, he had 'damaged some of the cargo but saved the ship.'[2] The leaders of the Jamaica Committee were united round an interpretation of evolution which did not yet condone imperialism, though significantly, perhaps, the correlation between science and the anti-Eyre faction was not absolute; John Tyndall and Joseph Hooker sided with the heavy artillery of Victorian literature, Thomas Carlyle, Alfred Tennyson, Charles Kingsley, John Ruskin, and Charles Dickens in defence of Eyre, Hooker on blatantly racialist grounds.[3] Yet the political breach was considered insufficient cause for a permanent severance of friendships, and when, in 1868, the case for a prosecution of Eyre was thrown out by a Grand Jury, normal social relations were resumed.

Spencer alone seemed unable to dissociate the social and intellectual compartments of his existence. The political inclinations of the Morley-Mill circle, expressed in their journalistic enterprises, soon alienated him from them. The foundation of the *Pall-Mall Gazette* in 1865 had brought together John Morley, William Rathbone Greg, Leslie Stephen, and George Lewes, but under the editorship of Frederick Greenwood it embraced an independent Toryism. In January 1867 Morley became editor of the *Fortnightly Review*, which began to preach a very practical radicalism and soon enjoyed

[1] F.W. Hirst, *The early life and letters of John Morley*, (London, 1927), i. 53.
[2] B. Semmel *The Governor Eyre Controversy* (London, 1962), p. 106.
[3] Ibid., p. 125.

a high prestige.[1] While retaining their allegiance to Darwin the *Fortnightly* radicals were to be found 'following Mill beyond the bounds of *laissez-faire*' and attempting to 'quicken the social conscience of England: to make Liberalism come alive.'[2] They championed national education and organized labour; their adherents soon included the young and ambitious Joseph Chamberlain. Significantly it was the *Fortnightly* which published Thomas Huxley's assault on Spencerism ('Administrative Nihilism') in 1871, but by this time Spencer had broken his association with the *Fortnightly* fraternity, confining his social forays to a small, scientific coterie.

In November 1864 this circle of intimates became institutionalized as the 'X-Club', in its inception an agency of the struggle of scientists against theologians; Joseph Hooker saw in it a means of 'bringing about more unity in our efforts to advance science.'[3] It incorporated a group of friends, all scientists newly recognized as distinguished in their fields, of middle-class origin and mildly radical. Membership was limited to men 'of adequate mental calibre and . . . on terms of intimacy with the existing members.'[4] The 'X' was spoken of with bated breath, but there was nothing conspiratorial in its nature, and despite its collective eminence its purpose was primarily recreational and its meetings 'spent chiefly in lively talk, of which *badinage* formed a considerable element.'[5] Among his close friends Spencer could indulge his vestigial sense of humour, and described himself as 'ever ready to laugh' at their high-powered witticisms. (Example: Lewes: I never hesitate, I get up steam at once, in short, I boil at low temperature'. Huxley: That implies a vacuum in the upper regions'.) Spencer's own speciality was the epigram, for instance; 'Talking: a race run by the tongue against time, in which generally the smaller the weight carried the greater the speed'. On a grimmer note he defined 'Time' as 'that which

[1] F.W. Hirst, op.cit., p. 87.
[2] F.L. Knickerbocker, *Free Minds: John Morley and his friends* (Cambridge, Mass., 1943), p. 90.
[3] R.M. MacLeod, 'The "X-Club": a social network of science in late-Victorian England', *Notes and Records of the Royal Society*, xxiv, 1970, p. 305.
[4] *Aby* ii. 115.
[5] *Aby* ii. 116.

Man is always trying to kill, but which ends up killing him.'[1] Contrived and sometimes morbid, these recorded examples confirm the observation that 'Mr. Spencer had no great native fund of wit.'[2] Nevertheless, although the 'X-Club' has been described as 'a powerful instrument for wielding scientific opinion in winning political battles,'[3] its crucial importance for Spencer lay in providing the stable nucleus of a social life, combining intelligent companionship with refreshing levity.

The 'X-Club' apart, there emerges a seasonal pattern to Spencer's recreational activities, with late summer and autumn devoted to vacations, the apparently extravagant duration of which reflected their essential regenerative function. When pressure of work overwhelmed him, two havens were particularly attractive. One was Ardtornish in the tranquillity of the Highlands, where he declared 'most of the happiest days of my life have been spent.'[4] At Standish, by contrast, Spencer found rejuvenation in his relations with the children of Richard Potter. Beatrice Webb's account of one visit does something to dispel his severe image:

'You can go out this morning, my dears, with Mr. Spencer', said the governess to her pupils, after listening to one of the philosopher's breakfast tirades against discipline, 'and mind you follow his teaching and do exactly what you have a mind to.' . . . The philosopher found himself presently in a neighbouring beech-wood pinned down in a leaf-filled hollow by little demons, all legs, arms and dancing dark eyes, whilst the elder and more discreet tormentors pelted him with decaying beech-leaves. 'Your children are r-r-rude children' exclaimed the 'Man versus the State' as he stalked into my mother's boudoir. But for the most part we were firm friends.[5]

Excursions of this sort provided an essential safety-valve for a mind perpetually wrestling with evolutionary complexities. Richard Potter understood Spencer's predicament, and warned Beatrice of the impending tragedy: 'Spencer's intellect is like a machine racing along with raw material; it is wearing out his body. Poor Spencer . . . he lacks instinct—you will discover that instinct is as important as intellect.'[6] She

---

[1] Spencer Papers, University of London Library.
[2] 'Two' *Home Life with Herbert Spencer* (Bristol, 1906), p. 41.
[3] R.M. MacLeod, op.cit., p. 312.
[4] *L.L.* i. 253.   [5] Webb, p. 26.
    Webb, p. 24.

took the lesson to heart, always regarding her debt to Spencer as one of deterrence as much as example. In later, grimmer years she was to be his greatest consolation.

Pressure of work began to have serious repercussions during the early 1870s. In 1873 Spencer circulated a lithographed, all-purpose reply to unwanted correspondence: 'Mr. Herbert Spencer regrets that . . . he has decided to cut himself off from every engagement that is likely to compel attention, however slight.'[1] He was now compelled to withdraw from all gatherings at which he would feel constrained to dispute with strangers, unprotected by the solicitude of his friends. Francis Galton testifies to his incapacity to suppress disagreement: 'His disposition was acknowledged by himself to be contentious; I would venture to consider it as being sometimes a little perverse',[2] but noted that 'he was very thin-skinned under criticism, and shrank from argument; it excited him overmuch, and was really bad for his health.'[3] Spencer was finding more and more difficulty in reconciling his need for companionship with his need for relaxation.

Death had already begun to decimate his friends. Octavius Smith died in January 1871, and Mrs. Smith in July 1878, though their children, Valentine and Flora, continued to invite him to Ardtornish. John Stuart Mill, a cordial friend and disputant over many years, died in 1873. When George Lewes died in 1878 Spencer, out of respect for George Eliot's feelings, broke a lifetime rule of abstention from religious ceremonies to attend the funeral, a rare triumph of emotion over principle. George Eliot herself died in 1881.

Spencer's everyday existence, allowing for the vagaries of health, was not unpleasant, although in some respects a little strange. He continued to reside in lodging-houses as a matter of policy, but craved the companionship of a domestic environment, however artificial. The inmates of 37 Queen's Gardens, Lancaster Gate, his domicile from 1866 until 1887, hardly comprised a stimulating menage:

There was a retired government officer belonging to the stores department—a Mauritian of French extraction, honourable in feeling, a great

[1] *Aby* ii. 249.
[2] F. Galton, 'Personal reminiscences of Herbert Spencer', *L.L.* ii. 262.
[3] *L.L.* ii. 263.

snuff-taker and one who regretted that duelling had ceased. Next to him came an admiral, who every day drank the Queen's health, and displayed piety and militancy in a not unusual combination. Another naval officer there was who uttered radical sentiments, fostered in him, I fancy, by disappointment in his profession, for which he was evidently incompetent; and there was also a captain in the army, occupied in some philanthropic work in London. Then came a maiden lady, between 70 and 80, who had acquired a certain stock of information, ideas and feelings in her teens, and had never since added to or modified them.[1]

Alfred Russell Wallace professed astonishment that Spencer could tolerate this 'rather commonplace set of people', but it was explained to him that 'he had purposely chosen such a home in order to avoid the mental excitement of too much conversation . . . he found that when his evenings were spent in commonplace conversation, hearing the news of the day or taking part in a little music, he had a better chance of sleeping.'[2] Small wonder that Wallace should be surprised to find the champion of industrial society playing the flute to a small group of retired military men; a curious obverse to his literary *persona*.

The passage of Spencer's London days was dominated by the Athenaeum Club, to which he was elected in 1868. Finding the atmosphere extremely congenial, he virtually made it his home. Having spent his mornings at work at a rented study in Leinster Place, his resources of energy exhausted, he would spend his afternoons there 'miscellaneously' talking, playing billiards, and cursorily reading. Books of travel attracted him as sources for his *Sociology*. He also took in the reviews: 'To observe the current of opinion was one motive; and another motive was to make myself acquainted with criticisms passed on my own views, which I not infrequently found objects of attack.'[3] He walked home for dinner at seven, and spent his evenings, when not engaged, 'killing time'. This leisurely cycle characterized his existence during middle age.

At the Athenaeum he was in his element. His membership spanned thirty-seven years, and his election was the only

[1] *Aby* ii. 145.
[2] A.R. Wallace, op.cit., ii. 25.
[3] *Aby* ii. 225.

recognition of merit he ever accepted. His friend and fellow-member, Francis Galton, described him as a 'model Club-man', invariably behaving with the 'studied decorum of one who is living, not in his own house, rather in the house of a friend.'[1] Spencer, who lived out his life in other people's houses, was an impeccable guest. He was elected to the club committee in 1874, there to remain, in defiance of the constitution, for seven consecutive years: 'He loved', said Galton, 'to discuss the art of tea-making according to philosophical principles.'

There were, however, less congenial aspects to Spencer's life, not least his celibacy and continued lack of domestic security. At the age of forty, with marriage still not inconceivable, he had consigned himself to the *Synthetic Philosophy*. At sixty he had become reconciled to permanent bachelorhood, but the problem of loneliness was only partially alleviated by contact with friends, clubmates, and fellow *pensionnaires*, and became more insistent with the passage of time. He lacked an avenue of escape from the closed circuit of his overtaxed mind which family life or even occasional debauchery might have afforded him. His self-absorption was becoming claustrophobic and few acquaintances could be expected to treat it with George Eliot's tolerance: 'We have given up vain expectations of him . . . He comes and consults us about his own affairs, and that is his way of showing friendship. We never dream of telling him OUR affairs, which would certainly not interest him.'[2]

Spencer's uncompromising rationalism, furthermore, prevented his escape into the unselfconscious enjoyment of art. Having once declared that 'pleasure is coy, but must be caught unawares',[3] he consistently flouted this principle. The trouble with most people, he once remarked, is that 'little given to mental analysis', they 'fail to discriminate among their sources of pleasure',[4] but as J.S. Mill observed, 'the enjoyments of life are sufficient to make it a pleasant thing

---

[1] *L.L.* ii. 255–6.
[2] Q.G. and R. Tillotson, *Mid-Victorian Studies* (London, 1938), p. 75.
[3] H.S., 'Manners and Fashions', *Essays*, iii. 41.
[4] *Aby* ii. 85.

when they are taken *en passant* . . . ask yourself whether you are happy, and you cease to be so.'[1] Spencer had no capacity for the willing suspension of disbelief. He applied rigorous scientific criteria to art; if a picture, however beautiful, contained faulty perspective, he denounced it as fraudulent. Of the opera he wrote: 'That serving-men and waiting maids should be made poetical, and prompted to speak in *recitative*, because their masters and mistresses happened to be in love, was too conspicuous an absurdity; and the consciousness of this absurdity went far towards destroying what pleasure I might otherwise have derived from the work.'[2]

Health, too, was becoming a source of nagging anxiety. Chronic insomnia and 'sensations in the head' whenever he concentrated beyond his limit, were complicated by physical annoyances of advancing middle age, rheumatism, sciatica, and pyrexia. His worst torment, however, was hypochondria, aggravated by a semi-educated medical expertise, prompting the diagnosis of improbable diseases from imaginary symptoms and the prescription of irrelevant 'cures'. He imagined himself at the mercy of changes in atmospheric pressure, avoiding 'enervating' beaches but seeking out 'bracing' cliff-tops. These fluctuations in health, however, were not yet drastic: 'There were the usual perturbations of health, and short absences of a week or so to obtain, partly by fresh air and partly by quiet, better nights and restored powers of working.'[3]

Literary success (a wide readership and a wider reputation) brought new trials, including the escalation of controversy. Spencer's attitude to 'fighting' fluctuated according to mood, circumstance and the antagonist. He praised John Stuart Mill, who disputed in a 'gentlemanly' manner, without malice, but warned that 'opponents as candid and conscientious as Mill, in whom the love of truth predominates over the love of victory, are rarely met with.' Controversy often dragged on, consuming precious time and energy, beyond the point at which the pursuit of victory outweighed objective enquiry, and in some cases, such as Spencer's correspondence with

[1] *Aby* i. 274.   [2] *Aby* ii. 284.
[3] J.S. Mill, *An Autobiography* (London, 1879), p. 142.

Edward Tylor in *Mind* over the copyright to an anthropological concept, degenerated into open abuse. Spencer was cheerfully ambivalent on the virtues of public debate. He could claim that he had 'never felt aggrieved by criticisms, however trenchant, when fairly made',[1] but 'fairness' is the crucial qualification. Spencer tended to welcome those criticisms which he could effortlessly deal with; those he could not he denounced as 'misprepresentations'. He occasionally displayed unsavoury attitudes to conflict, now retreating with cries of 'Unfair!', now hovering in combative glee over the mangled and vulnerable carcase of a critic: 'Tait will very likely show fight. I hope he will, I shall be down on him still more heavily if he does.'[2]

The obsession with misrepresentation reflected a wide-ranging persecution complex. Spencer conceived himself prey to a variety of tyrannies; the 'tyranny of resolution, once formed' (the completion neurosis which chained him to the *Synthetic Philosophy*), the tyranny of his nervous disorder, the tyranny of social convention, personified in the menacing figure of 'Mrs. Grundy'. He feared a conspiracy to confute his claim to originality, and to undermine the integrity of his system by falsification and plagiarism. He scorned recognition and public acclaim, yet exhibited a well-developed sense of grievance when, for example, his pioneering work on mental evolution was pirated without acknowledgement in Henry Maudsley's successful *The Physiology and Pathology of Mankind*,[3] or Charles Darwin's *The Descent of Man*.[4] At the root of the conspiracy there lurked the press, placing false emphases on his work, misconstruing his doctrines, or ignoring him altogether.

Spencer's tragic isolation, which intensified with age, shows through in this neurotic vision of injustice, falsehood, and misconstruction. The problems which beset him during the first two decades of the *Synthetic Philosophy* were thus largely of his own imagination, though none the less burdensome for that. Not until the 1880s and 1890s, however, did they assume intolerable and disastrous proportions.

---

[1] H.S. to the Earl of Pembroke, 2 May 1883, *L.L.* i. 308-9.
[2] *Aby* ii. 219.   [3] *L.L.* i. 195.
[4] H.S. to E.L. Youmans, 5 June 1871, *L.L.* i. 197.

During 1882 Spencer broke the steady, methodical routine imposed by the *Synthetic Philosophy*, and as a consequence disastrously overreached himself. The first diversion occurred when he helped to found the Anti-Aggression League, and attempt to bring under control by pacific propaganda the imperialistic and militaristic currents dominant in foreign policy and public opinion. The damage inflicted by his exertions in this cause was compounded by an arduous excursion to America in the same year. Together, these efforts left Spencer completely broken in health, a relapse which marked the beginning of the end: 'There had commenced a series of descents, severally caused by exceeding my diminished strength and making it still less, which brought me down in the course of subsequent years to the condition of a confirmed invalid, leading little more than a vegetative life.'[1] His remaining years contained but one landmark, the completion of the *Synthetic Philosophy*; otherwise the thread of narrative slackens into a morbid case-history of progressive senile deterioration.

Spencer's involvement in the Anti-Aggression League reflects a deep concern; no other cause moved him to waive his self-imposed rule of abstinence from politics. A discussion at Lord Airlie's house in 1881 'on the subject of the antagonism between industrial progress and war' led to Spencer's initiative in forming the League, aimed at 'checking the aggressive tendencies displayed by us all over the world'. Its programme diverged sharply from the non-resistant pacifism of the Peace Society: 'My belief is that all the difficulties hence arising may be excluded by having in place of the principle of non-resistance the principle of non-aggression, which for all practical purposes would prove equally efficient.'[2]

Spencer's first duty lay in the recruitment of famous names. On the strength of *The word of an English republican on the Muscovite crusade* he attempted to enrol Algernon Swinburne, but without success. He managed, however, to recruit John Bright, whose lonely stand against the Crimean War and latterly against the bombardment of Alexandria

[1] *Aby* ii. 380.
[2] H.S. to Bright, 2 July 1881, *L.L.* i. 294.

placed him in much the same position of high-minded obsolescence as Spencer. Even Gladstone was canvassed, and conceded that 'our aims were in harmony with the progress of
Liberalism at large.'[1] Spencer also laboured to attract the
support of sympathetic organizations, like the International
Arbitration Co-operative Society, and the Workingmen's
Peace Association, with a view to harnessing the traditional
antipathy of Dissenters for the aristocratic and ecclesiastical
establishment. A public meeting at the Westminster Palace
Hotel on 16 June 1882 passed off quite successfully, Spencer
making a rare and 'much complimented' foray into public
speaking. Press coverage of the event, however, underlined
the apathy which foredoomed the movement to early extinction: 'While continental nations were bristling with arms,
and our own was obliged to increase its defensive forces and
simultaneously foster militant sentiments and ideas, it was
out of the question that an "Anti-Aggression League" could
have any success.'[2] The League folded soon after the first
meeting. The quixotic nature of the task renders Spencer's
decision to tackle it all the more praiseworthy, and illustrates
the sincerity of his concern for human betterment. He continued throughout the remainder of his life to prod others
into a show of enthusiasm, emphasizing that in view of
ecclesiastical complicity in the imperialist consensus, 'the
preaching of justice and mercy has to be undertaken by
rationalists.'[3]

During 1881, meanwhile, Spencer had finally consented
to Edward Youmans's importunate invitations to America.
Negotiations were protracted by the philosopher's fastidi-
ousness; he felt obliged to gratify his American admirers,
but could accept no financial assistance from them, and
refused to 'make myself a show' by giving public lectures at
200 dollars a time. The tour itself, thus delayed until 1882,
passed uneventfully. He was greeted everywhere with lavish
hospitality and accorded celebrity status, culminating in a
sumptuous reception at Delmonico's, in New York, where

[1] *L.L.* i. 298.
[2] *Aby* ii. 378.
[3] H.S. to A. Herbert, 30 Sept. 1888, *L.L.* i. 381.

John Fiske, in a warm farewell oration, ranked Spencer with Aristotle and Newton for his contribution to human enlightenment. Spencer himself remained largely preoccupied with the avoidance of publicity, and the visit had little significance for a reputation already showing signs of wear. Physically and mentally, however, it proved devastating; the combined effects of stormy crossings, a cabin directly beneath the ship's fog-horn and the stress of public appearances left Spencer 'a wreck, fit for nothing and for no society.'[1]

Two weeks at Standish, however, restored him sufficiently to contemplate another significant break in the sequence. Early in 1883 he was approached by the editor of the *Contemporary Review* to reply to an article by Lord Salisbury on the provision of dwellings for the labouring poor. The outcome was *The Man versus the State*, which more than anything else sums up Spencer's political creed. Its publication brought a new lease of public life: a renewed, if slightly invidious recognition as the spokesman of an archaic brand of Liberalism.[2] On the strength of it he was offered the Liberal candidacy of Leicester but, perhaps mindful of the parliamentary fate of John Stuart Mill, declined. In any case, the strain of writing these polemics proved excessive, and nothing must now be allowed to impinge upon the slow, laborious construction of *The Principles of Sociology*.

The summer of 1886 found Spencer feeling old and depressed, full of wild schemes to improve his health, which included sailing daily to and fro across the English Channel, dictating on board ship. His nervous decrepitude was by this time chronic; Beatrice Potter described his existence as 'one continuing touching of his pulse to see how it fares with himself—a torturing self-analysis of all his physical feelings.'[3] His secretary relates how Spencer 'asked me to go and look at the barometer and on learning that there had been a fall, exclaimed "Ah I thought so. That's what makes me feel so wretched.'[4] Irrationality had begun to pervade his behaviour;

---

[1] H.S. to Mrs. F. Smith, 11 Aug. 1883, *L.L.* i. 315–16.
[2] H.S.'s definition of 'Liberalism' is discussed below in Chap. 7, esp. pp. 165–8.
[3] Webb, p. 295.
[4] Memoir by J. Troughton in the Spencer Papers, University of London Library.

his temporary estrangement from Thomas Huxley over the Land Question,[1] his quest for domestic comforts, his overwhelming sense of persecution and conspiracy all confirm this. The hardening of some attitudes proceeded to extremes; he refused a subscription portrait of himself, thinking it a 'grave social abuse' that people should be 'taxed' for a picture of him.

He spent the winter of 1887 at Bournemouth with the Potters, where Beatrice recorded his pitiable condition: 'The old philosopher downstairs . . . the victim of a strange disease of mind and body, sits in his chair not daring to move body or mind; one day passes like another, and still no improvement.'[2] He clearly nurtured no hopes of completing his life's work, and did not expect a prolonged dotage. His verdict on the Anti-Aggression League was that 'by an imprudent effort I . . . have disabled myself from completing the undertaking I might otherwise have completed.'[3]

Beatrice Potter was very much the prop of Spencer's declining years, their close relationship surviving even the shock of her marriage to the notorious socialist Sidney Webb, and Spencer acknowledged that her insight into his personality and problems was unique. Her account of him is objective yet sympathetic. She imputed his terrible loneliness to the deficiency of his emotional faculties: 'Strange—a nature so perfect in intellect and little else, save friendliness and the uprightness of a truth-loving mind. He has sometimes told me sadly that he has wondered at the weakness of his feelings. . . that he thought it came from his mind being constantly busied with the perfection of this one idea—never once doubting the value of it.'[4] She realized too that self-analysis crippled his capacity for enjoyment: 'To me there is a comic pathos in his elaborate search after pleasurable "sensations", as if sensations can ever take the place of emotion.' She understood that his haughty, forbidding demeanour disguised 'a capacity for deep feeling, a capacity which is now covered up with crotchety ideas presenting a hedgehog's

---

[1] This issue is discussed in Chap. 5, pp. 119–29.
[2] Webb, p. 31.
[3] H.S. to B. Potter, 21 Nov. 1887, in the Passfield Collection, II. i (ii).
[4] Webb, p. 31.

coat to the outer world, a surface hardly inviting contact.'[1]

What sort of man was Herbert Spencer? His apologists and expositors dutifully list his moral accomplishments: scrupulous honesty, fixity of purpose, expansive, if slightly academic altruism, before passing hurriedly on to his theories. His detractors take his public behaviour at face value, characterizing him as humourless, dry, hypochondriac, and vindictive. In later life, certainly, his command of the social graces was not enhanced by the effects of declining health, which made him unstable, sharp-tongued, and persistently morbid. Even David Duncan was forced to admit that Spencer, 'like all the finer natures, shrank from parading the more attractive aspects of his character.'[2]

This superficial unattractiveness concealed qualities best measured by balancing his achievements against his disabilities. During a loveless lifetime, tormented by insomnia and other disorders no less real to him for being partly imagined, and without much formal education, he produced, single-handed, in fourteen large volumes, a philosophical system which preoccupied thinking men for fifty years. He contributed originally and significantly to the bodies of psychological, sociological, and political theory, and exerted an over-all influence not yet completely dissipated.

Spencer's personality abounds with contrasts. He was a pitiless advocate of natural selection who loved children, a seeker after recognition who refused all honours, a misogynist who craved female companionship. These apparent paradoxes may be related to the peculiarly high level of self-consciousness at which he lived. Every action was calculated; he seldom responded to impulse. The exacting moral standards derived from the application of evolution to ethics he applied most severely to himself. Spencer was, above all else, a stringent moralist. He was driven by a strong intellectual intensity and a fierce moral intensity: 'He was a man who in everything he did, even in trivial matters, was guided by principle, the principle being in each case that which by a process of reasoning he had found to be valid.'[3] Spencer was

---

[1] Webb, p. 30.   [2] *L.L.* i. viii.
[3] *L.L.* ii. 270.

a very good man, whose goodness, however, owing to his inability to laugh at himself hardened into asceticism.

This continuous restraint of the emotions over the intellect not only rendered Spencer an unlovely acquaintance but set a limit to the penetrative depth of his philosophy. Severed, like Jeremy Bentham, from the emotional experiences which might have tempered his mechanistic account of human behaviour, he became an archetypal 'closet-philosopher', a brilliant intellect caged in an inadequate experience. The emotional poverty of his existence shaped the content and structure of his thought in two significant ways.

First, it denied him a dispassionate approach to his work; he was unable to view it in any perspective but its own. Hence his fanatical regard for internal consistency, and his semi-neurotic obsession with criticism. With tortured ingenuity Spencer wove the whole fabric of observable phenomena into the pattern of his slender evolutionary premises. Beatrice Webb likened him to a spider, 'sitting alone in the centre of his theoretical web, catching facts and weaving them again into his theory.'[1] The monolithic character of his system, and its convenience as a target, explains Spencer's exaggerated sense of threat whenever critics, however obscure or deferential, ventured to call it into question. In the conduct of controversy the detached tone of his normal prose is forsaken for a shrill, near-hysterical dogmatism.

Second, emotional narrowness had a fundamental influence on the theory of social evolution itself. As a logical, original thinker Spencer is impressive enough, but his experience was too restricted to enable him to formulate a philosophy of conduct embracing all human needs. The missing ingredient in Spencerian theory is compassion. Brought up, like so many of his generation, on self-help and the proportioning of rewards to merits, he had no occasion to think of suffering as anything other than unfortunate but probably deserved aberrations from the comfortable middle-class norm. His popularity stemmed largely from the fact that he imparted a gloss of 'scientific' incontrovertibility to the ethos of expanding capitalism and its bourgeois virtues

[1] Webb, p. 31.

of self-sufficiency. His conception of philanthropy is a vestigial, patronizing one, designed to 'foster the unfortunate worthy' to the exclusion of those who deserve poverty. For Spencer, even charity could not free itself from the grip of moralism. In its monolithic integrity and moral austerity, therefore, the Spencerian system of thought faithfully reflects the man.

Back in London in 1890 Spencer undertook by far his most peculiar experiment in domestic settlement, a *ménage à trois* consisting of himself and two elderly maiden ladies. The artificial domesticity thus contracted for effected an ephemeral improvement; the sisters found him a 'genial tyrant', capable of occasional demonstrations of affection, but his idiosyncrasies of conduct and his irritability soon began to wear them down. Despite his 'fatherly care' he proved an exacting companion, and they complained that 'few men were so oblivious of the trouble and inconvenience they cause',[1] while Spencer for his part became obsessed with the anxiety that they were spreading rumours about him. In April 1893 the ladies revolted against their financial terms, causing Spencer 'dreadful worry'. Protracted negotiations failed to produce a satisfactory settlement, and after a year the agreement was terminated.

The 'X-Club' was pronounced dead in May 1895, most of the members being either deceased or too infirm to attend. It had long since lost its conviviality. A meeting of 1889 is thus described by Joseph Hooker: 'There was Hurst, Frankland, and Lubbock. Poor Spencer, looking the ghost of misery, dined apart.'[2] John Tyndall's death on 6 December 1893 caused Spencer to observe that 'Had I finished my task I should be very willing to promptly pass away in the same quiet manner.'[3] The only redeeming feature of an otherwise torpid existence was 'that slightly pleasurable excitement given to me by the trifling amount of work I do daily'. He could sustain dictation for ten minutes at a time, five times a day. The conservation of nervous energy enjoined an almost

---

[1] 'Two', op.cit., p. 71.
[2] R.M. MacLeod, op.cit.
[3] H.S. to Mrs. J. Tyndall, 6 Dec. 1893, *L.L.* ii. 62.

complete withdrawal from any aspect of his environment requiring attention or stirring interest; he spent the long hours
of inactivity 'letting my thoughts ramble in harmless ways,
avoiding as much as possible exciting subjects . . . watching
the passage of clouds, listening to birdsong.'[1] Soporific
drugs, almost an addiction by this time, deepened his somno-
lence. It became an obsession to 'exclude superfluities from
my environment . . . I shut out the presence of books by
curtains, that I may be free from the sense of complexity
which they yield.'[2] Similar devices included ear-muffs to
obliterate conversation while taking tea, and a vast woolly
over-garment in which he could, if necessary, enswathe himself to the complete exclusion of his surroundings.

Thus, painfully slowly, but with undiminished resolve,
Spencer pressed on towards the culmination of his life's
work. On 13 August 1896, he dictated the last lines of the
Synthetic Philosophy to his secretary, who duly recorded
the scene:

Rising slowly from his seat . . . his face beaming with joy, he extended
his hand across the table and we shook hands on the auspicious event.
'I have finished the task I have lived for' was all he said, and then resumed his seat. The elation was only momentary, and his features
quickly resumed their customary composure.[3]

The completion attracted a flood of congratulation from men
of all political and philosophical persuasions. A committee
was formed consisting, in Beatrice Webb's words, of 'everybody in the intellectual world', and a document drawn up
expressing the awe and admiration of a concourse of writers,
critics, scientists, dons, and savants:

Not all of us agreeing in equal measure with its conclusions, we are all
at one in our estimate of the great intellectual powers it exhibits and
the immense effect it has produced in the history of thought; nor are
we less impressed by the high moral qualities which have enabled you
to concentrate those powers for so many years upon a purpose worthy
of them and, in spite of all obstacles, to carry out so vast a design.[4]

---

[1] *Aby* ii. 454.
[2] H.S. to F.H. Collins, 9 Dec. 1895, *L.L.* ii. 117.
[3] *L.L.* ii. 95.
[4] Signatories to H.S., 16 Dec. 1896. *L.L.* ii. 98. A full list of the signatories
appears in *L.L.* ii. 99–102.

Among the signatures appended were those of Alexander Bain, Arthur Balfour, Bernard Bosanquet, Leonard Hobhouse, Joseph Hooker, William Lecky, John Lubbock, James Martineau, John Morley, General Augustus Pitt-Rivers, David Ritchie, Henry Sidgwick, Leslie Stephen, and Sidney Webb. William Gladstone, who disapproved of signing circulated documents, sent a personal note of recognition, and a fresh sprinkling of honorary degrees and fellowships was proferred. A portrait by Hubert von Herkomer entered the National Portrait Gallery. Spencer paused momentarily to savour the taste of hard-earned recognition.

5

SPENCER'S LAST YEARS AND THE
'DRIFT TO CONSERVATISM'

Longevity was Herbert Spencer's worst enemy; he outlived his vigour, his concentration, his friends, and ultimately his reputation. His last years were sad and pointless as the descent into infirmity coincided with literary oblivion, for, despite the plaudits of eminent intellectuals, Spencer, acutely sensitive to changes in the intellectual atmosphere, detected an evaporation of his influence. His identification of peace and progress was drowned in xenophobia, jingoism, and frenzied colonial expansion; his individualistic Liberalism was challenged by the 'neo-Hegelianism' of Thomas Hill Green and Bernard Bosanquet.[1] Beatrice Webb wrote that Spencer 'felt he had dropped out and was no longer of much consideration.'[2] It can have been little consolation to see an article devoted to himself entitled 'Herbert Spencer: last of the great Victorians'.

How far Spencer's pessimism was justified it is difficult to assess in retrospect, but it received some contemporary corroboration. William Hudson, writing in 1904, recounted his almost complete obliteration from the public mind: 'Life moves rapidly in these days, and it is safe to say that for the present generation Herbert Spencer has been little more than a name.'[3] In the long term, however, his ideas retained considerable force and became widely diffused, especially in America, where his influence on ideology was broad-based and pervasive.[4] The socialism of the Webbs borrowed from him the model of an industrial society free of class antagonism, and the advancement of the species as its objective, while his influence on the development of sociological theory

[1] See below, Chap. 7, esp. pp. 186–8.
[2] Webb, p. 39.
[3] W.H. Hudson, 'Herbert Spencer: a character-study', *Fortnightly Review*, 1904, p.17.
[4] See R. Hofstadter, *Social Darwinism in American Thought*, (Boston, 1955).

was immense. Even his individualism survived; in politics as a component of modern conservatism, and in political theory in the work of F. Hayek, who argues that totalitarianism is the inescapable destiny of any political system that becomes infected by 'socialism' or state interference.[1]

This chapter relates Spencer's physical decline and obsolescence to the developing conservatism detectable in his later political thought. Spencer's political thought reflects the developmental antithesis which he perceived between the first and second halves of the nineteenth century, the first a golden age of peace, prosperity, and individual freedom, the second a period of regression, war, chauvinism, state interference, and bureaucratic tyranny. It is evident in the contrast between the soaring optimism of his early writings and the haunted pessimism of his later works, in the progressive hardening of his attitudes which prompted his renunciation of universal suffrage, land nationalization, and natural rights, and in what Spencer himself called the 'conservatism of advancing years'. The whole of Spencerian thought evinces this simple parabolic development from the buoyant expectancy of youth to the sour disillusionment of old age.

The completion of the *Synthetic Philosophy* saved Spencer the anxiety of not living to accomplish it, but complicated his life by leaving him without incentive. His obsession with rumour and misrepresentation partly filled the vacuum, as his eccentricities, real and fictitious, became public property. It was, for instance, once seriously alleged that he devoured tallow candles to nourish his brain. At a more serious level it is legitimate to question how far his last years were poisoned by a crisis of faith in his own doctrines, and the consequent fear of death. Beatrice Webb affirmed this:

To me he seemed in these last years to be stumbling in total darkness, hurting himself and then crying aloud in his lonely distress, clinging to his dogmas, but without confident faith . . .[2] Indeed it is a favourite speculation of mine that Herbert Spencer himself eventually discovered that there was no evidence in the findings of physical science for any such assumptions of essential beneficence in the working of natural forces; and that the mental misery of his later years was not altogether

[1] See especially F.A. Hayek, *Individualism and Economic Order* (London, 1949).
[2] Webb, p. 37.

unconnected with the loss of the inspiring creed with which he began his *Synthetic Philosophy*.[1]

In *Facts and Comments* Spencer faced the Nemesis of rationalism, the prospect of the obliteration of his consciousness:

After contemplating the inscrutable relationship between brain and consciousness, and finding that we get no evidence of the last without the activity of the first, we seem obliged to relinquish the thought that consciousness continues after physical organisation has become inactive. But it seems a strange and repugnant conclusion that with the cessation of consciousness at death, there ceases to be any knowledge of having existed. With his last breath it becomes to each the same thing as though he had never lived.[2]

Similar anxieties, and the psychological tensions associated with them, were common to many Victorian writers of Spencer's generation, a generation which had taken the brunt of the onset of doubt. Raised in faith, they had embraced agnosticism; nurtured on belief in the rationalist millenium, they had outlived its optimism. W.E. Houghton ascribes the astonishing literary output of men like Herbert Spencer, John Stuart Mill, Charles Kingsley, and Thomas Huxley to a therapeutic impulse: 'For the Victorians, intense activity was both a rational method of attacking the anxieties of the time, and an irrational method of escaping them.'[3] Doubt overhauled them in the end. William Mallock, in a work pessimistically entitled *Is Life Worth Living?* described a generation paralysed by *ennui*: 'We admit nothing now without question; we have learned to take to pieces all motives to actions . . . we not only know more than we have done before, but we are perpetually chewing the cud of our knowledge.'[4] James Froude openly mourned the erosion of his faith: 'I would gladly give all I am . . . but for one week of my old child's faith, to go back to calm and peace again, and then to die in hope.'[5] Spencer came to an uneasy compromise with the unknown:

[1] Webb, p. 90.
[2] H.S., *Facts and Comments*, pp. 202-3.
[3] W.E. Houghton, *The Victorian Frame of Mind* (New Haven, Conn., 1957), p. 262.
[4] ibid., pp. 71-2.
[5] Ibid., p. 86.

It seems to me that our best course is to submit to the limitations imposed by the nature of our minds, and to live as contentedly as we may
in ignorance of that which lies beyond things as we know them. My
own feeling respecting the ultimate mystery is such that of late years
I cannot even try to think of infinite space without some feeling of
terror, so that I habitually shun the thought.[1]

There seemed nothing left but retirement and death, but
Spencer, though he conceded that life in the capital was too
much for him, and moved to Brighton in 1898, could not be
reconciled to permanent inactivity. Having at last found a
simulacrum of domestic security, he went on to produce two
further books, *Various Fragments* (1897) and *Facts and
Comments* (1902) which added little to his reputation and
consisted of miscellaneous short pieces and letters, some
previously published, some showing evidence of intellectual
wear and tear. They bore witness, however, to his determination not to succumb to senility without a fight.

Despite the nervous symptoms which dominated his private
correspondence to the exclusion of almost all else, he retained an outward-looking interest in the affairs of a world in
which he found himself less and less at home. Requests for
support reached him daily from organizations, many of them
representing lost causes, eager to recruit as 'figurehead' this
elder statesman of an outmoded Liberalism. They included
the South African Conciliation Committee, the Aborgines
Protection Society and the Anti-Vaccination League, and his
replies, though sympathetic, convey the sadness, half resignation, half bitterness, which contemplation of his own time
stirred in him. The Boer War provided him with a last, demo-
ralizing spectacle of social atavism, coupled with a last gleam
of vindictive hope: 'A little pressure on the market, a bank
failure or two and a consequent panic may open people's
eyes and make them repent. However heavy the penalty they
have to bear, it cannot be too heavy to please me.'[2] His very
last act, appropriately enough, was to allow his name to be
added to the subscription list of the *Bibliothèque Pacifiste
Internationale*.

[1] H.S. to the Countess of Pembroke, 26 June 1895, *L.L.* ii. 83.
[2] H.S. to W.S. Blunt, 5 Sept. 1901, *L.L.* ii. 192.

During his last summer, his last book complete, his health visibly failing, Herbert Spencer busied himself in dictating answers to a motley stream of inconsequential correspondence, every reply interspersed with expostulations on the need to conserve his powers. Hitherto free from pain, he now began to experience 'spasms', and reluctantly consigned himself to the care of a doctor, whose diagnoses he none the less contested, and whose prescriptions he frequently ignored. He accepted the imminence of death with comparative equanimity, and made the arrangements for his own funeral with characteristic thoroughness. He requested John Morley to deliver his funeral oration, but excused him in advance if he thought he would incur any damage to his election prospects. In the event, Morley was abroad when Spencer died, and so unable to attend.

More harrowing than physical discomfort was the bleak despair to which Spencer now fell victim. An utter despondency overwhelmed him which resulted from the firm conviction that his achievements would be buried with him. His life seemed more desolate, in retrospect, for having been pointlessly sacrificed to an unproductive enterprise, a 'hard bargain' to which he constantly referred. 'If pessimism means that you would rather not have lived,' he confided to Beatrice Webb, 'then I am a pessimist.'[1] She did her best to reassure him; 'it may be that in time some other method of attacking the great problem will be adopted, which will be neither wholly yours, nor wholly ours.' 'Yes,' agreed Spencer, 'it may be.'[2]

During November 1903 Spencer's condition deteriorated rapidly. He exhibited only occasional interest in his surroundings, and ventured only occasional reassertions of his will. He was often delirious; his last words expressed the incongruously Nelsonian wish that his body should be 'taken by sea to Portsmouth'. He entered a coma on Monday 7 December, and at 4.40 a.m. on 8 December he died. He was cremated, and the remains interred at Highgate Cemetery,

[1] Webb, p. 35.
[2] Quoted by Lord Courtney during his oration at H.S.'s funeral, *L.L.* ii. 233.

where his simple, unadorned tomb faces the glowering effigy of Karl Marx.

SPENCER'S PESSIMISM AND HIS 'DRIFT TO CONSERVATISM'

Spencer's personal disintegration produced a deepening em-bitterment in his view of the world, which in turn was re-flected in his thought. While little was added to or subtracted from the central consistencies of individualism and evolution, the more immediately political aspects of his doctrine under-went a significant transition from apparent radicalism to apparent conservatism. Just as Spencer's radicalism con-formed to his youthful faith in human rationality, so his latter-day conservatism can be seen as a facet of the ageing process.

Spencer had begun his literary career convinced of the inevitability of uninterrupted social progress. The com-pelling but as yet ill-defined 'development theory' treated him to visions of an inexorable upward curve of human betterment, with the millenium of rationality just round the corner: 'Always toward perfection is the mighty movement— toward a complete development and a more unmixed good.'[1] This confidence was bolstered by the historical situation of the 1840s:

The signs of the times are indicating the near approach of that era of civilisation when men shall have shaken off the soul-debasing shackles of prejudice . . . the long-acknowledged rationality of man and the ob-vious corollary that he is to be guided by his reason rather than by his feelings, is at length obtaining a practical recognition.[2]

The confidence resulted from a belief in the omnipotence of natural laws and the power of Reason to comprehend them, unqualified as yet by consideration of the fits and starts, pro-gressions and retrogressions of evolution. Social development proceeds under the benevolent guidance of the 'self-adjusting principle'; social evils would be smoothly eradicated. This optimism was reinforced by Spencer's confidence in the edu-cative power of 'correct' social theories. On the publication of

[1] S. Stat., p. 323.
[2] H.S., 'Programme for a projected magazine, Philosopher', 3 Jan. 1844, L.L. i. 59.

The Origin of Species, he wrote: 'Believing as I did that right guidance, individual and social, depends on the acceptance of evolutionary views of man and of society, I was hopeful that its effects would presently be seen on educational methods, political opinions, and men's ideas about human life.'[1]

The remainder of Spencer's life was spent in disillusionment. The state extended its tentacles with unseemly haste over the brave new world of industrial Britain, while the reasoned philosophy of individualism was overtaken by indiscriminate philanthropy as the guideline of social policy:

Sympathy which, a generation ago, was taking the shape of justice, is relapsing into the shape of generosity; and the generosity is exercised by inflicting injustice. . . . Along with that miserable *laissez-faire* which calmly looks on while men ruin themselves in trying to enforce their equitable claims, there goes activity in supplying them, at other men's cost, with *gratis* novel-reading.[2]

With a bitterness tinged with resignation, Spencer charted this regression through his century:

If we contrast the period from 1815 to 1850 with the period from 1850 to the present time, we cannot fail to see that along with increased armaments, more frequent conflicts, and a revived military sentiment, there has been a spread of compulsory regulations. While nominally extended by the giving of votes the freedom of the individual has been in many ways actually diminished; both by restrictions which ever-multiplying officials are appointed to insist on, and by the forcible taking of money to secure for him, or for others at his expense, benefits previously left to be secured by each for himself. And undeniably this is a return towards that coercive discipline which pervades the whole social life where the militant type is predominant.[3]

Spencer's pessimism was reinforced by consideration of the two mainstays of his thought, social evolution and individualism. The 're-barbarisation' of which he complained is explained in terms of the violation of both evolutionary and liberal precepts.

Spencer's grasp of the principles of evolutionary sociology convinced him that growth, if firmly consolidated, needed to be imperceptibly slow:

[1] *Aby* ii. 50.
[2] *Justice*, p. 44.
[3] *P. Soc.* i. 575.

So far as a doctrine can influence general conduct . . . the doctrine, in its social applications, is calculated to produce a steadying effect, alike on thought and action . . . [1]

As between infancy and maturity there is no short cut by which may be avoided the tedious progress of growth and development through insensible increments; so there is no way from the lower forms of social life to the higher, but one passing through small successive modifications. [2]

The old may not safely be discarded until the new has evolved to replace it; if this is attempted, the universal principle of rhythm in natural development will assert itself to produce a violent reaction. Because institutions depend for their soundness on the prevailing climate of morality, furthermore, it follows that substantial development of the human personality must precede institutional change:

Before there arise in human nature and human institutions, changes having that permanence which makes them an acquired inheritance for the race, there must go innumerable recurrences of the thoughts, the feelings, and actions, conducive to such changes. The process cannot be abridged, but must be gone through with due patience. [3]

For Spencer, the eclipse of his radical convictions was explained in terms of his growing awareness of sociological precepts: 'In youth, my constitutional repugnance to coercion, and consequent hatred of despotic forms of rule, had involved a belief . . . that free forms of government would ensure social welfare. . . . These and allied prejudgements were destroyed or greatly modified by contemplation of the facts. [4]

'Contemplation of the facts' revealed to Spencer the vital formula which rationalized the conservative drift of his political thought, the correspondence between institutions and character. Electoral reform and land nationalization are impractical because they are 'in advance of character'; 'The goodness of these or those institutions is purely relative to the natures of the men living under them.' [5] This explains 'the greater contentment I feel now than of old with established governmental forms'. Even monarchy, derided in

[1] *Stud. Soc.*, p. 400.
[2] Ibid., p. 402.   [3] Ibid., pp. 402–3.
[4] H.S., 'The Filiation of Ideas', *L.L.* ii. 7.
[5] H.S. to the Earl of Dysart, 27 May 1892, *L.L.* ii.7.

Social Statics, is rehabilitated: 'Institutions of every kind must be regarded as relative to the characters of citizens and the conditions under which they exist . . . it would be no more proper to deprive them of their king than it would be proper to deprive a child of its doll.'[1] The sweep towards 'socialism', then, is a consequence of a premature relaxation of social restraints.

The principal feature of this social regression was 'over-legislation', to which *The Man versus the State* (1884) was Spencer's lively response. Overlegislation assumes there a menacing ability to perpetuate itself: 'the more numerous governmental interventions become, the more confirmed does this habit of thought grow, and the more loud and perpetual the demands for intervention.'[2] Successive legislative concessions to popular demands create the impression that social evils are rectifiable by Act of Parliament. More and more social conduct is thus drawn into the net of state super-intendence, diminishing the self-reliance of the population. Social disequilibrium is created as the increased demand for officials, inspectors, and commissioners heightens the danger of bureaucratic hegemony. Using the inappropriately mechanical analogy of a pair of scales, Spencer describes the dangers of transferring individuals from the 'regulated mass' of society to its 'regulating structures', until at a given point the scales will tip, and society be left wriggling impotently in the grip of officialdom:

An organization of officials, once passing a certain stage of growth, becomes less and less resistible. . . . We are on the highway to Communism, and I see no likelihood that the movement in that direction will be arrested. Contrariwise, it seems to me that every new step makes more difficult any reversal; since the reactive portion of the public seems likely to become weaker.[3]

Factors which might be expected to deflect this process only intensify it. The failure of legislation to achieve its objectives stimulated 'more insistent demands for recourse to the same remedy, reflecting an inexhaustible credulity.'[4] If failure

[1] *Aby* ii. 465.
[2] *M.v.S.*, p. 34.
[3] *M.v.S.*, pp. 35–6.
[4] H.S. 'Political Fetishism', *Essays* iii. 395.

exercised no check, then neither did success; the mitigation of social evils increased the outcry for their eradication, since partial rectification reinforced faith in the possibility of a total cure:

During the time when the mass of people were profoundly ignorant, there was no recognition of their ignorance; but when they became partially instructed, there arose an outcry that the nation was perishing for lack of knowledge, and that state-agency was needful to spread it . . . now that distress is far less than it used to be, there comes at outcry that things will come to a crash unless it is stopped.[1]

A source of latter-day pessimism, therefore, can be isolated in Spencer's obsession with 'over-legislation'. Even the terminology he employed, 'waves', 'tides', and 'floods', imparts a sense of overwhelming hopelessness: 'The numerous socialistic changes made by Act of Parliament, joined with the numerous others presently to be made, will by and by be all merged into State-Socialism—swallowed in the vast wave which they have little by little raised.'[2] His response alternated between despair and resignation:

I am hopeless of any good to be done. The drift of things is so overwhelming in the other direction, and the stream will, I believe, continue to increase in volume and velocity, simply because political power is now in the hands of those whose *apparent* interest is to get as much as possible done by public agency, and whose desires will inevitably be pandered to by all who seek public functions.[3]

Having heralded the catastrophe in *The Man versus the State* he expressed 'a certain satisfaction in the thought that I shall soon be out of it all, and leave no posterity.'[4]

Although incidental to his theoretical system, the modifications which Spencer introduced as a consequence of this gloomy prognosis had the important effects of damaging his credibility as a philosopher of intellectual integrity, and of isolating him from progressive political movements. *Social Statics* (1851) contained a triumphant and exhaustive affirmation of individual rights, inalienable and inviolable. *Justice*

---

[1] H.S. to T.H. Huxley, 5 Feb. 1888, Hux. Coll. vii.
[2] *M.v.S.*, p. 41.
[3] H.S. to A. Herbert 16 June 1890, *L.L.* i. 402.
[4] H.S. to E.L. Youmans, 15 May 1884, *L.L.* i. 325.

(1891) largely repudiated them. *Social Statics* included among these the right of universal suffrage; *Justice* spoke of 'political rights—so-called'. *Social Statics* talked confidently of the restoration of all land to the community; *Justice* pleaded that such a measure would be both unethical and impractical. Spencer, the radical iconoclast of 1851, had become the establishment philosopher of 1891, and his doctrine, in Henry George's graphic phrase, had been 'disembowelled, stuffed and then set up in the Garden of the Spencerian Philosophy, where it may be viewed with entire complacency by Sir John and His Grace',[1] George's satirical personification of the patrons of the Liberty and Property Defence League.

The disparity between his pronouncements of 1851 and those of 1891 is not at issue. Criticism of Spencer, by converts to his former radicalism, was levelled rather at the mode of his retreat, and the motives underlying it. In George's estimation, Spencer had abandoned his principles in full flight from their radical implications. Where Spencer indicated a gradual modification of his views to accord with the logical requirements of the mature evolutionary theory, and the *laissez-faire* premises which had always governed his thinking, his detractors saw a sudden and less honest betrayal. Examination of the chronology of the process shows that, whereas Spencer's view is vindicated with respect to the question of political reform, on the Land Question he retracted his earlier conclusions less decorously, and with apparent haste.

SPENCER'S CONSERVATISM AND ELECTORAL REFORM

The young Spencer's advocacy of electoral reform was based on the desirability of allowing the impulses of radicalism a restricted freedom in order to forestall violent change, since 'new institutions obtained by violence are of necessity premature.' His mature opposition to it was founded on two objections. First, according to the requirements of social

---

[1] H. George, *Herbert Spencer: a perplexed philosopher, being an examination of Mr. Herbert Spencer's various utterances on the Land Question* (London, 1892), p. 132.

evolution, political institutions must match the collective character of the citizens regulated by them, a conviction implicit in his verdict that 'the forms which freedom requires will not in themselves produce the reality of freedom in the absence of the appropriate national character.'[1] The second objection concerned overlegislation. The extension of democracy is desirable only where it can be guaranteed that the newly enfranchised will not pursue legislation in their own interests. Spencer had only to prove that legislative meddling was on the increase, which posed no problem to an inveterate individualist of his ingenuity, and reform is discredited. The two disqualifications of electoral reform, therefore, stemmed from the two main sources of Spencerian theory; an evolutionary imperative of the appropriateness of political institutions to national character, and the individualist imperative which made reform conditional on the continued passivity of the state.

Spencer withdrew his support for electoral reform by slow degrees. In 'Representative Government; what is it good for?' (1857)[2] which enumerated the shortcomings of contemporary democracy, he undermines the reformers' case without directly challenging it. If, as he asserts, representative government is vitiated by the venality and ignorance of voters (on which he approvingly quotes Thomas Carlyle, of all people) then there can be no strong argument for enlarging their political rights. Representative government, furthermore, is guilty of presuming itself to be omnicompetent: 'Both the theory and the practice of this English government implies that it may do whatever it pleases.'[3] Even if the theory were convincing, the practice conclusively disqualified it. Spencer declared that 'for administrative efficiency autocratic power is the best', but swiftly adds the qualification 'IF you would have society actively regulated by a staff of state agents.'[4] Representative government succumbs to inefficiency only when it assumes too wide a jurisdictional scope; none of its short-

---

[1] H.S., 'Parliamentary Reform: its dangers and safeguards', *Essays,* iii. 381.
[2] *Westminster Review,* Oct. 1857.
[3] H.S., 'Representative Government: what is it good for?', *Essays,* iii. 305.
[4] *Essays,* iii. 302.

comings unfit it for discharging 'the comparatively simple duty of protector'. At this point, *laissez-faire* begins to encroach on the extension of the franchise.

Interventionist tendencies in the ministries of Palmerston and Derby awakened Spencer's disquiet during the years 1857-9. Congratulating John Stuart Mill on *On Liberty*, he wrote:

The strong tendency there is on the part of the working-class to Over-legislation has given me the only qualms I have had of late respecting the effects of increased popular power. . . . I hope for great effects from it in mitigating that mania for meddling which has been the curse of recent legislation, and I know of no more important service to the time than to reform public opinion on this matter.[1]

This anxiety is expressed, and the argument extended, in 'Parliamentary Reform: its dangers and safeguards'[2] (1860). The cautionary prerequisites of extended democracy now impinge directly upon the admissibility of reform. Spencer welcomed some of the immediate consequences of popular power, but 'besides ideas likely to eventuate in changes which we would regard as beneficial, the working class entertain ideas that could not be realised without gross injustice to other classes and ultimate injury to themselves.'[3] The urgent need for middle-class tutelage is pointed by dangerous proclivities among the workers; their 'prevailing enmity towards capitalists', their belief that 'machinery acts to their damage', and their espousal of the Nine-Hour Bill, 'believing, as they have been taught by Act of Parliament to believe, that the relation between the quantity of labour given and the wages received is not a natural but an artificial one.'[4]

Here are neatly interwoven both individualistic and evolutionary strands of the anti-reform argument. Not only do the workers favour an undue invocation of legislative authority, but their behaviour reveals them, as yet, unfitted for democracy:

[1] H.S. to J.S. Mill, 17 Feb. 1859, *L.L.* i. 121.
[2] *Westminster Review,* Apr. 1860.
[3] *Essays*, iii. 363.
[4] *Essays*, iii. 363.

It becomes a grave question how far we may safely give political power to those who entertain beliefs so erroneous respecting fundamental social relations; and who so pertinaciously struggle to reinforce these erroneous views. Men who render up their private liberties to the despotic rulers of Trade Unions seem scarcely independent enough rightly to exercise political liberties. . . . When, in short, they prove themselves ready to become alike slaves and tyrants, we may well pause before giving them the franchise.[1]

Two important modifications of Spencer's reformist viewpoint as set forth in *Social Statics* are evident here. First, electoral rights, from being the inalienable rights of free men, have become by implication conferable, something that 'we' may well pause before 'giving'. Second, the equivalent ignorance of upper-class protectionists goes unmentioned. In *Social Statics* Spencer argued that the franchise could not consistently be withheld from the working class on the grounds of a political ignorance common to all strata of society. Here, the alleged homogeneity of national judgement is set aside; working-class ignorance is anti-capitalist, Trade Unionist, Luddite ignorance, and must be contained beyond the electoral pale. It is also interventionist ignorance; the workers look to the state not only for industrial regulations but for wider social benefits, as their poverty and consequent sense of injustice make fertile soil for the seductive schemes of Lord Shaftesbury, Edwin Chadwick, and the National Association for the Promotion of Social Sciences: 'Led by philanthropists having sympathies stronger than their intellects, the working classes are very likely to employ their influence in increasing social legislation.'[2]

To counteract these dangers, Spencer devised a system of 'safeguards'. To forestall 'artificial' restrictions on labour he enjoined 'the spread of sounder views among the working classes, and the moral advance which such sounder views imply.'[3] Social legislation can be prevented by a widening of the incidence of direct taxation, thus exploding 'the superstition that the law can give *gratis* benefits':[4]

[1] *Essays*, iii. 365–6.
[2] *Essays*, iii. 370.
[3] *Essays*, iii. 375.
[4] *Essays*, iii. 371.

The connection between all governmental action and the demand for taxes . . . is becoming less and less familiar to the working-class mind. I feel very much inclined to think *that representation may be safely extended so fast only* as taxation becomes direct and equally distributed.[1]

The notion of 'equally distributed' is dubious in the light of Spencer's argument, in the same essay, that benefits conferred by the state, although directly financed by tax- and rate-payers, are ultimately financed by the working class through inflated prices charged by the capitalist to protect his profit, and higher rents to compensate the landlord for his rates. If direct taxation is also levied on income, the working class will then be paying twice over for benefits equally available to the middle-class taxpayer. Despite the punitive character of these sanctions, Spencer did not, in 1860, repudiate electoral reform in principle. He supported the 1867 Reform Act, but his commitment cannot long have survived this measure.

First to be relinquished was the principle of female suffrage. In *Social Statics* Spencer argued for a comprehensive equality of the sexes, but became disturbed by his perception of developing female emancipation. Disliking all changes, even those prophesied by himself, he complained that 'what were originally concessions have come to be claimed as rights, and in gaining the character of rights have lost much of the grace they had as concessions.'[2] He seems almost to have reverted to the archaic conception of the 'woman's place', arguing that 'if women comprehended all that is contained in the domestic sphere, they would ask no other.'[3] From a close friend of George Eliot this is an astonishing remark, although Spencer always regarded her as something of a freak, too clever to be naturally a woman.

Accordingly, when John Stuart Mill canvassed his support for female suffrage, Spencer withheld it: 'while I should advocate the extension of the suffrage to women as an *ultimate* measure, I do not approve of it as an *immediate*

[1] H.S. to J.S. Mill, 25 Mar. 1859, *L.L.* i. 123.
[2] *P. Soc.* i. 755–6.
[3] *P. Soc.* i. 757.

measure, or even as a measure to be shortly taken.'[1] Voting
exists to maintain equal freedom, 'the unhindered exercise of
the faculties by each limited by the equal claims of others'.
Would female suffrage strengthen or impair this freedom?
Regretfully, Spencer decided that it would impair it, for
'women as a mass are habitually on the side of authority.'
This alleged predilection derives from a 'psysiological
necessity', a constitutional power-worship which only evolution could eradicate. Their authoritarianism notwithstanding, women are naturally the nurturers of the young, so
that their sympathies gravitate towards the weak. They
would tend, therefore, to view social questions in a maternal
light, resulting in 'a more general fostering of the worse at
the expense of the better',[2] were they to be endowed with
the franchise. Spencer's political misogyny later hardened to
the extent that he denied women the right to vote until such
time as they paid taxes and served in the armed forces along-
side their menfolk, an argument to which, in the late-nine-
teenth century, even the formidable Mrs. Mill would have
found no answer.

Justice (1891) contained the comprehensive repudiation of
the electoral principle. The franchise, extended to protect
rights, is falsely identified as a right *per se*. On the contrary,
the right to vote is seen as being conditional on its usage: 'the
franchise . . . gives the citizens in general powers of checking
trespasses upon . . . their rights; powers which they may or
may not use to good purpose.'[3] A universally-enfranchised
community may establish a tyrannical regime; the franchise
itself is no guarantee of the liberty of the individual. In
England, for example:

While the outside form of free government remains, there has grown up
within it a reality which makes government not free. The body of professional politicians, entering public life to get incomes, organising their
forces and developing their tactics have, in fact, come to be a ruling
class quite different from that which the constitution intended to secure; and a class having interests by no means identical with public

[1] H.S. to J.S. Mill, 9 Aug. 1867. *L.L.* i. 181.
[2] *P. Eth.*, i. 196.
[3] *Justice*, p. 177.

interests. This worship of the appliances of liberty in place of liberty
itself, needs continually exposing. There is no intrinsic virtue in votes.[1]

Spencer's overriding concern was now with the protection
of minorities. In *Social Statics* 'our tender regard for the
minority' is not allowed to obscure the priority of majority
rights, but he was unhappy about the forcible subjection of
the minority to the majority will: 'The very existence of
majorities and minorities is indicative of an immoral state . . .
implies that the desires of some cannot be satisfied without
sacrificing the desires of others.'[2] The submission of the
minority is not axiomatic, as Rousseau alleged, but merely an
interim solution. Spencer's misgivings grew with his experience
of the railway boardroom: 'Our popular form of government
has so habituated us to seeing public questions decided by
the voice of the majority . . . that there has been produced in
the general mind an unhesitating belief that the majority's
right is unbounded.'[3] On the contrary, the majority decision
is conditional upon observance of the contractual limits of
the incorporated body, be it limited company or state.
Minority rights are intrinsically bound up in the limits of
state intervention:

The general principle underlying the right government of every incorporated body is that its members contract with each other severally
to submit to the will of the majority *in all matters concerning the fulfilment of the object for which they are incorporated, but in no others.*
If there exists no expressed or understood contract between the union
and the members respecting unspecified objects, then for the majority
to coerce the minority into undertaking them is nothing less than gross
tyranny.[4]

This statement has obvious bearings on electoral reform. The
enfranchisement of the working class would create a majority
interested in the promotion of legislation not catered for in
the original governmental terms of reference (as understood
by Spencer) and financed by the propertied minority.

Spencer regarded the theory of majority government as an

[1] *Stud. Soc.,* p. 278.
[2] *S. Stat.,* p. 234.
[3] H.S., 'Railway Morals and Railway Policy', *Essays,* iii. 89.
[4] *Essays,* iii. 91.

authoritative principle equivalent to the monarchical theory of Divine Right, and an equivalent threat to democracy:

The great political superstition of the past was the divine right of kings. The great political superstition of the present is the divine right of parliaments. The oil of anointing seems unawares to have dripped from the head of the one on to the heads of the many, and given sacredness to them and to their decrees.[1]

Nevertheless, he was prepared to invoke this principle where occasion arose. His objection to the demolition of the Great Exhibition buildings at the instigation of local residents illustrated how 'a small body of men deeply interested and able to cooperate' conspired to deprive millions of 'refining pleasure.'[2] In denouncing Charles Parnell's obstructionist tactics during the sessions of 1885 he arraigned the government for 'tacitly allowing the system of government by minority within the House . . . the 584 are traitors to free institutions if they let themselves be ruled by the 86.'[3] These examples are introduced, not to berate Spencer for his inconsistency, but to reinforce the suggestion that he was not afraid to invoke the rights of majority or minority where over-legislation was the issue. Intervention is the fixed criterion of his judgement on all issues; all else is variable, and is adjusted in conformity with its dictates.

Spencer's repudiation of electoral reform is therefore merely a manifestation of the consistency of his thinking. The equation in Spencer's mind of popular power with administrative tyranny is a major theme of his later political writings: 'instead of the powerful rule of political classes, men are elaborating for themselves a rule of official classes which will become equally powerful. . .'[4] 'The drift towards socialism, now becoming irresistible, has resulted from giving to the masses not a due proportion of power but the supreme power.'[5] It derives from the competition between politicians and parties to capture the mass vote by promising to meet expectations of social amelioration: 'Every candidate for parliament is prompted to propose or support some new

[1] M.v.S., iii. 91.   [2] Aby i. 374.
[3] The Times, 21 Dec. 1885.   [4] P. Soc. iii. 597.
[5] Aby i. 221.

piece of *ad captandum* legislation . . . Each seeks popularity by promising more than his opponent has promised.'[1]

Spencer's view articulated the anxieties of propertied men faced with parliamentary reform since before 1832. He conjured up for their alarm a vicious spiral of expensive legislation culminating in a monstrous bureaucratic monopoly of power. Political theory itself is corrupted by 'an identification of freedom with the political appliances set up to maintain freedom . . . and possession of political power by all is supposed to be the same thing as freedom.'[2] At the root of the problem lies the crude materialism of the masses, who 'appreciate nothing but material boons, better homes, shorter hours, higher wages, more regular work.'[3] The overt objectives of working-class electoral agitation were undeniably materialist; reform of representation was only a means to the end of greater physical well-being, and Spencer was neither the first nor the last to scold them for it. In so doing, however, he neglected the fact that physical comfort and security were essential prerequisites of the fine and civilized existence which he predicted as the outcome of social evolution. George Orwell might have been thinking of Spencer when he excoriated

The damned impertinence of these politicians, priests, literary men and what-not, who lecture the working-class socialist for his materialism! All that the working man demands is what these others would consider the indispensable minimum without which human life cannot be lived at all . . . How right the working classes are in their materialism! How right they are to realise that the belly comes before the soul, not in the scale of values, but in point of time.[4]

The 'dangers' of mass power were evident to others besides Spencer. Robert Lowe, a Benthamite Whig, opposed successive reform bills on the grounds that mass legislation would undermine the mid-Victorian constitutional balance, an argument posited on the political *naiveté* of the new voters. Most Victorian Liberals drew a careful distinction between democracy and liberty, and held that liberty might be imperilled by too rapid an extension of democracy. Walter Bagehot

[1] *M.v.S.*, p. 38.   [2] *Aby* i. 439.
[3] *Aby* ii. 368.
[4] G. Orwell, *Homage to Catalonia* (London, 1962), pp. 244–5.

expressed the fear that 'both our political parties will bid for
the support of the working man'; 'both of them will promise
to do as he likes if he will only tell them what it is.'[1] John
Stuart Mill, in *On Liberty*, set out to circumscribe 'the
tyranny of the majority', though he later looked to socialism
to close the educational gap and make democracy safe. Most
English Liberals feared the extension of popular power, a fear
which Harold Laski attributed to their championship of a
propertied minority, and their acceptance, after David
Ricardo, of the logic of inequality under capitalism. For
them the state existed 'to enable rich men to sleep peacefully in their beds.'[2]

Thus Liberals from Thomas Babington Macaulay through
Henry Maine to A.V. Dicey consistently opposed extensions
of the franchise. The democratic spirit which inspired
Spencer's participation in the Complete Suffrage Movement,
itself tempered by a preventive perspective, was finally stifled
by the logical necessities of individualism. In openly allying
himself with the opponents of reform, however, Spencer was
not straying far from the Liberal consensus.

SPENCER'S CONSERVATISM AND THE LAND QUESTION

The consistency of Spencer's thinking is less apparent in his
volte-face on land nationalization, which gained him un-
welcome publicity and embroiled him in a bitter and exhausting controversy. His reputation as a serious thinker was
at this stage sufficiently solid to have enabled him to shrug
off attacks from relatively obscure visionaries. Instead, his
querulous self-justification drew attention to his equivocacy.
John Tyndall advised him sensibly: 'Relying upon merits
which the whole world acknowledges, you ought, I think, to
be able to say "Damn consistency" in respect of these scraps
and fragments of your views',[3] but Spencer's sensitivity to
criticism overruled this wise counsel.

In *Social Statics* the right of property in land is declared to
be invalid, a deduction from the 'law of equal freedom'

---

[1] W. Bagehot, *The English Constitution* (London, 1867), p. 22.
[2] H. Laski, *The Rise of European Liberalism* (London, 1936), p. 254.
[3] Tyndall to H.S., 25 Nov. 1889, *L.L.* ii. 30.

which 'made sad havoc with the pretensions of landlords.'[1]
Each man is 'free to use the earth for the satisfaction of his
wants, provided he allows all others the same liberty'.
'Equity', therefore, 'does not permit property in land.'[2]
Historically the original communal possessors of the soil
were forcibly ousted by the ancestors of current owners. No
intervening lapse of time can eradicate this injustice: 'How
long does it take for what was originally a *wrong* to grow
into a right?'[3] Spencer admits of no compromise: 'Either
men *have* a right to make the soil private property, or they
have not.'[4] This verdict enjoins 'a protest against every
existing pretension to the individual possession of the soil;
and dictates the assertion that the right of mankind at large
to the earth's surface is still valid; all deeds, customs and laws
notwithstanding.'[5]

Land nationalization is the means of resolving the contradiction of existing private ownerships, in that 'separate
ownerships would merge into the joint-stock ownership of
the public',[6] owners would become tenants and the community their landlord. A crucial difficulty now arises in the form
of compensation; the present holders themselves are not
brigands, and would incur considerable loss. Spencer, however, in his zeal for public ownership, is dismissive about their
claims: 'In our tender regard for the vested interests of the
few, let us not forget that the rights of the many are in abeyance; and must remain so, as long as the earth is monopolised
by individuals.'[7]

The core of Spencer's analysis, then, is a powerful vindication of land nationalization, but it includes the rudimentary loopholes which he later enlarged and, in his own
estimation at least, slipped through. Compensation is one;
another is the dichotomy between absolute and relative ethics.
Richard Hutton, reviewing *Social Statics*, noted that all its
boldly radical pronouncements could be swiftly nullified by
the invocation of this simple formula: 'if a consequence of
his theory is absurd, impractical, unsupported by a shadow

---

[1] *Leader*, 15 Mar. 1851.
[3] *S. Stat.*, pp. 133-4.
[5] *S. Stat.*, p. 134.
  S. Stat., p. 142.
[2] *S. Stat.*, pp. 131-2.
[4] *S. Stat.*, p. 139.
[6] *S. Stat.*, p. 141,

of argument, moral or otherwise, he has a theory ready to account for the failure of the theory . . . that it only states the rights and duties of perfect men.'[1] Relative ethics, by contrast, deals in a hierarchy of lesser evils. In a society of imperfect men conduct cannot be evaluated by reference to absolute ethics, since pure rectitude cannot be expected of them: 'no guiding principle, no method of estimation, enables us to say whether a proposed course is ever relatively right, as causing, proximately or remotely, specially or generally, the greatest surplus of good over evil.'[2]

This statement has two important implications for the Land Question. First, the relative claims of community and landlord cannot be adjudicated, since no one is qualified to discriminate between shades of injustice. Spencer does so, however, in declaring that the rights of the community should prevail. Second, the conclusions of the chapter, deriving from a hypothetical perfection at odds with prevalent injustice, are inapplicable to the current social state (a disqualification stated in *Social Statics*, though not in the specific chapter, and having no declared connection with it).

Another loophole is Spencer's theory of property. He also deduces from the law of equal freedom that no man may rightfully deprive another of his property, a simple deduction which avoids the important issue of whether the title to property is itself valid. If the acquisition of property involves the infringement of communal rights, then it must be lawful for the culprit to be deprived of his 'property' (i.e. that which he *holds* as opposed to that to which he is *entitled*). The strictly deductive approach, therefore, apparently yields two incompatible ethical precepts; the community is rightfully proprietor of the soil, yet the landowner cannot rightfully be deprived of it.

This disquieting discrepancy arises out of the ambiguity of the term 'equal freedom' in Spencer's usage. It has three possible meanings: (1) equal opportunities to pursue ends (assuming the right to pursue them, which may or may not be universally enjoyed); (2) equal lack of institutional restraint in the pursuit of ends; (3) equal *rights* to ends, subject

[1] *L.L.* i. 77.
[2] *D. of E.*, p. 231.

to their availability, which in turn depends on whether the objectives have already been pursued and attained by other men so as to forestall further attempts.

Spencer's general argument was that equal freedom in sense (2) provides a logical premise for equal rights (3). This works out logically with respect to private property in land, where the unrestrained pursuit of the object, land, by some men has effectively excluded the rest, though the rest still have, technically, the right (3) to land. In *Social Statics*, however, he had argued that communal proprietorship of the soil, based on 'equal freedom' in senses (1) and (2) precludes individual proprietorship, so that freedom in sense (3) does not pertain. In *Justice*, conversely, individual proprietorship, based on freedom in sense (3), makes a meaningless technicality of 'equal freedom' in senses (1) and (2).

Is the landlord's relation to the soil authentically proprietorial? Spencer apparently thinks so. Following John Locke, he attributes property to the mixture of labour with natural resources, and ascribes to the human race an innately acquisitive mentality which makes property a 'natural' institution. Initially the fruits of the earth were freely available to all, but since all men have equal opportunities to exploit it the emergence of a propertied élite reflects their 'natural' superiority, and is no infraction of natural justice:

If, therefore, out of many starting with like fields of activity, one attains, by his greater strength greater ingenuity or greater application, more gratification and sources of gratification than the rest, and does this without in any way trenching on the equal freedom of the rest, the moral law assigns him an exclusive right to all those extra gratifications and sources of gratification.[1]

The Lockean explanation of property, however, allows equal access to a Marxist interpretation. If expended labour is the origin of property, then property should continue to accrue to those whose labour produces it: the worker rather than the entrepreneur; the peasant rather than the landlord. The property-based privileges of Spencer's 'natural' élite should persist for no longer than a generation. If, by hereditary acquisition, the actual production of value by labour and its

[1] *S. Stat.*, p. 150.

ownership by inheritance are divorced, then the social distribution of property is inequitable.

In *Social Statics* Spencer was alive to this predicament, and
questioned the validity of the labour theory of property itself: 'the question at issue is, whether by labour so expended,
he has made his right to the thing caught or gathered greater
than the pre-existing rights of all men put together.'[1] He
returned to land nationalization as a compromise; proprietory
ownership of the soil and expropriation are equally inequitable, therefore nationalize it, invest ownership in the
community and return it to its present owners as rented lots.
Private tenure of land replaces private ownership; landlords
become tenants and continue to enjoy the proceeds of their
tenure with the blessing of the community.

Spencer's critics attributed his repudiation of this scheme
to a sudden change of heart, motivated by timidity and concern for a respectable reputation. Spencer argued that it was
the product of a gradual evolution beyond juvenile radicalism,
and that the explicit repudiation of common ownership
merely formulated a conviction of long standing. *Political
Institutions* (1882), however, had reaffirmed the principle,
and suggested that evolution might eventually re-establish
the communal mode of ownership:

With the passage from a nomadic to a settled state, ownership of land
by the community becomes qualified by individual ownership; but
only to the extent that those who clear and cultivate portions of the
surface have undisturbed enjoyment of its produce . . . There is reason
to suspect that while private possession of things produced by labour
will grow even more definite and sacred than at present; the inhabited
area, which cannot be produced by labour, will eventually be distinguished as something which may not be privately possessed.[2]

The revelation that some of his pronouncements of 1851
were still taken seriously caught Spencer unawares. In 1881
he received an effusive invitation from fellow-evolutionist
Alfred Russell Wallace to join the Land Nationalisation
Society, as 'the first eminent Englishman of Science to establish the doctrine of Land Nationalisation upon the firm basis
of social justice.'[3] Spencer replied that he 'fully sympathised

[1] *S. Stat.*, p. 146.   [2] *Pol. Inst.*, pp. 645-6.
[3] A.R. Wallace, op.cit., ii. 240.

in the general aims' of the Society, but demurred that before committing itself to a specific programme, 'it is needful to generate a body of public opinion on the general issue.'[1] None the less his endorsement of the principle was contrasted by Wallace with the later 'most impotent conclusion' repudiating it in *Justice*.

In 1883 Henry George published *Progress and Poverty* and *The Irish Land Question*, socialist polemics in which Spencer was extensively and approvingly quoted. *The Edinburgh Review* commented that 'Writers like Mr. George and Mr. Spencer are at war, not only with the first principles of political economy and law, and social order and domestic life, but with the elements of human nature.'[2] In reply Spencer wrote to the ultra-conservative *St. James' Gazette* (14 Feb. 1883) dissociating himself from 'a book which I closed after a few minutes on finding out how visionary were its ideas'. Spencer listed four substantive reasons for his recantation. First, the discrepancy between absolute and relative ethics: 'the views on land tenure set forth in *Social Statics* . . . were purely ethical in their derivation'; second, his admission to having been overtaken by events ('I had no conception that the question of State-ownership would be raised in our time'); third, the amount of compensation, determined by the incremental value conferred on the soil by generations of cultivation, and obviously a prohibitive sum; and, fourth, predictably, the undesirability of governmental administration of the land, once appropriated. The transfer of ownership would be 'made in the interests of Communism'.

The controversy reopened in 1889, when *The Times* reported a political meeting during which *Social Statics* was quoted in support of Land Nationalisation. Spencer's letter of retraction was followed by a lengthy correspondence in *The Times*'s letter columns with Spencer and Auberon Herbert ranged against a phalanx of antagonists which included Thomas Huxley. Spencer retreated further; he claimed to have disowned *Social Statics*, interdicted translations and waived further editions. His proposals in any case went no further than the symbolic resumption of land ownership by

[1] Ibid., ii. 27.
[2] *Edinburgh Review*, Jan. 1883.

the community, currently expressed in the nominal proprietorship of the Crown. The tortuous affiliation of absolute and relative ethics was thrashed out anew. Compensation
was described as not only obligatory (even for a 'symbolic'
resumption) but exorbitant: 'whereas in 1850 I supposed
that resumption of land ownership by the community would
be economically advantageous, I now hold that, if established
with due regard to the existing claims, as I have always contended that it should be, it would be disadvantageous.'[1]

Spencer's embroilment attracted the invidious approval of
the Liberty and Property Defence League, who invited him
to become a member. The disillusionment of his alienated
disciples, a constant theme of the controversy in *The Times*,
was voiced by Henry George: 'the name of Herbert Spencer
now appears with those of about all the dukes in the kingdom as the director of an association formed for the purpose
of defending private property in land.'[2] Spencer, attentive to
his Liberal reputation, took the point:

I think it would be politic neither for the League nor for myself that I
should join it. Rightly or wrongly, it has acquired the repute of a Tory
organisation; and as I have recently been exasperating the Liberal Party
by my criticisms, were I to join the League, the inference would be
drawn, and apparently with very good ground, that I had turned tail.
Now were this inference to be drawn and widely asserted as it would
be, such effect as may be presently produced by papers I am now
writing would be in large measure destroyed. The press of the Liberal
party would have a seemingly valid reason for pooh-poohing all I say.[3]

Nevertheless, he remained in clandestine touch: 'Though I am
quite willing to aid pecuniarily, I am desirous that my aid
should not be publicly interpreted into membership of the
League.'[4] He regarded it as a bulwark against 'State Socialism',
shared its concern for the autonomy of the ratepayer and
quoted its deliberations with approval in *Justice*.[5] In a recent
article entitled 'The Liberty and Property Defence League
and Individualism'[6] E. Bristow gives a fascinating account of

---

[1] *The Times*, 11. Nov. 1889.
[2] H. George, op.cit., p. 201.
[3] H.S. to the Earl of Wemyss, 1 Mar. 1884, *L.L.* i. 323.
[4] H.S. to the Earl of Wemyss, Feb. 1890, *L.L.* i. 400.   [5] *Justice*, pp. 90-1.
[6] E. Bristow, 'The Liberty and Property Defence League and Individualism',
Historical Journal, xviii no. 4 (1975), pp. 761-89.

the League, and of the individualistically motivated pressure-groups which sprang from it. The young activists involved in them regarded Spencer as their mentor, and even formed 'Spencer circles', while Spencer himself played a marginal role in their activities by giving his endorsement and occasionally his advice.

Justice contains Spencer's definitive statement on the Land Question. Communal ownership of the land is still considered to be valid in principle:

It appears to be a corollary from the law of equal freedom, interpreted with strictness, that the earth's surface may not be appropriated absolutely by individuals, but may be occupied by them only in such manner as recognises the ultimate ownership by other men; that is—by society at large.[1]

However, since the Crown is nominally proprietor of the soil, and since monarchical power has been superceded by popular power, the community is already effectively the supreme landlord. The Land Nationalisers are asking for something they already have.

Any more practical form of land nationalization encounters the insuperable obstacle of compensation: 'Were the direct ownership to be resumed by the community . . . without purchase', therefore, 'the community would take, along with something which is its own, an immensely greater amount of something which is not its own.'[2] In addition, landowners must be reimbursed for rates, poor-law contributions and other property-levies amounting, by Spencer's inscrutable arithmetic, to £500 000 000. The community, furthermore, is entitled only to 'the surface of the country in its original, unsubdued state',[3] so that nationalization implies the payment of a gigantic sum for 'prairie-style' land. The seizure of the commons, furthermore, took place in barbaric times. 'Restoration' is therefore an illusion since the descendants of the deprived cannot be distinguished from those of the predators. Demographic history obscures identification of the 'rightful claimants'; 'the only imaginable form of the

---

[1] *Justice,* p. 81.
[2] *Justice,* p. 91.
[3] *Justice,* p. 92.

transaction would be a restoration of Great Britain bodily to the Welsh and the Highlanders.'[1] A final warning is sounded of the perils of allowing the land to fall under bureaucratic control.

In 1892 Henry George replied with *Herbert Spencer: a perplexed philosopher*, a thorough but not unduly vindictive examination of Spencerian contortions on the Land Question. Its theme is that the conclusion that 'treatment of land as private property cannot equitably be interfered with' is 'a position the reverse of which he once ably asserted.'[2] Far from consigning the question to a rosier future, George insists that it is 'already passing into the domain of practical politics, and soon to become the burning question of the time'. Whether Spencer liked it or not, *Social Statics* contained an important contribution to a controversy very much alive.

Its shortcomings, according to George, arise from Spencer's failure to distinguish between value as utility (by which a golden spade is equivalent to an iron one) and value as exchange (in which a golden spade purchases more). The basis of the second, relative value, is labour, which artificially increases the value of land in terms of the excess of produce it yields over the most worthless land in use (basically the Ricardian rent theory). Spencer believed that labour conferred some intrinsic, utilitarian value to the land, inalienable and transferable by bequest. This confusion led him to regard private tenancy from the state as the only equitable form of land nationalization. Nevertheless, *Social Statics* was a great leap forward, and George acclaims Spencer as iconoclast of 'the sacred white elephant of English respectability', private property in land.

His retraction seemed thereby all the more reprehensible. Spencer publicly disowned *Social Statics*, 'yet at the time he thus wrote, the book was being published in the United States, and continued to be for years afterwards.'[3] This is true; *Social Statics* was published in America in 1864, and without revision (on Edward Youmans's advice that radical

[1] *Justice*, p. 266.
[2] H. George, op.cit., p. 5.
[3] H. George, op.cit., p. 83.

discourse sold well). A preparatory note was appended explaining changes in Spencer's position on the rights of women and children, and disclaiming his occasional invocations
of the Almighty in support of his arguments, but the Land
Question was not mentioned, and the book was not substantially revised until 1892. Spencer's letter to the *St.
James' Gazette* was designed, in George's view, to salvage a
respectable reputation from the taint of 'communism'.
George particularly resented the denunciation of himself in
The Man versus the State (1884) as 'the movement for land
nationalization which, aiming at a system of land-tenure
equitable in the abstract is, as all the world knows, pressed
by Mr. George and his friends with avowed disregard for the
just claims of existing owners, and as the basis of a scheme
going more than half-way to State Socialism.'[1] The correspondence of 1889 compounded the betrayal; Spencer had
become the 'valued ally of the Liberty and Property Defence
League'.

To Spencer's mortification these accusations gained a wide
acceptance. *The Times* loftily observed that 'Spencer had
abandoned the necessary inference from motives less abstract
and considerably less creditable than those founded on sound
logic and the truth of things.'[2] Further skirmishes took place
between Spencer and the English Land Restoration League
in the columns of the *Morning Chronicle*, and it was not until
January 1895 that he resolved, wisely if tardily, to 'wash my
hands entirely of the whole George business.'[3]

Spencer's claim to consistency rests on two propositions:
that he never relinquished the principle of communal proprietorship in the soil, and that the resumption of this right
would be impractical and unethical in its treatment of
current landowners. Absolute ethics demands that the land
be owned by the community. 'Equitable' is the key word,
and in context its meaning is frequently obscure. Spencer
states, for instance, that expropriation of landowners in
'inequitable' (in relative ethics), but landowners' 'rights' are
inequitable in the first place (in absolute ethics). Spencer

[1] *M.v.S.*, pp. 38–9.
[2] *The Times* 12 Jan. 1894.
[3] H.S. to A. Skilton, 22 Feb. 1895, *L.L.* ii. 44.

employs 'inequitable' without these necessary qualifications, in a purely dyslogistic sense, rather than as a strict definition of the ethical status of an action. It cost him nothing to denounce individual property-rights in land as 'absolutely' inequitable, provided that relative ethics and practical considerations combined to invalidate all attempts to remove them. Spencer's inconsistency lies in his selection of the 'least wrong'; in 1851 expropriation is the least wrong, while in 1891 the least wrong is to leave well alone.

Spencer's changed attitude to land nationalization turns on the question of compensation. For the community to disburse £500 000 000 for virgin land is obviously impracticable, yet the justification of this transaction is less obvious. Spencer enjoins compensation for the additional value created by generations of landowners through tillage, drainage etc., but if it is to be restored to the community in its natural state, as Spencer recommends, it will have no such additional value. Conversely, the owners ought to compensate the community for generations of income of which they have been as wrongfully deprived. Ignoring this implication, Spencer concentrates on reimbursing the owners for their rates, poor-relief, and taxes (exacted directly or indirectly from the peasants who actually worked the land), and for this fraction of the income of which they have deprived the community and grudgingly repaid as public dues, he first demands a price of £500 000 000, and then triumphantly declares that it is too high. The Land Question, then, is the least creditable aspect of Spencer's developing conservatism.

The questions of the franchise and of land nationalization reflect a dramatic shift of emphasis within Spencer's system of 'natural rights'. The Land Question involved a clash of communal and private rights in which individual proprietorship is accorded priority. A similar transformation is evident on the suffrage question; at first the 'natural' right of each to a share of political power overrides pragmatic considerations, but fear of the infringement of property rights through overlegislation ultimately dictates a reversal of priorities. The whole complex of natural rights set out in *Social Statics* had suffered a severe erosion in *Justice*, a process, however, which left intact the right to individual property. Yet rights, according to Spencer, defined the limits of the individual's freedom of action, and their authority rested on their being logically deduced from the first principles; 'If it be shown to follow . . . that he is free to act up to a certain limit but not beyond it, then the implied admission is that it is right he should have the particular freedom so defined.'[1] Rights, then, are strictly corollaries of the law of equal freedom, but rights deduced, with impeccable logic, from this law in *Social Statics* are denied in *Justice*.

Rights of a non-proprietorial nature are mutilated or excluded altogether. The 'right to life and personal liberty' becomes 'the right to physical integrity', conditional upon social requirements in the prevailing climate of 'political burglary'. The 'right to free motion and locomotion' is similarly qualified. The rights of women and children are severely curtailed. All individual human rights are now held subject to evolutionary imperatives and significantly, the 'right to ignore the state', which in *Social Statics* affirmed the autonomy of the individual even against the majority of his fellows, is in *Justice* conspicuously absent. The state, normally treated by Spencer as the antithesis of individual self-determination, is here regarded as the agency of species preservation. The conflict between idealistic individualism and social evolution is nowhere more clearly demonstrated.

Whereas *Social Statics* is claimed to refute equally Jeremy Bentham's conception of conferred rights and Jean-Jacques Rousseau's contractual theory, the more radical of Spencer's 'logical' deductions from the law of equal freedom were disqualified by practical policy and evolutionary gradualism. Rights are to be held in abeyance until the moral transcendence of mankind makes it safe to release them. As Sir Ernest Barker puts it: 'Spencer tantalises the individual with glimpses of jewels of freedom, which he can only wear in the days of perfection',[2] and what is left is a recital of individualist privileges. The right of private property is affirmed and extended to cover two of Spencer's personal preoccupations; the right of property in the produce of the mind ('property

[1] *Justice*, p. 62.
[2] E. Barker, *Political Thought in England, 1848–1914* (London, 1942), p. 102.

in ideas') and to reputation ('property in character'). Free disposal of property is guaranteed by the rights of 'gift and bequest' and 'free exchange'. Economic *laissez-faire* acquires 'natural' status as 'the right to free industry'.

It becomes clear, therefore, that Spencer's reconsideration of the franchise and land questions reflects a significant modification of his view of personal and political rights in which private property has come, by 1891, to outweigh the strict logic of the derivation of the original catalogue of 'natural rights' from the 'law of equal freedom'. Possessive individualism has become the premise of Spencer's political thought, to which justice, strictly interpreted, must be deferred, a shift of emphasis rather than a departure from principle, but none the less significant to the explanation of Spencer's developing conservatism.

PART II

INDIVIDUALISM AND EVOLUTION —
SPENCERIAN SOCIAL AND POLITICAL
THEORY

6

THE LIMITS OF STATE INTERVENTION

Spencerian evolution and Spencerian individualism are closely interdependent. The limitation of the state to the purely negative duty of the protection of citizens, and the proscription of positive interference in their affairs is, in one sense, a corollary of the thesis that society is an evolving organism, continually undergoing a metamorphosis over which men have no control. Chronologically, however, Spencer was an individualist first and an evolutionist second. Whilst his scientific education and his politico-ethical indoctrination proceeded together, his individualism was substantially formulated in 'The Proper Sphere of Government' (1842), while the perfected statement of evolution materialized in the revised edition of *First Principles* in 1864. Sir Ernest Barker says of Spencer that 'he was already charged with political preconceptions when he approached science, and he sought to find in science examples or analogies to point a moral already drawn.'[1] M. Harris, too, places his sociological theory firmly in a political context; 'to appreciate Spencer's contribution we must see him as the most effective scientific spokesman of early industrial capitalism.'[2] If, as Beatrice Webb suggests, his faith in the validity of evolution deserted him, he persisted in his anti-interventionism with almost fanatical consistency. 'Over-legislation' is the dominant theme of Spencerian political theory.

The apparent simplicity of this concept is deceptive, and this chapter sets out to define the limits of the state's jurisdiction as Spencer conceived them, and to elucidate and assess the arguments which he used in support of them. It shows that, far from assigning to the state an enforced impotence, he looked to it for the performance of vital tasks. The extent of these tasks gives us, by exclusion, an accurate

[1] E. Barker, op.cit., p. 85.
[2] M. Harris, op.cit., p. 124.

description of the forbidden territory beyond, but Spencer was especially preoccupied with certain specific instances of 'undue state interference', and these are briefly discussed. The chapter concludes by reviewing Spencer's anti-interventionist arguments, which include the inefficiency of the state, the ignorance of legislators, the imperatives of natural selection in society, and the priority of 'natural rights' over state supervision, and suggests that Spencer's case for 'administrative nihilism' is in fact weakened by the amassing of contradictory arguments in support of it.

The positive duty of the state is that of protection, internal and external. The state may direct citizens for their own security against all external hostility, and legitimately appropriate some of their income and resources to this purpose. Internal aggression, however, is more complex. For example, non-fulfilment of the terms of a contract constitutes aggression, and falls within the scope of law. Commercial competition, however, in which rivals are ruined and employees reduced to starvation, does not. Spencer observed a clear distinction between these types of aggression: 'If we define the primary state duty to be protecting each individual against others, then all other action comes under the definition of protecting each individual against himself—against . . . his own incapacity for doing something or other which should be done.'[1]

'Protection', then, is defined in terms of natural competition. Between an individual and the fulfilment of his desires lie two sets of obstacles; the desires of other men for the same goals, and his own incapacity to achieve them. If he fails either through the legitimate competition of others, or through his own disabilities, then the state should afford him no protection; only if competition is unfairly pursued should it intervene on behalf of the aggrieved. There are practical, as well as theoretical reasons why the state should observe these limits. Like all organisms, it obeys the law of 'increasing specialization of function.'[2] Progress, applied to government, is expressed as a tendency towards exclusive specialization in

---

[1] H.S., 'Over-legislation', *Essays,* ii. 36.
[2] H.S., 'Representative government: what is it good for?', *Essays,* iii. 323.

the tasks for which it was instituted: 'A government cannot gain ability to perform its special work without losing such ability as it had to perform other work.'[1] Since the assumption of extraneous tasks requires excessive taxation, furthermore, levied on the successful for the benefit of the unsuccessful, the state's role as preserver of social harmony is negated: 'Not a single supplementary service can it perform without producing dissent; and in proportion to the amount of dissent produced by it, the state defeats the end for which it was established.'[2] Conversely, he often cited the failure of the state to execute its legitimate tasks against its assumption of further duties: 'Had we . . . proved its efficiency as judge and defender, instead of having found it treacherous, cruel and anxiously to be shunned, there would be some encouragement to hope for other benefits at its hands.'[3]

For Spencer the state existed to subserve the requirements of the moral law. This entails the creation and maintenance of an environment as nearly as possible conforming to the 'law of equal freedom', where 'every man has freedom to do all that he wills, provided he infringes not the equal rights of every other man.'[4] 'Freedom' is enjoyed by men who reap the rewards and suffer the consequences of all their actions. The state should confer nothing, beyond the opportunity to compete freely, for, 'it is one thing to secure to each man the unhindered power to pursue his own good; it is a widely different thing to pursue the good for him.'[5] The state is constituted, then, 'simply to defend the natural rights of men—to protect person and property, to prevent the aggression of the powerful on the weak; in a word, to administer Justice.'[6] Prevention of 'the aggression of the powerful upon the weak' was subsequently elided, and Spencer, in stricter conformity with natural selection, endorsed 'those shoulderings aside of the weak by the strong' as part of a natural upward development:

The prosperity of the species is best subserved when—among adults each experiences the good and evil results of his own nature and consequent conduct . . . This, which is the ultimate law of species life as

[1] *Essays*, iii. 324.   [2] *S. Stat.*, p. 306.
[3] *Essays*, iii. 323.   [4] *S. Stat.*, p. 121.
[5] *Essays*, iii. 325.   [6] 'Proper Sphere', 11 June 1842.

qualified by social conditions, it is the business of the social aggregate, or incorporated body of citizens, to maintain.[1]

This socio-biological statement furnishes a definition of 'interference'; it includes 'any arrangements which in considerable degree prevent superiority from profiting by the rewards of superiority, or shield inferiority from the evils it entails.'[2]

None the less, Spencer repeatedly urged on the state a more conscientious discharge of its legitimate duties, dismissing as 'a persistent misunderstanding' the suggestion that he advocated a passive government:

While *laissez-faire*, as I understand it forbids the stepping between . . . private acts and their consequences, it is quite consistent with the doctrine that a government should, far more effectually and minutely than at present, save such individuals from suffering evils or claiming benefits due to the acts of others . . .[3]

In its special sphere, the maintenance of equitable relations among citizens, governmental actions should be extended and elaborated.[4]

'The fundamental requirement', declared Spencer, 'is that the life-sustaining actions of each shall severally bring him the amounts and kinds of advantage naturally achieved by them; and this implies firstly that he shall suffer no direct aggression on his person and property, and secondly that he shall suffer no indirect aggressions by breach of contract.'[5]

To prevent such aggressions is the function of the judiciary. Legal corruption and inefficiency, therefore, were targets of recurrent attacks throughout his writings. In *Social Statics* he marvels 'that we, the independent, determined, self-ruling English, should daily behold the giant abominations of our juridical system, and yet do nothing to rectify them.'[6] In *The Man versus the State* he denounces a legal system operating beyond the financial reach of the huge majority, incomprehensible even to the litigants and ethically rooted in the medieval laws of battle: 'the result being less a question of equity than a question of pecuniary ability and forensic skill . . . and not infrequently the wronged man, who sought protection or restitution, is carried out of court pecuniarily

[1] *Justice*, p. 213.   [2] *P. Eth.* i. 189.
[3] H.S. to J.E. Cairns, 21 Mar. 1873. *L.L.* i. 213.
[4] *Contemporary Review*, Jan. 1853.   [5] *D. of E.*, p. 128.   [6] *S. Stat*, p. 284.

dead.'[1] He dismissed the argument that cheaper justice would trigger 'a rush of litigation' as implying 'that it is better to have no administration of justice at all.'[2] Judicial reform and a wider availability of justice, accordingly, were priorities in Spencer's demand for a more dynamic approach by government to its legitimate role.

Having ensured perfect competitive freedom, the state must abdicate all responsibility for the outcome and refrain from 'delivering happiness to the front doors'. Those who achieve their aims, given freedom of manoeuvre, are by definition those 'best fitted' to do so. Where 'justice' reigns, success is its own reward, and is, for all practical purposes, equated with virtue.

Whenever it exceeds this protective jurisdiction, government is the trangressor. Spencer's composite term for all such excesses was 'over-legislation':

We conceive that the great family of ills that have been for so long preying on the national prosperity . . . are all the offspring of one primary, and hitherto almost unsuspected evil—over-legislation . . . We can discover no radical remedy for our social maladies but a stringent regulation which shall confine our governors to the performance of their primitive duty—the protection of person and property.[3]

Although this dictum proscribed all undue intervention, Spencer's individualism was initially formulated in response to certain specific categories of legislative transgression. These afford an instructive catalogue of his preoccupations.

1. Disestablishment

True to his Dissenter's upbringing, Spencer advocated the disestablishment of the Established Church. The association of Church and State, an 'essentially Popish' arrangement, impinges on the free exercise of the faculties connected with worship. John Locke's contention, in Spencer's words, that 'there must be something of the sort to keep the people in order',[4] is rejected on the grounds that a religion which depends for its social acceptance on governmental compulsion

---

[1] *M.v.S.*, p. 57.
[2] *S. Stat.*, p. 286.
[3] H.S., 'The Machinery Outcry' (unpublished, composed in 1843), *L.L.* i. 48.
[4] *S. Stat.*, p. 338.

can hardly be propagating social cohesion or ensuring stability. It was not, however, one of Spencer's principal concerns, since he considered it substantially resolved. By 1850 the bonds of union are said to have been 'shaken loose': 'Dissent has long been organizing a mechanism for religious control, wholly independent of law.'[1] Thereafter the issue is rarely encountered.

2. Currency and banking

'State tampering with money and banks' impedes freedom of exchange and expresses an unnecessary solicitude towards 'hard-headed men of business', according to Spencer. If the law of bankruptcy is rigorously applied, the self-interested prudence of bankers and traders would guarantee against the circulation of unsound paper bills, provided that the money-market were allowed to find its own level: 'The state's duty in the case of currency, as in other cases, is sternly to threaten the penalty of bankruptcy on all who make engagements which they cannot meet, and sternly to inflict the penalty when called upon by the aggrieved. If it falls short of this, mischief ensues. If it exceeds this, mischief ensues.'[2]

3. Free trade

Spencer adopted an uncompromising Free Trade position, roundly condemning colonialism, monopolies, and protectionism, and celebrating the repeal of the Corn Laws: 'When the crutches which state quacks had provided were taken away, when the *ennui* which idleness and indulgence had created was no more permitted, then did health begin to return.'[3] Faithful to the teaching of Harriet Martineau's *Tales of Political Economy* he followed a Ricardian line on all matters of economic policy: 'Political Economy has shown us in this matter . . . that our wisest plan is to let things take their own course.'[4]

---

[1] H.S., 'Manners and Fashions', *Essays,* iii. 11.
[2] H.S., 'State tampering with money and banks', *Essays,* iii. 335.
[3] *Pilot,* 23 Nov. 1844.
[4] *S. Stat.,* p. 334.

4. Labour relations

Spencer denounced all agencies, public or voluntary, tending to impinge on the autonomy of the labour-market. The establishment of 'artificial' maxima of hours and minimum wages he saw as both presumptuous and ineffective, and about their advocates he wrote: 'A fly seated on the surface of the body has about as good a conception of its internal structure as one of these schemers has of the social organization in which he is imbedded.'[1] On this issue Spencer went further, castigating not only the state, but also the parallel efforts of Trade Unionists.

His distaste for Trade Unionism verged on hysteria. He dismissed the activities of Trade Unions as futile, 'permanent rates of wages are determined by other causes than the wishes of either employers or employed', yet he attributed price inflation to their 'artificial' wage increases. He accused of paramilitary terrorism the primly respectable 'New Model' unions, steeped as they were in the doctrine of self-help, and agreed with Richard Cobden's cheerful suggestion that the freedom of the labour market could be secured by every workman willing to save £20,[2] to serve him as a basis of financial security from which to negotiate with employers and obtain himself the most favourable terms available. *Laissez-faire*, a comforting ideal for the self-sufficient, was less so for those condemned to the precarious, marginal existence of the factory towns. Nevertheless, the combination of thrift, sobriety, and self-improvement disseminated by most craft unions diverged from it only in enjoining some equality of opportunity. It opposed only 'that system of individualism which gives Praxiteles his due and Arkwright, Brunel and Stevenson "full scope for the exercise of their extraordinary skill", but leaves the thousands less skilful to scramble through a selfish world as best they can.'[3]

5. Sanitation and public health

Spencer regarded the public health agitation as a subversive

[1] *P. Soc.* iii. 403.
[2] J. Morley, *The Life of Richard Cobden* (London, 1920), p. 935.
[3] Cited in A. Briggs, *Victorian People* (London, 1967), p. 193.

conspiracy to foist upon the unsuspecting public the tyrannous restriction of disease. Its instigators, the *Lancet*, the *Journal of Public Health*, and the *Medical Times* were in his view cynically distorting the evidence to over-emphasize the magnitude of the problem. England, Spencer asserted, was the healthiest country in Europe and getting healthier: 'One would have thought that less excuse for meddling existed now than ever. Now that spontaneous advance is being made at an unparalleled rate . . . to interfere *now*, of all times is surely as rash and uncalled-for a step as was ever taken.'[1] Spencer had two further objections to health regulations. First, the growth of a medical bureaucracy would give free licence for the manufacture of sinecures for the genteel unemployed. Second, diseases, 'insofar as they do exist . . . are among the penalties Nature has attached to ignorance and imbecility, and should not therefore be tampered with.'

6. Poor Relief

'Poor laws are bad in principle and have, in their effects, operated most injuriously.'[2] The young Spencer opposed the Old Poor Law, believing, like Edwin Chadwick, that 'every penny bestowed, that tends to render the condition of the pauper more eligible than that of the independent labourer, is a bounty on indolence and vice.'[3] The New Poor Law, however, proved no better; half a century later Spencer alleged that it had brought into being 'a permanent corps of tramps who roam from union to union', that poor-rates had quadrupled, that the alleviation of the poverty of large families had fostered a disregard of the need for carnal self-discipline, and that natural selection had been obstructed. The survival of the fittest apart, Spencer's opposition to state-organized poor relief was based on firm Ricardian principles. Society produces a fixed quantity of commodities. Upper- and middle-class consumption is constant, so that if production falls, the poor, who buy the surplus with their

---

[1] *S. Stat.*, p. 418.
[2] *Bath and West of England Magazine*, Mar. 1836.
[3] Cited in J.R. Poynter, *Society and Pauperism: English ideas on poor relief, 1795–1834* (London, 1969), p. 320.

labour, bear the deficit. Poor Laws therefore aggravate economic hardship:

Manifestly, out of a given population, the greater the number living on the bounty of others, the smaller must be the number living by labour; and the smaller the number living by labour, the smaller must be the production of necessaries, and the smaller the production of necessaries, the greater must be the distress . . . to crown all, we find not only that a poor-law must necessarily fail to diminish popular suffering, but it must inevitably increase that suffering, both directly by checking the production of commodities, and indirectly by causing a retrogression of character, which painful discipline must at some future day make good.[1]

7. Education

Spencer was at his most ambivalent in his examination of state education. He condemned it for a number of reasons. First, it stimulates uniformity, where variety conduces to progress. Second, it cultivates 'great veneration of authority, a higher respect for superiors and implicit faith in the opinion of the great.'[2] Third, the state's power to mould children into a moral and intellectual pattern assumes totalitarian implications:

Legislators exhibit to us the design and specification of a state-machine, made up of masters, ushers, inspectors and councils, to be worked by a due proportion of taxes, and to be plentifully supplied with raw material in the shape of little boys and girls, out of which it is to grind a population of well-trained men and women who shall be 'useful members of society.'[3]

Fourth, it violates the rights of the taxpayer: 'in as much as the taking away of his property to educate his own or other people's children is not needful for the maintenance of his rights; the taking away of his property for such a purpose is wrong.'[4] Last, it interferes with natural selection: 'if those of the lower ranks are left to get culture for their children as best they may . . . it must follow that the children of the superior will be advantaged.'[5] Education, therefore, is best left to private enterprise, to be bought and sold in the

[1] S. Stat., pp. 359–60.
[2] 'Proper Sphere', 26 Oct. 1842.
[3] S. Stat., pp. 366–7.   [4] S. Stat., p. 361.
[5] H.S., Facts and Comments, p. 67.

market-place where 'price is a tolerably safe index of value,'[1] though this last conclusion contrasts sharply with what Spencer had to say about tendencies observable in the Public Schools.[2]

With regard to electoral reform, however, Spencer struck a different attitude. Literacy alone is no guarantee against political ignorance: 'nine out of ten people read what amuses them or interests them, rather than what instructs them; and . . . the last thing they read is something which tells them disagreeable truths or dispels groundless hopes.'[3] The working class read to obtain 'confirmation of their errors', hence the wide circulation of subversive authors like John Ruskin and William Morris, and the rise of socialism. Spencer's remedy is to saturate the working class with his own brand of political 'cultivation': 'The establishment of a true theory of government, a true conception of what legislation is for and what are its proper limits.'[4] 'Did the upper classes understand their position', he concluded, 'they would, we think, see that the diffusion of sound views on this matter more nearly concerns their welfare, and that of the nation at large, than any other thing whatever.'[5]

In some instances of putative state interference, Spencer was beset by doubts. Should the state intervene to secure honourable business dealings? Apropos of railway investment, he concluded that the state might insist that funds should not be diverted from a specified purpose to an unspecified one, for if it behoves the state to enforce contracts, then it must ensure that their limits are observed, and since these limits define the object of investment, legislation to protect the shareholder is just. Should proxy-voting at shareholders' meetings, by which 'in the hands of interested manipulators the ignorance of the many is used to extinguish the knowledge of the few'[6] be subject to legislative control? Should legislation guarantee the veracity of company prospectuses? He eventually admitted that 'I have never been

[1] S. Stat., p. 369.
[2] See below, Chap. 10, p. 245.
[3] M.v.S., p. 37.
[4] 'Parliamentary Reform: its dangers and safeguards', Essays, iii. 378.
[5] Essays, iii. 379.
[6] H.S., Facts and Comments, p. 169.

able to decide whether the implied check on transactions in shares would be theoretically legitimate or practically beneficent.'[1] Such speculations raised broader issues, for if investors are to be granted legal protection, should the factory operative, the under-employed rural labourer, the urban pauper be subject to unrestricted competition? Spencer's lapse from consistency rationalizes a class interest, a desire to protect his own, including his father and uncle,[2] from the rigorous discipline of natural selection so heartily recommended to the rest of society in all his subsequent works.

As he grew older, and his 'administrative nihilism' hardened, Spencer became increasingly suspicious of interference with the 'natural' workings of social processes, from whatever source. Innocuous organizations like the National Society for the Prevention of Cruelty to Children, founded in 1891, were regaled with dark prophecies that 'movements of this kind, begun with the best of objectives, are apt to degenerate into undue interference.'[3] In 1892 he refused to sign a petition to secure a charter for the British Nurses' Association, because it constituted 'a restriction upon individual liberty to which I am strongly opposed.'[4] He saw in every innovation a potential spawning-ground of official restriction, and carried his mistrust of state agencies to the extent of carrying his proofs to the printers personally rather than commit them to the clutches of the (state-controlled) G.P.O.

SPENCER'S CASE FOR NON-INTERVENTION

Spencer's individualism rested on two main propositions: that state intervention was impracticable and immoral. Because the state lacks the theoretical knowledge, technique, and organization to execute its complicated designs, its endeavours result at best in failure, and at worst in the aggravation of existing problems. At the same time the state is ethically debarred from attempting to rectify social evils,

---

[1] *Aby* i. 290.
[2] Both of them suffered from unwise investments; see above pp. 3 and 21.
[3] *Pall Mall Gazette*, 16 May 1891.
[4] H.S. to T. Buzzard, 15 Mar. 1892, *L.L.* ii.6.

since this involves harmful and presumptuous usurpation by human agency of the processes of nature. These propositions will be examined in turn.

The failure of legislation to achieve its objectives and its tendency unwittingly to intensify evils which it was designed to abolish are recurrent themes in Spencer's writings. A project which never saw fulfilment was the compilation of an exhaustive record of nineteenth-century legislation, enabling interested researchers to calculate the ratio between the volume of legislation and its ill effects. 'The chief difficulty' Spencer warned 'would be that of getting within any moderate compass the immense number of cases in which the benefits anticipated were not achieved, while unanticipated disasters were caused.'[1] Between 1872 and 1890, 3,352 Acts of Parliament were amended or replaced, 'the inference being that their repeal indicates their failure.'[2] As late as 1894 he was trying to recruit volunteers for this undertaking, without success. Meanwhile he drew consolation from the Report of the Poor Law Commission of 1880: 'Scarcely one statute connected with the administration of public relief . . . has produced the effect desired by the legislature, and . . . the majority of them have created new evils, and aggravated those which they were intended to prevent.'[3]

His favourite specific example was that of building regulations. The Metropolitan Buildings Act had laid down minimum criteria of structural soundness and sanitation for working-class dwellings, but fixed rents so that additional costs could not be recouped from tenants. The response of builders was to move into more profitable sectors of the market, neglecting working-class housing for the lucrative business of rehousing the middle class in expensive residential suburbs. In the working-class areas, therefore, hardship was redoubled. The scarcity of new homes disinclined sitting tenants to leave, thus removing the competitive incentive for landlords to keep their property in good repair; by 1883 21 000 Londoners had been rendered homeless by compulsory demolition, and only 12 000 housed, at a cost to the

[1] H.S., 'Political Fetishism', *Essays*, iii. 399.
[2] *M.v.s.*, p. 61.
[3] *M.v.S.*, p. 71.

ratepayer of £1 500 000. The imposition of these standards, therefore, 'having, by successive measures, produced first bad houses and then a deficiency of better ones . . . has at length provided for the artificially-increased overflow of poor people by diminishing the house-capacity which already could not contain them.'[1]

Spencer's brief was to demonstrate the inevitability of such failures and aggravations. His first point was that the 'meddlers' legislate out of an ignorance which forever precludes the achievement of their goals. 'What is the statute-book', he asks,

but a series of unhappy guesses? Or history, but a narrative of their unsuccessful issues? . . . the expediency-philosophy, however, ignores this world full of facts. Though men have so constantly been baulked in their attempts, by legislation, to secure any desired constituent of that complex whole 'greatest happiness', it nevertheless continues to place confidence in the unaided judgement of the statesman. It asks no guide, it possesses no eclectic principle . . . but . . . it assumes that after an inspection of the aggregate phenomena of national life, governments are qualified to concoct such measures as shall be 'expedient'. It considers the philosophy of humanity so easy, the constitution of the social organism so simple, the causes of people's conduct so obvious, that a general examination can give to 'collective wisdom' the insight required for law-making.[2]

While the specific targets of this tirade are the 'expediency-philosophers' (Benthamite Philosophical Radicals), the wider implication is that predictive calculation is beyond political intelligence, and that nature should accordingly be left to take its course.

Subsequent essays, including 'The Collective Wisdom' (1865) and 'Specialised Administration' (1870) purported to show 'how utterly beyond the conceptions of common-sense, literally so-called, and even beyond the conceptions of cultivated common-sense, are the workings of sociological processes.'[3] Even the scientific approach is deemed inadequate, since the object of science is prevision, which postulates a recurring and easily perceptible relation between cause and effect. Social causation, on the contrary, defies analysis:

[1] *M.v.S.*, p. 67.
[2] *S. Stat.*, p. 21.   [3] *S. Stat.*, pp. 22–3.

'Evidence thrust before us every morning shows throughout the body politic a fructifying causation so involved that not even the highest intelligence can anticipate its aggregate effects.'[1] Legislators, manifestly not characterized by the highest order of intelligence, will never be able to employ the techniques of social science in order to render their law-making more effective.

Elsewhere the opposite is implied: 'The legislator is morally blameless or morally blameworthy, according as he has or has not acquainted himself with these several classes of fact'[2] . . . 'successfully to prescribe for society, it is needful to know the structure of society . . . If there be not a true understanding of what constitutes social development . . . un-foreseen disasters will ensue.'[3] It is here ignorance of socio-logy, rather than the impenetrable complexity of social causation, to which Spencer attributes the persistent failure of social legislation. The lawmaker is likened to a medical quack, prescribing treatments from a cursory and superficial knowledge of the symptoms without an inkling of their cause: 'that which is really needed is a systematic study of natural causation as displayed among human beings socially aggregated.'[4] Legislators, therefore, are morally indictable for their ignorance of the principles of social pathology.

Lawmaking, 'unenlightened by social science', can aggra-vate entrenched evils and create new. By contrast, Spencer occasionally indicated the total impotence of legislators to alter the naturally determined course of events. Referring to 'that beautiful self-adjusting principle which will keep every-thing in equilibrium',[5] he chided the reformers for their in-ference that 'every little evil that springs up is to be con-demned by Parliamentary enactment.'[6] All 'natural' pheno-mena resist artificially-induced change, and society is no exception:

It is impossible for man to create force. He can only alter the mode of its manifestations, its direction, its distribution . . . Moral feeling is a

[1] *Justice*, p. 249.
[2] Loc.cit.
[3] *M.v.S.*, p. 93.   [4] *M.v.S.*, p. 74.
[5] 'Proper Sphere', 15 June 1844.
[6] *Pilot,* 28 Sept. 1844.

force by which men's actions are restrained within certain prescribed bounds, and no legislative mechanism can increase its results one iota.[1]

The 'incidence of mischief', then, may be directed by legislation, but 'the amount of it must be borne somewhere.'[2] The governmental 'creation' of happiness, knowledge, and wealth thus amounts to the redistribution of misery, ignorance, and hardship.

This impotence is compounded by the paramount influence of 'national character' upon institutions. The framing of social reforms seemed to presuppose a perfect humanity; building regulations, for example, assumed that the restrictions of builders' profit margins would not drive them to seek greener pastures. The promptness with which they did so demonstrated to Spencer's satisfaction that visionary reforms were foredoomed by their incompatibility with the current level of social altruism: 'No philosopher's stone of a constitution can produce golden conduct from leaden instincts.'[3] On the contrary, 'the defective natures of citizens will show themselves in the bad acting of whatever social structure they are arranged into.'[4]

Human frailty equally undermines the probity and efficiency of the governmental machine itself. Spencer called 'modern fetishism' the 'idolatry which . . . expects by moulding a mass of this humanity into a particular form, to give it powers and properties quite different from those it had before it was moulded.'[5] If the raw material is defective the design of the machine is equally inappropriate. Spencer had an engineer's shrewd eye for the functional potentialities of organizations: 'that is the best mechanism', he stated, 'which contains the fewest parts.'[6] In government, power is systematically dispersed; an impulse is repeatedly subdivided by delegation until most of its force is dissipated in the effort of setting the machine in motion, each new directive activating a series of 'levers', 'each of which absorbs in friction and inertia part of the moving force.'[7] Analogies apart, Spencer subjected officialdom to a penetrating functional

[1] S. Stat., p. 295.
[2] Stud. Soc., p. 23.
[3] S. Stat., p. 295.
[4] M.v.S., p. 52.
[5] M.v.S., p. 71.
[6] H.S., 'Over-legislation', Essays, iii. 246.
[7] Loc.cit.

analysis. It is stupid, ignoring talent as a qualification for promotion and insisting on deference to hierarchical superiority. It is extravagant, the enormous resources theoretically at its disposal and the remoteness of the taxpayer encouraging a careless attitude to expense. It is unresponsive to change: 'it lumbers on under all varieties of circumstances through its ordered routine at its habitual rate . . . By its very nature it is fitted only for average requirements.'[1] It is corrupt; Spencer baldly asserts that the payment of salaries unrelated to effort entails bribery, a statement supported not by evidence but by generalization: 'In all social agencies in which the duty done and the income gained do not go hand in hand, the like corruption is found.'[2] The placid, permanent security of civil servants, furthermore, induces a dangerous stagnation: 'exposed to no such antiseptic as free competition . . . all law-made agencies fall into an inert, overfed state, from which to disease is a short step.'[3] It is, lastly, obstructive, resisting innovations which threaten its interests, thus conforming to a Spencerian law that 'every organized body of men tends to grow, and tends to magnify its own importance.'[4] This analysis, although unrelievedly destructive and limited in objective, anticipated much subsequent sociological criticism of bureaucracy, including Max Weber's.

Private enterprise displays all the corresponding virtues. The constant spur of competition, cost-efficiency and the profit-motive steel private organizations into a dynamic efficiency from which they lapse at their peril, for 'immediately, every private enterprise is dependent on the need for it.'[5] The malaise of public agencies is weeded out with the feeble, inefficient corporations; talent rises sharply to positions of command; extravagance is eradicated in the drive for competitive efficiency; the organization is tailored to meet fluctuations and emergencies; corruption is purged, and change welcomed as the life-blood of the competitive system. Private enterprise, furthermore, is appropriate to an imperfect humanity: 'Given a race of men having a certain proclivity to misconduct, and the question is, whether a society of these

[1] 'Over-legislation', *Essays,* iii. 249.   [2] *S. Stat.,* p. 72.
[3] 'Over-legislation', *Essays,* iii. 251.   [4] H.S., *Facts and Comments,* p. 156.
[5] 'Over-legislation', *Essays,* iii. 254.

men shall be so organized that ill-conduct directly brings punishment, or whether it shall be so organized that punishment is but remotely contingent on ill-conduct.'[1] Private enterprise is omnicompetent: 'Even were there no other form of spontaneous cooperation among men than that dictated by self-interest, it might rationally be held that this, under the negatively-regulative control of a central power, would work out, in proper order, the appliances of satisfying all needs.'[2]

The past and potential exploits of spontaneous organization are not merely commercial. Private philanthropy could with advantage supplant public relief, not least because it would be applied selectively. Spencer would have approved of Richard Cobden's definition of philanthropy: 'Mine is that masculine species of charity which would lead me to inculcate into the minds of the labouring classes the love of independence, the privilege of self-respect, the disdain of being patronized, the desire to accumulate and the ambition to rise.'[3] Spencer was careful to point out that he had no quarrel with 'aid given to the inferior by the superior in their individual capacities', which 'associated with a greater sense of responsibility, would, on the average, be given with the effect of fostering the unfortunate worthy rather than the innately unworthy.'[4] Such discriminating benevolence he regarded as 'adequate to achieve all those mitigations that are proper and needful.'[5] In philanthropy, as in commerce, freedom of the market is sufficient guarantee of the efficient apportionment of resources according to sound moral criteria.

In his eagerness to demonstrate the impracticality of state intervention, Spencer overstated his case. The nineteenth-century bureaucracy, slow, inefficient, and vulnerable to corruption (though considerably improved after the reforms of 1854) was the graveyard of much well-intentioned social legislation, but it is questionable whether all state intervention

---

[1] *Idem.*
[2] 'Specialised Administration', *Essays,* iii. 432.
[3] Cited in J. Morley, op.cit., p. 954.
[4] *M. v. S.*, p. 81.
[5] H.S. to Count Goblet d'Alviella, 7 Jan. 1895, *L.L.* ii. 76.

thereby stands condemned. Scorning the fetishism of government, Spencer went to the opposite extreme in extolling
private enterprise. His scathing accounts of the machinations
of railway enterprise and the 'morals of trade'[1] would seem
to indicate that the 'antiseptic' of competition was a poor
defence against human venality. Ruthless competition, while
weeding out the weak and the scrupulous, tended to sharpen
up the vices of the predatory. The only difference is that the
business world, then as now, had fewer pretensions to
morality, and that it kept itself well hidden. As Thomas
Huxley pointed out: 'The state lives in a glasshouse—we see
what it tries to do, and all its failures, partial or total, are
made the worst of. But private enterprise is sheltered under
good opaque bricks and mortar.'[2] In private, Spencer had
few illusions; in a letter to Richard Potter he expressed himself 'extremely impatient' of 'this condition of things, under
which the fraudulent minnows come in for severe punishment, while the fraudulent Tritons escape without harm.'[3]

Spencer's ethical case for non-intervention has twin bases
in social evolution and the theory of natural rights. Over-
legislation is, first of all, presumptuous. The politician,
seeking to direct social development after his own image, sets
his face against nature: 'by a commission, a staff of officers
and a parliamentary grant, every deficiency shall be made
good, and the errors of Omniscience be rectified.'[4] The
cardinal sin of these 'self-appointed nurses to the Universe'
was less their temerity than their perversion of the natural
order of events. 'Mischievous meddling' entailed 'disastrous
neglect' in diverting resources from their natural priorities:
'If some social progress does not seem to them to be going
on fast enough, they stimulate it; where the growth is not in
the direction they think most desirable, they alter it; and so
they seek to realize some indefinable ideal community.'[5]
Spencer saw no intrinsic virtue in suffering. In opposing
vaccination, for example, he was not advocating a resurgence

---

[1] See above, Chap. 2, pp. 41-4.
[2] T.H. Huxley, 'Administrative Nihilism', *Fortnightly Review,* Nov. 1871.
[3] H.S. to R. Potter, 4 Dec. 1874, in the Passfield Collection, II (I) ii.
[4] *S. Stat.*, pp. 321-2.
[5] 'Representative Government: what is it good for?', *Essays,* iii. 302.

of smallpox; indeed he published a letter, anonymously, on improving the means of cure. The reforms of which Spencer disapproved were designed to relieve individual suffering or deprivation. In his view racial preservation was the primary concern, and up to a point inconsistent with individual welfare. Until the two become compatible, the individual remains expendable. As for reform, 'until spontaneously fulfilled, a public want should not be fulfilled at all . . . it must be a general law of society that the chief requisites of social life—those necessary to popular existence and multiplication will, in the natural order of things, be subserved before those of a less pressing kind.'[1] The unforgivable transgression of legislators was their subversion of the natural *order* of human achievement in accordance with their own priorities, thus artifically diverting resources of benevolence and wealth from their 'natural' outlets, and so deferring the age of peace, harmony, and plenty which Spencer promised.

Premature reform incurs the dangers of social regression: 'it is in the order of nature . . . that man's habits and pleasures are not to be changed suddenly. For any PERMANENT effect to be produced it must be produced slowly—better tastes, higher aspirations must be developed, not enforced from without.'[2] Oliver Cromwell's policy of 'dragooning men into virtue' merely provoked the licentiousness and mayhem of the Restoration. The history of the latter half of the nineteenth century appeared to Spencer as a similar case of barbaric reaction to a premature increment of freedom.

State intervention, then, interferes with the evolutionary process. Spencer exhorted lawmakers to look beyond their proximate aims to the remote evolutionary repercussions of their actions:

The highest aim ever to be kept in view by legislators and those who seek for legislation is the formation of character . . . If, generation after generation, their conduct in all its details is prescribed for them, they will more and more need official control in all things.'[3]

Social legislation is condemned above all for seeking to alleviate

[1] 'Over-legislation', *Essays,* iii. 265–6.
[2] 'Representative Government: what is it good for?', *Essays,* iii. 315.
[3] H.S. to Mrs. J. Butler, 3 Sept. 1899, *L.L.* ii. 149.

suffering, without which there would be no evolutionary motivation. Mankind competes, not to attain comfort, but to avoid pain. Just as physical pain warns of physiological malfunction, so social pain is an index of social conduct: 'Adversity is, in most cases, the only efficient school for the transgressor.'[1] Despite the Spartan implications of this law, its objective is, eventually, a better world. Spencer's education in Dissent had schooled him to look to remote, rather than immediate gratifications as the rewards of good conduct. Suffering is a necessary evil, and its justification ultimately humanitarian: 'Fostering the good-for-nothings at the expense of the good-for-somethings is an extreme cruelty. It is a deliberate storing-up of miseries for future generations.'[2]

Complete adaptation to the perfect state is only feasible given the prior elimination of those unfit to attain it. It was this 'weeding-out' which the misguided philanthropist threatened to sabotage. Evolution is

a felicity-pursuing law, which never swerves for the avoidance of partial or temporary suffering. The poverty of the incapable, the distresses that come on the improvident, the starvation of the idle, and those shoulderings aside of the weak by the strong, which leave so many 'in shallows and in miseries' are the decrees of a large, far-seeing benevolence.[3]

The suffering thus incurred is justified in terms both of the intrinsic demerits of the sufferers and of the ultimate perfection of the race.

Artificial preservation of the evolutionary non-elect amounts to 'lowering the average type of constitution to a level of strength *below that which meets without difficulty the ordinary strains and perturbations and dangers.*'[4] If the improvident, idle and incapable are allowed to multiply, their descendants will exhibit the same weaknesses and vices, and present the same problems to their better-endowed neighbours: 'the quality of a society is lowered, morally and intellectually, by the artificial preservation of those who are least able to take care of themselves.'[5] It was for the welfare

[1] 'Proper Sphere', 27 July 1842.
[2] *Stud. Soc.*, pp. 344–5.
[3] *S. Stat.*, pp. 353–4.
[4] *Stud. Soc.*, p. 342.   [5] *Stud. Soc.*, p. 343.

of a hypothetical posterity, therefore, that Spencer denounced the

spurious philanthropists who, to prevent present misery, would entail greater misery on future generations. Blind to the fact that under the natural order of things society is constantly excreting its unhealthy, imbecile, slow, vacillating faithless members . . . in their eagerness to prevent the really-salutary sufferings that surround us, these sigh-wise and groan-foolish people bequeath to posterity a continually-increasing curse. [1]

Such impulses cannot even be condoned as 'natural'. Nature exhibits two modes of the organization of resources designed to preserve the species, those respectively of childhood and adulthood. During childhood, benefits are related directly to weakness. At its youngest and most helpless, the small creature receives the maximum gratuitous aid from its parents. As it gradually attains a measure of self-sufficiency this aid is decreased until, at maturity, the scale is tipped, and the benefits it receives relate directly to its own ability to secure them. Paternalism, which Spencer was brought up to despise, is the social manifestation of the misapplication of family ethics. Evolutionary self-reliance can proceed only if this distinction is preserved throughout social relations, and adult rewards made to accord to merits:

Nature's modes of treatment inside the family group and outside the family group are diametrically opposed to one another . . . the intrusion of either mode into the sphere of the other would be fatal to the species either immediately or remotely . . . [2]

The radical distinction between family-ethics and state-ethics must be maintained . . . while generosity must be the essential principle of the one, justice must be the essential principle of the other. [3]

State intervention, lastly, is negated according to the precepts of absolute ethics. Spencer's formulation of a system of ethical principles from the fundamentals of human conduct was no merely semantic exercise. It had the specific purpose of 'influencing conduct', and of constructing, in absolute ethics, an unshakeable foundation for the limits of state interference:

[1] S. Stat., p. 354.   [2] M.v.S., p. 80.
[3] M.v.S.,p. 81.

Written as far back as 1842, my first essay, consisting of letters on 'The Proper Sphere of Government' vaguely indicated what I conceived to be certain general principles of right and wrong in political conduct; and from that time onwards my political purpose, lying behind all proximate purposes, has been that of finding for the principles of right and wrong in conduct at large a scientific basis.[1]

The limitation of state activities, therefore, is substantiated by reference to the law of equal freedom, upon which depends the ethical classification of all types of conduct.

This principle in turn is rooted in hedonistic assumptions: 'Conduct is good or bad according as its total effects are pleasurable or painful.'[2] The primary requisite of social life is that each shall conduct himself so as neither to burden nor injure his fellows, and positively, that each shall obtain pleasure by increasing the pleasure of his fellows, thereby 'completing one another's lives'. The happiness which it is the purpose of social conduct to fulfil consists in 'the due satisfaction of all desires, that is, happiness consists in the due exercise of all the faculties.'[3]

To the self-sufficient human being, state aid is worse than superfluous. It confers nothing he cannot achieve for himself, but robs him in order that others, less well-endowed, may obtain the same facilities *gratis*. Taxation was seen by Spencer as the main mechanism by which the state vitiates the evolutionary selection process. The taxpayer and ratepayer, declared Spencer, might reasonably argue that 'no-one is justified in forcing him to subscribe towards the maintenance of persons whom he does not consider worthy of relief.'[4] He guarded the distinction between deserving and undeserving poverty with an almost Elizabethan asperity. His theory of punishment forcibly expresses the causal association of unemployment and crime: 'The criminal classes being thus recruited in great part from the idle class, and idleness being a source of criminality it follows that a successful discipline must be one that shall cure the idleness.'[5] In Spencer's vocabulary 'idleness' and 'vice' are almost synonymous: ' "They have no work", you say. Say rather that they either

---

[1] *D. of E.*, p. v.   [2] *D. of E.*, p. 22.   [3] *S. Stat.*, p. 92.
[4] 'Proper Sphere', 22 June 1842.
[5] 'Prison Ethics', *Essays*, iii. 179.

refuse work or quickly turn themselves out of it. They are simply good-for-nothings who in one way or another live on the good-for-somethings—vagrants and sots, criminals and those on the way to crime.'[1] State charity, by taking from the thrifty money which they can ill afford, forces them into poverty: 'Protection of the vicious poor involves aggression on the virtuous poor . . . Is it not cruel to increase the sufferings of the better that the sufferings of the worst may be decreased?'[2] Spencer objected, lastly, to the bureaucratic tyranny implicit in taxation for social purposes, characterizing the official attitude thus: 'Hitherto you have been free to spend this portion of your earnings in any way which pleased you; hereafter you shall not be free so to spend it, but we will spend it for the general benefit.'

The artificial supply of gratification is equally damaging to the higher sentiments: 'National character will only improve by that daily exercise of the higher sentiments and repression of the lower, which results from keeping men subordinate to the requirements of orderly social life—letting them suffer the inevitable penalties of breaking those requirements and reap the benefits of conforming to them.'[3] The end product of this social discipline is a state in which positive beneficence ('helping to complete one another's lives') will supplement the negative benevolence of voluntarily respecting the rights of others. The first stirrings of this positive benevolence are perceptible in the growth of philanthropic and humanitarian movements. As the trend gathers momentum it will provide more and more opportunities for the exercise of the beneficent sentiments, which will in turn gather strength. State intervention, which seeks to 'make men pitiful by force', starkly disrupts this upward tendency. The warm glow of generosity experienced by the volunteer philanthropist is replaced by bitter resentment as his charity is forcibly wrenched from him as taxation, and distributed without his consent or direction: 'Being kind by proxy—could anything be more blighting to the finer instincts?'[4]

[1] *M.v.S.*, p. 22.
[2] *M.v.S.*, p. 89.
[3] *Stud. Soc.*, pp. 372-3.
[4] *S. Stat.*, p. 351.

Social justice requires that opportunities for the pursuit of individual satisfaction be equally available for all. The first assumption is freedom of action; the second is equality of opportunity, hence 'the liberty of each limited by the like liberty of all . . . is the rule in conformity with which society must be organised.'[1] More dogmatically expressed, this deduction becomes the 'law of equal freedom': 'Every man is free to do all that he wills, provided he infringes not the equal freedom of every other man.'[2]

State interference infringes the 'rights' logically deduced from this first principle. It restricts the 'right to life and liberty' by preventing due exercise of the altruistic impulses. It threatens the 'right to free industry' by regulating the hours and conditions of labour, the 'right to free exchange' by monetary and economic intervention, and the 'right to free worship' by maintaining an Established Church. Taxation, above all, impinges on the right to private property where it is exacted for any schemes which fall outside the legitimate governmental spheres of justice and protection. The 'law of equal freedom' and its dependent clauses, therefore, hold out the ultimate ethical sanction against state intervention beyond the prescribed limit.

To summarize: Spencer's definition of the legitimate duty of the state restricts it to the 'negative' roles of the protection of its citizens from external attack, the maintenance of justice internally and the enforcement of contract by legal sanction.

'Positive' state intervention is incapable of producing 'artificially' the desired amelioration of social problems for the following reasons. Legislators fail to take account of the complexities of social causation, incomprehensible even in terms of social science (of which they are in any case culpably ignorant), while social evolution, 'naturally' determined, is impervious to their meddlings. State agencies are clumsy, ill-adapted to their task and lack the 'antiseptic' of competition. Their activities broaden the scope for bureaucratic entrenchment. State intervention is also ethically reprehensible; it presumes a superhuman wisdom on the part of

[1] *S. Stat.*, p. 106.   [2] *S. Stat.*, p. 121.

the legislator, which is not supported by the legislative record; it usurps the natural order in which evils are rectified by according individual welfare a higher priority than that of the species; it obstructs the evolution of human self-reliance and delays the development of the 'higher type' of man by seeking to mitigate suffering (which is the mainspring of social evolution) and the elimination of the 'unfit'; it violates absolute ethics by artificially extending the liberty of some men, while constricting that of others, and by taxing the latter into the bargain. Spencer leaves state intervention with nothing to commend it but its misguided good intentions.

Spencer's argument that the role of the state should be restricted in conformity with the law of equal freedom ignores the possibility that other influences at work in society, besides the state, might prevent it from operating freely. The inescapable paradox of possessive individualism, as stated by C.B. MacPherson, is relevant here: 'A market society generates class differentiation in effective rights, yet requires for its justification equal rights . . .'[1] Spencer saw the emergence of a class structure as a dimension of 'natural' inequality, yet expected it to have no modifying effect on the continuing struggle. Class is unique in Spencerian theory as being acknowledged to exist, but being accorded no function.

It is relevant at this point to compare Spencer's disregard of the social function of class with the role assigned to it by Karl Marx. Marxian sociology suggests that stratified inequality, incorporated in a class system, undermines the 'equal freedom' of each man to pursue his own goals. This element of the socialist critique gained acceptance among later nineteenth-century Liberals.[2] Second, it reinterprets the function of the state. In Spencer's theory, granted his individualistic premise, the state ought not to emerge from its prescribed neutrality and assert itself as a positive social force. Marxists, however, view the state as integral to a 'class society', and therefore incapable of neutrality between

---

[1] C.B. MacPherson, *The Political Theory of Possessive Individualism* (Oxford, 1970), p. 269.
[2] See below, Chap. 7, pp. 178–91.

classes; where class is defined by position in the economic structure, government is the 'executive' of the ruling class. The state, the laws it passes and enforces, and the ideology which underpins it reflect and preserve existing property relations. Spencer's state is the 'referee' in the struggle of life, an authority erected by the consent of all to guarantee their freedom; Marx's state is ever strong upon the stronger side. It is therefore ironical that both believed the state to be a transitional feature of social development, destined eventually to 'wither away'.

It is a basic precept of Spencerian theory that no essential conflict of interest can exist between capital and labour. The 'class struggle' did not exist for him; even Trade Unionism was viewed in terms of the supposed contravention of 'free' contractual relations. Like Samuel Smiles he saw in the capitalist 'merely a man who does not spend all that is earned by work', and defined his social stratification in moral terms: 'Society consists mainly of two classes—the savers and the spenders, the provident and the improvident, the thrifty and the thriftless.'[1] The economic relations of capitalism—the appropriation of the surplus-value of labour by the owners of capital on which the Marxian class-structure rested—were regarded by Spencer as perfectly equitable. Marx designated Spencer part of the ideological superstructure of capitalism; Spencer would probably have dismissed Marx as another misguided collectivist. The premises of their respective analyses of human behaviour in industrial society diverge so widely that it is scarcely worth pursuing a critique of Spencer's individualism from a Marxist viewpoint.

Spencer's ethical system, furthermore, furnishes no adequate definition of 'aggression'. The formula of equal freedom is a safe enough introductory gambit for any theoretical system, yet no limits are specified for it. The absence of such a specification throws the interpretation of equal freedom open to whim.

In treating of rights Spencer ignored the plurality of sectional interests within a society, even leaving aside the

---

[1] K. Fielden, 'Samuel Smiles and self-help', *Victorian Studies,* xii (1968), pp 160-1.

question of class. In any advanced society exhibiting a
plurality of interests the rights of contending individuals and
groups must be expected to clash with one another, yet this
notion of a conflict of equally valid rights is rarely acknowledged by Spencer. All situations of social conflict, in which
the arbitration of the state is required entail such a collision
of rights. Spencer's denunciation of sanitary regulations, for
example, asserts the right of property (of the owner not to
render his property more salubrious) as prevailing over the
right to life (of the tenant to be free of disease).[1] Adjudica-
tion of such conflicts in a systematic manner is the legitimate, if thorny, task of governments.

Spencer preferred to define aggression by the agency
committing it, which afforded a simple solution to all problems. If the state enforces a regulation or generalizes a decision it is wrong. If private impulses are at work they are justified in doing whatever they wish, within vestigial limits. The
simplicity of this approach tempted Spencer into self-evident
contradictions. State philanthropy is bad; private philanthropy
is good. National education is pernicious; private schemes
organized by panels of altruistic businessmen are to be encouraged. In every case where a conflict of rights is detectable the crucial factor is the identity of the interests involved.

An instructive exception to this rule is Spencer's inveterate
opposition to Trade Unionism: a spontaneous organization of
individuals for a mutual objective. In castigating not only
state interference in the 'freedom' of the labour-market, but
also the parallel attempts of Trade Unionism to regulate
hours, conditions, and wages, he implicitly denied the right
to free association. His individualist formula for industrial
relations was based on a model of perfect competition which,
if it ever existed, had been outgrown by the capitalism of the
late nineteenth century, with its trusts, cartels, price-rings,
and political pressure-groups. The growth of 'organized' as
opposed to 'anarchic' capitalism took Spencer by surprise; he
'did not seriously face one of the inevitable consequences of
free economic competition, that the success of the victors
is used to eliminate the possibilities of further competition.'[2]

[1] For Huxley's critique of this position and H.S.'s defence of it, see below, Chap.
7, pp. 184–5.
[2] D.G. Macrae, op.cit., p. 43.

Spencer was profoundly alarmed by the rise of the Trade Union movement, which cut across his vision of a deferential and grateful working class. A shrill note of outrage and incredulity enters his writing whenever it is alluded to. His definition of 'freedom of contract' in the context of industrial bargaining took no account of the inequalities in wealth, power or influence between the parties (i.e. the individual master and the individual employee). As the Belgian economist Emile de Laveleye pointed out:

When the labourer . . . deprived of all property, is forced to choose between the wages offered by his employer . . . and starvation, he is no more 'free' than the traveller when requested to deliver up his money or his life. It is a mockery to call a man free who, by labour, cannot secure to himself the necessities of existence.[1]

The myth of 'free negotiation', furthermore, ignored the operation of the law as a framework of social action. Law, as Spencer repeatedly demonstrated, favours the rich; wealth purchases legal facilities and access to the law out of reach of the majority, and the substance of the legal system is the protection of property. Spencer's freedom of contract, therefore, left the worker at the mercy of his employer.

Yet Spencer himself had encountered the realities of imperfect competition. Bookselling in London during the 1840s had been controlled by the Booksellers' Association, whose members received a discount in return for assurances that they would retail at no less than 90 per cent of the recommended price. John Chapman fell foul of this consortium by selling imported books, for which he claimed exemption, at cost price plus commission, a misdemeanour for which he was 'blacked' by his fellow-publishers. In an angry article entitled 'The Commerce of Literature' (*Westminster Review*, Apr. 1852) Chapman appealed to authors, suggesting that the arrangement, by restricting circulation and keeping prices high, was detrimental to their interests. Spencer responded by convening a meeting of authors, chaired by Charles Dickens, to protest at their exploitation by booksellers.[2] A committee was formed which successfully took the Association to arbitration in 1853.

[1] E. de Laveleye to H.S., 2 Apr. 1885, *L.L.* i. 328.
[2] G.S. Haight, *George Eliot, a biography* (Oxford, 1968), p. 110.

Although theoretically re-establishing the autonomy of the market, this struggle was conducted by two institutions representing conflicting sectional interests, indicating a disharmony within capitalism. Spencer remained closely interested in the rewards of authorship, joined the Society for the Repeal of Taxes on Knowledge and gave evidence to the Copyright Commission in 1877. He even advocated a law protecting international copyright, inconsistently claiming that such a law would encourage good conduct among the regulated: 'far from its being needful . . . that the necessity is the diffusion of knowledge at the expense of dishonesty, it is, contrariwise, needful that there should be some diffusion of honesty, even should there be some consequent impediment to the spread of knowledge.'[1]

Analysis of a governmental system implies three basic questions: (i) who rules? (ii) to what ends? and (iii) within what sphere? Spencer's political theory is almost exclusively concerned with the third of these questions, and his opposition to state intervention is based on his answer to it. He rightly shows that democracy does not always entail liberty, yet he persists in describing the alternative to his narrowly-conceived state jurisdiction as a 'regime' of bureaucrats and officials. His invocation of 'socialism' further confuses the issue; sometimes it describes the supposed goal of the collectivist conspiracy, at others the expanding scope of governmental intrusion itself. The identity of the governing agency and its objectives are irrelevant because Spencer's individualism is exclusively focused upon the scope of governmental action: 'the real issue is whether the lives of citizens are more interfered with than they were; not the nature of the agency which interferes with them.'[2] In introducing these extraneous concerns in order to strengthen his case, Spencer thereby obscures it.

It is possible to see a certain degree of arbitrariness in Spencer's classification of 'legitimate' state functions. If 'natural' competition denotes the ideal society, why then not jettison the state altogether, and choose the Hobbesian mode

[1] H.S. to E.L. Youmans, 10 Jan. 1882, *L.L.* i. 210.
[2] *M.v.S.*, p. 17.

of struggle? Can the validity of some functions be logically explained, while others are excluded? Spencer would rightly consider this criticism unjust, and claim that his scheme is based on the ethics of reciprocity; if everyone's rights are to be accorded equal importance, an impartial state agency invested with regulatory powers is obviously necessary. The question is important, however, as foreshadowing the central problem of Spencer's political theory: the clash between a rational, hedonistically-based theory of social justice, and a naturalistic explanation of social development based on the 'survival of the fittest'. No reasonable hedonist would wish to live in a jungle; but if society *is* a jungle, then the laws of the jungle should, strictly speaking, pertain.

7

SPENCERIAN LIBERALISM AND ITS LIBERAL CRITICS

Herbert Spencer's individualist theory incurred contemporary criticism from two sources: from fellow-Liberals who questioned his definition of freedom and perception of the interplay of natural rights, and from fellow-evolutionists who challenged its basis in the ethical inferences from natural selection. This latter body of criticism is examined in Chapter 8; this chapter seeks to isolate the content of Spencerian Liberalism, and to explain Spencer's condemnation both of the Liberal Party and of its leading theoreticians as having reneged upon the fundamental principles of the faith as he interpreted it. It then goes on to discuss his allegation that the political practice of Liberalism degenerated during the nineteenth century from a pure individualism to a corrupt collectivism motivated by electoral expediency, an assertion that is examined in the light of the historical actualities of the period. Finally, it recounts the criticisms levelled at Spencer's Liberalism by spokesmen of the 'mainstream' of the Liberal movement, who concentrated upon his theory of 'natural rights' and his neglect of the problem of inequality of opportunity in a society characterized by competition, both arguments which indicate the degree to which Spencerian Liberalism had, by the end of the century, aged to the point of anachronism.

SPENCER'S LIBERALISM

Spencer was a 'Liberal' in that he saw the fundamental problem of political theory in the reconciliation of the maximum individual freedom with the bare essentials of social stability and coherence. 'Equal freedom' was his device for balancing them out. This simple antithesis between 'self-love and social' presupposed an atomic society in which needs are experienced and gratified in an individual context, requiring only community of restraint. In this Spencer conformed to the basic assumptions comprising possessive individualism. Humanity is freedom from the constraint of other wills; the individual is therefore proprietor of his person and capacities. If his freedom is inalienable (a controversial point) his capacities are not, least of all his capacity to labour, which he may sell. Thus human society consists of a series of market relations, and the state is the contrivance whereby equitable transactions are guaranteed. Yet this interpretation drew a barrage of criticism from thinkers who, as sincerely as Spencer, considered themselves Liberals. This paradox can only be resolved by examining Spencerian Liberalism in the political and social context in which it was developed, and by relating it to the broad and variegated stream of political thought for which 'Liberalism' is a convenient collective term.

Spencer's lifelong belief was that his 'principled Liberalism' had been betrayed by the Liberal Party. As early as 1846 he demonstrated that he held no brief for the Whigs: 'I have no objection', he wrote, 'to a whole host of Churchmen and Protectionists getting into the next parliament . . . The great thing to be wished is the crippling of Lord John Russell to disable him from carrying out his education and endowment measures.'[1] Parliamentary Liberalism, having embraced state intervention, had lost its way:

the notion of liberty has been so mixed up of late with that of organic reforms that, with the mass of men, it has come to be synonymous with democratic government; and many of those who think themselves its warmest advocates are above all others inclined to increase the tyranny of the state over individuals.[2]

Spencer was resolved to reset Liberalism on its true path. In 1881 he even considered launching an alternative party, incorporating remnants of the anti-Corn Law League and the Peace Society. The immediate need was for a redefinition of political affiliations:

In our day Toryism and Liberalism have become confused, and the line between them has to be drawn afresh. Toryism stands for the coercive power of the state *versus* the freedom of the individual. Liberalism stands for the freedom of the individual *versus* the power of the state.

[1] H.S. to W.G.S., 3 Sept. 1846, *L.L.* i. 70.
[2] H.S. to J.S. Mill, 17 Feb. 1859, *L.L.* i. 70.

At present the Liberal Party has lost sight of their essential principle, and a new Liberal Party has to be formed to re-assert it.[1]

Spencer's disillusionment with the Liberal Party led him on occasion to advocate the abolition of parties altogether. Party allegiance and political principle, he argued, were incompatibles. If political conduct is ethically motivated, then the party, which demands the abdication of individual conscience and judgement, must disappear: 'Good government can only be assured by basing our political institutions on principles. The party distinction between Whig and Tory must perish . . . While either of these great factions rule, our best interests are imperilled.'[2] Spencer voted at a parliamentary election only once, in 1865, thereafter feeling no temptation to distinguish between two parties equally tainted by state intervention. In 1902 he was still arguing that parliamentary voting should be governed by individual conscience: 'A ministry would become that which its name implies, a servant, instead of what it is now, a master . . . . At present that which we boast of as political freedom consists in the ability to choose a despot or group of oligarchs.'[3]

In 'The New Toryism' Spencer declared that 'most of those who now pass as Liberals, are Tories of a new type.'[4] To identify the individualistic essence of true Liberalism he traced its origins back to Whiggery, drawing heavily on Henry Bolingbroke's *Dissertation on Parties*. The struggle of the Whigs against Charles II and the Cabal reflected the greater conflict between militarism and industrialism, Toryism and Liberalism being, respectively, the system of government appropriate to each. Popular political discrimination, however, has lost sight of this distinction. Early Whig-Liberal measures, like the repeal of the Combination Laws, the removal of legal restrictions on Dissenters, and the abolition of the East India Company's monopoly, were measures which 'permitted revival of the industrial regime' after the militancy of the Napoleonic era. They were also, however, 'abolitions

---

[1] H.S. to W.C. Croft, Dec. 1881, *L.L.* i. 219.
[2] *Pilot*, 9 Nov. 1844.
[3] H.S., *Facts and Comments*, pp. 101–2.
[4] *M.v.S.*, p. 1.

of grievances suffered by the people'; 'and since, in the minds of most, a rectified evil is equivalent to an achieved good, these measures came to be thought of as so many positive benefits; and the welfare of the many came to be conceived alike by Liberal statesmen and Liberal voters as the aim of Liberalism.'[1]

Liberal objectives, then, were being pursued by dangerously un-Liberal methods. The essential difference between a free and an unfree political system is expressed in the relation between individual autonomy and state power. The fact that government is formally democratic is inconsequential: 'the liberty which a citizen enjoys is to be measured, not by the nature of the governmental machinery he lives under, whether representative or not, but by the relative paucity of the restraints it imposes on him.'[2] 'The New Toryism' comprehensively sums up Spencer's political priorities:

I now, in 1884, reach what seems a sufficiently completed view—the politico-ethical doctrine set forth in this article being a presentation in a finished form of the theory gradually developed during those forty-two years. It will, I think, eventually form a new departure in politics. The definite conclusions reached, alike concerning the legitimate powers of governments and the reasons why, beyond a certain range, their powers cannot be legitimately exercised, and along with them the definite conception presented of the nature of true Liberalism for the future may, I think, serve presently to give a positive creed for an advanced party in politics.[3]

No new party emerged, and the creed was assimilated into the ideology of twentieth-century conservatism.

SPENCER AND THE NINETEENTH CENTURY

Spencer's notion of the 'betrayal' of Liberalism is based on his highly-selective account of nineteenth-century administrative history, which closely resembles that described in A.V. Dicey's *Law and Public Opinion in England in the Nineteenth Century*. Dicey, who severed his connection with the Liberal Party over Home Rule, spent the rest of his life, like Spencer, bemoaning its interventionist tendencies. His work

[1] *M.v.S.*, p. 8.
[2] *M.v.S.*, p. 19.
[3] H.S. to E.L. Youmans, 13 May 1884, *L.L.* i. 324.

postulates three phases 'during which a different current or stream of opinion was predominant, and in the main governed the development of the law of England.'[1] They were the age of Old Toryism or 'legislative quiescence' (1800–30), the age of 'Benthamism, or Individualism' (1825–70), and the age of 'Collectivism' (1865–90), which 'favours the intervention of the state, even at some sacrifice of individual freedom, for the purpose of conferring benefit upon the mass of the people.'[2] Two criticisms levelled at Dicey are that his political recollection extended only as far back as 1848, and that his hypothesis is unsupported by factual evidence. For Spencer, whose political consciousness dated from about 1836, and who likewise tailored the data to fit his interpretation, the compartmentalization of the nineteenth century was similarly a political, rather than a scholarly exercise.

Spencer's vision of a 'pure' Liberalism suddenly corrupted in 1850 by electoral pressure ignores two solid facts. First, all the social legislation of which he complained originated before 1850; subsequent acts elaborated and extended regulations already established. Second, 'Liberalism', the emergent party and its theoreticians, comprised a confused, heterogenous coalition of incongruous political allies, and contained contradictory tendencies never fully reconciled. The Liberal Party itself was inchoate and heterogeneous; parties were created at Westminster by fortuitous alignments on crucial but isolated issues, and were constantly dispersing and re-forming. The Liberal Party of 1859 contained a mixture of Manchester radicals, conservative Whigs, and disillusioned Peelite Tories, including William Gladstone. Spencer's account of the process is a thing of labels and theoretical logic: its reality was far more complex.

The Poor Law Amendment Act of 1834, a measure of economy rather than philanthropy, set the pattern for future legislation, entailing a Royal Commission, and a bureaucratic establishment. By 1849 there had been over 100 Royal Commissions; Spencer himself railed against them in the

---

[1] A.V. Dicey, *Law and public opinion in England in the Nineteenth Century* (London, 1914), p. 62.
[2] Ibid., p. 64.

Pilot (1844). The first state grant to elementary education was voted in 1833, and two years later the Municipal Corporations Act empowered local authorities to assume responsibility for urban improvements. The Poor Law Amendment Act was extended in 1839, 1840, and 1842, and in 1848 the irrepressible Edwin Chadwick engineered the passage of the Public Health Act. In the sphere of factory reform no fewer than ten 'coercive' bills had become law before 1850, including the 1833 act which established the Factory Inspectorate. Enforcement was uneven; officials were appointed through the network of official patronage, prosecutions were infrequent, and penalties light, but the principle of state intervention in social procedures was firmly entrenched before 1850, and institutionalized in the Poor Law Commission, the Education Committee of the Privy Council, and the Board of Health. These, ironically for the Dicey thesis, have been seen as the political realization of Jeremy Bentham's blueprint for an administrative state.[1]

Spencer neglected the important distinction between the provision of services and the practice of public inspection. What he denounced as 'over-legislation' was in fact 'a technique for reconciling freedom with an efficient and active government.'[2] The social by-products of industrialization offended the Victorian conscience and stimulated the fear of revolution. The problems of the factory, the slum, and the insanitary conurbation were too big for local authorities, yet the sanctity of local autonomy precluded central management. Central inspection of local organization, then, was the compromise designed (as by Bentham) to ensure that men did with their own what was consistent with the social good. Far from being a doctrinaire tyranny, the 'Victorian administrative state' can be seen as 'a political contrivance, shaped by men with various persuasions, all of whom were disturbed at the existence of ignorance, disease and misery in their changing society.'[3]

Considering Spencer's tidiness of mind, there is surprisingly

---

[1] See D. Roberts, 'Jeremy Bentham and the Victorian Administrative State', *Victorian Studies,* ii (1958–9).
[2] Ibid., p. 194.
[3] Ibid., p. 210.

little attempt in his work to discriminate between the forces of state interference. M.P.s, civil servants and philanthropic campaigners are treated as part of the same insidious network. As D.G. Macrae points out:

Spencer is never clear about the relation that subsists between the threatening tyranny of administrators and the excessive powers ascribed to parliaments and majority opinions. He seems to believe, contrary to the main flow of his sociology, that to limit the latter will necessarily abridge the former.[1]

The Liberal movement, secondly, contrary to Spencer's ascribed image of single-mindedness and concord, emerged out of an incongruous coalition of elements, united for the purpose of carrying the 1832 Reform Act and maintaining an effective parliamentary majority thereafter. The Whigs, led by Lords Grey, Melbourne, and Russell, subscribed to the necessity of a balanced constitution based on deference, but from Charles James Fox they had inherited a tradition of aristocratic radicalism, and were the patrons of Nonconformity, a connection which assured them the support of the emergent industrial and commercial middle classes. In 1832 they found themselves at the head of a collection of assorted radicals, including extremists like Daniel O'Connell, Francis Place, and William Cobbett, but whose main body was broadly aligned in two camps, the Philosophic Radicals and the Political Economists.

The personnel of early Philosophic Radicalism was at first indistinguishable from the adherents of Political Economy. The first agitation against the Corn Laws was instigated in 1826, in London, not Manchester, but the unanimity which accompanied it quickly evaporated, and radicalism began to split. John Stuart Mill found his father's utilitarianism mean-spirited and dessicated; Thomas Babington Macaulay reacted against Jeremy Bentham's dismissal of History, and became the spokesman of the Whig Interpretation. The most significant line of fracture, however, separated the Economists from the Philosophicals, and traced the division between state intervention and individualism. A.V. Dicey equated Benthamism with individualism in order to reconcile the mid-century as-

[1] D.G. Macrae, op.cit., p. 42.

cendancy of Benthamite thought with his proposition that individualism had given way to collectivism after 1865. In this he became 'the principal maintainer of the myth for others.'[1]

Bentham's Constitutional Code is acknowledged, even by Dicey, to contain substantial concessions to the interventionist principle. Its hypothetical cabinet includes ministries of health, education, and 'indigence'. Bentham is seen as 'the patriarch of British collectivism'; 'The Fabians were the direct descendants of Bentham, via Chadwick and Forster.'[2] Lionel Robbins argues that although there is no necessary contradiction between Benthamism and *laissez-faire*, utilitarian rather than doctrinaire considerations were responsible for the Free Trade hegemony of the 1840s and 1850s. Bentham advocated Free Trade, not, like Spencer, out of regard for abstract 'natural rights', but as part of the utilitarian framework of the efficient state, in accordance with prevailing conditions. The Benthamite principle prompted considerable extensions of Free Trade and state intervention simultaneously.[3] D. Roberts describes Bentham's 'administrative state' as 'a balance between local and central government and a belief in *laissez-faire*, reconciled by the principle of inspection.'[4] H. Parriss concurs that 'the question was not one of *laissez-faire* or state intervention but where, in the light of constantly-changing circumstances, the line between them should be drawn.'[5] Dicey, like Spencer, failed to distinguish between the economic and social implications of Benthamism.

The Economists took their cue from Adam Smith. Their chief spokesman, David Ricardo, rejected the Benthamite reconciliation of personal and social interests, and substituted an endemic conflict between landed aristocracy and industry, and, within industry, between capital and labour.

---

[1] See J.B. Brebner, '*Laissez-faire* and state intervention in the nineteenth century', *J.Econ.Hist.* (Supplement), viii, 1948.

[2] M.P. Mack, 'The Fabians and utilitarianism', *J.Hist.Ideas,* xvi, 1955.

[3] L. Robbins, *The Theory of Economic Policy in Classical English Political Economy* (London, 1952), pp. 117–26.

[4] D. Roberts, op.cit., p. 194.

[5] H. Parriss, 'The nineteenth century revolution in government; a re-appraisal re-appraised', *Historical Journal,* iii (1966), p. 37.

From the tripartite stress of this conflict he deduced his 'iron law of wages'; the standard of living of the worker is caught between the greed of his landlord and the legitimate interests of his employer in low labour costs. The permanent tendency of wages, therefore, is to sink to the minimum indispensable to the worker's existence. The lot of the labouring poor can be improved indirectly by technological improvements, voluntary birth control and, above all, by a reduction in the price of corn. Spencer's individualism is suffused with the encouraging certitude of Ricardian economics.

During the 1830s, therefore, Liberalism became divided between interventionism and individualism. Edwin Chadwick and his circle of professional administrators, in alliance with upper-class Evangelicals and humanitarians like Richard Oastler and Lord Ashley, invoked the power of the state and achieved, even before 1850, a substantial body of social legislation. Before Chadwick, vigorous reformist campaigns had been waged behind the scenes, by William Huskisson and Nassau Senior at the Board of Trade, by William Farr in the annual reports of the Registrar General, by Leonard Horner and George Howell in the factories, James Kay-Shuttleworth and John Morell in the schools, Frederick Hill in the prisons, and Stephen Tremenheere in the mines. After 1834 they began to integrate their activities, and to become aware of corporate aims. Even so, their interventionism was not motivated by single-minded philanthropy, as imputed by Spencer. Chadwick's initial motive in the Poor Law and sanitary movements was economy; poor relief was costing too much. In this he articulated the orthodox Whig enthusiasm for cheap government.[1]

Even the Political Economists were not uniformly anti-interventionist with respect to social questions. The issue was grossly oversimplified in popular indictments of social individualism from the pens of Thomas Carlyle and Charles Dickens. Adam Smith, describing the duties of the Sovereign, had acknowledged, as well as the functions of external protection and internal justice, the need of 'certain public works

---

[1] See M.W. Flinn, ed., introduction to *The Report on the Sanitary Conditions of the Labouring Population of Great Britain: 1842* (Edinburgh, 1965).

and certain public institutions which it can never be for the interests of any individual, or small number of individuals, to erect and maintain.'[1] Nassau Senior, a Free Trade extremist, stated in his report on hand-loom weavers, apropos of their living conditions:

With all our reverence for the principle of non-interference, we cannot doubt in this matter it has been carried too far. We believe that both ground landlord and the speculating builder ought to be compelled by law, though it should cost them a percentage of their rent and profit, to take measures which should prevent the towns which they create from being the centres of disease.[2]

Elsewhere, Senior issued what could almost be a specific repudiation of Spencer's 'administrative nihilism':

Many political thinkers . . . have declared that the business of government is simply to afford protection, to repel or punish internal or external violence or fraud, and that to do more is usurpation. This proposition I cannot admit. The only rational foundation of government is expediency—the general benefit of the community. It is the duty of a government to do whatever is conducive to the welfare of the governed.[3]

M.W. Flinn has remarked:

The Political Economists were, in short, too intelligent and too well-informed to advocate out-and-out *laissez-faire*. They were constantly being brought up short by the realities of the economic system in which they worked, and were only too conscious of the clash between the logic of pure theory and the demands of social morality. They did not invariably . . . insist on the priority of the former claim.[4]

This proposition implies for Spencer an even deeper isolation.

Individualism, meanwhile, drowning interventionism in its well-organized clamour, achieved its principal aim with the repeal of the Corn Laws, and rapidly assumed the status of a new Liberal orthodoxy. Spencer, bent on denouncing the legislative transgressions committed by Lord Palmerston and William Gladstone, ignored the broadly anti-interventionist guidelines of their policies. The repeal of the Corn Laws was

[1] A. Smith, *The Wealth of Nations* (London, 1904), ii. 185.
[2] M.W. Flinn, op.cit., p. 39.
[3] Cited in M. Bowley, *Nassau Senior and the Classical Economists* (London, 1937), p. 205.
[4] M.W. Flinn, op.cit., pp. 39–40.

by no means the zenith of individualism; Gladstone's budget of 1853 has been described as 'perhaps the best date for the *beginning* of a truly Free Trade economy,'[1] while in 1860 Richard Cobden negotiated the Free Trade treaty with France. The fiscal measures of Gladstone's budgets enshrined the very principle enunciated by Spencer in 'Representative Government: what is it good for?', that taxation be levied so as to assist the taxpayer to identify the sums exacted from his private income as the source of public expenditure, and therefore be motivated to maintain a persistent brake upon it. From 1860 until 1914, finally, successive British governments upheld an unflinching policy of overseas Free Trade, which gained them little popular respect and none at all from Spencer.

Gladstone's Liberalism, like Spencer's, was in direct line of descent from David Ricardo, Richard Cobden, and the Manchester School orthodoxy. On social issues he took only such measures as were necessary to placate evangelical pressure and the new idealistic radicalism within his own party. This is not to imply that he was indifferent to public misery; indeed he was gravely concerned. His response, however, was not instinctively legislative; he shared the anti-interventionist convictions of 'responsible' Liberal opinion, and the deep aversion among men of all political colours to public expenditure. Good government was cheap government, and although motivated by a social conscience which prompted him to spend his own money on 'fallen women', he was loath to commit anyone else's, a truly Spencerian sentiment. His watchwords, after all, were 'Peace, Retrenchment, and Reform'.

Intervention first became political policy in Benjamin Disraeli's administration of 1874, from which time Spencer is justified in describing a concerted sweep by all parties towards the legislative correction of social evils, if hardly towards Bismarckian 'state socialism'. He was palpably wrong, however, to accuse the Liberal Party of instigating it, for the old guard of Gladstonian Liberals were caught up and swept aside by it, just as Spencer was. Their fate is illustrated

---

[1] R.B. McCallum, op.cit., p. 58 (my italics).

by the downfall of John Morley, M.P. for Newcastle-upon-Tyne, and defeated in 1895 because he refused support for an eight-hour day in the mines. He was the biographer, not only of Gladstone, but of Cobden, and was chosen by Spencer to give the address at his funeral, 'because of the general likeness of ideas that distinguishes us from the world at large.'[1]

The trend towards over-legislation which, belatedly, 'infected' the Liberal Party, reflected a shift in the broad consensus of attitudes towards governmental responsibility. Even behind the facade of confident individualism contradictions persisted. Lord Shaftesbury's New Royal Commission on Child Labour (1842) stirred up the indigation of those who did not share the general complacency. The meliorative forces of Liberalism were beginning to break up, not the party itself, but the very interventionist issue. The distinction was coming increasingly to be drawn between individualism as vindicated in Free Trade and individualism as the adoption of a *laissez-faire* attitude to social problems. John Stuart Mill's *The Principles of Political Economy* was an ideological landmark in formulating this distinction.

As prosperity seemed firmly established, people began to notice problems which the triumphant expansion of capitalism had left in its wake. A reaction set in against the social thinking of 'Manchesterdom', intensified during the (controversial) 'Great Depression' of 1876–96, which left John Bright isolated in the Commons and Herbert Spencer in the reviews. In academic circles the doctrines of classical economics were beginning to be questioned, largely as a result of the efforts of J.E. Cairns and Henry Fawcett to defend them. A new-found concern for the plight of the poor permeated even the colums of *The Times*, where it was now authoritatively asserted that 'to employ women and children unduly is simply to run into debt with Nature.'[2] Samuel Smiles, architect of the doctrine of self-help, repudiated its use to rationalize the neglect of social problems, especially in the fields of sanitation and health:

[1] H.S. to Morley, 16 Sept. 1903, *L.L.* ii. 222.
[2] *The Times*, 4 Mar. 1867.

When typhus or cholera breaks out they tell us that Nobody is to blame. That terrible Nobody! How much he has to answer for. More mischief is done by Nobody than by all the world besides . . . Nobody poisons us with bad drink . . . Nobody supplies us with foul water . . . Nobody leaves our towns undrained . . . Nobody has a theory too—a dreadful theory. It is embodied in the two words: '*Laissez-faire*.'[1]

Even Spencer felt himself obliged to deny the imputation of 'vicious *laissez-faire*' and to emphasize the state's duty as preventer of injustice.

The development of this interventionist sentiment could not but produce echoes in Liberal thought, and ultimately in Liberal Party policy. Gladstone and his supporters, however, remained faithful, despite extreme pressure from inside and outside the Party, to individualist principles. It was the opportunism of Disraeli, whose 'Tory democracy' won over discontented workers and frustrated humanitarians, which capitalized on it. The election result of 1874 tempted the Liberals to follow suit, and Gladstone's intransigence split the party. Widespread disillusionment with social *laissez-faire* produced a parallel bifurcation of liberal thought. Some heretics wondered if higher standards of working-class life, artificially induced, might not in the long run increase productivity and prosperity, a hint to this effect having been dropped by the shrewd Chadwick on several occasions.

Underlying these speculations was a dash of simple humanitarianism, the 'spurious philanthropy' pilloried by Spencer. This trend towards the democratization of Liberalism left Spencer very much in the cold. He became an anachronism, divorced by his extremism in the orthodoxy of the 1840s from the mainstream of the 1880s. Free competition was no longer a sufficient guarantee of progress, and the harmony of individual interests was no longer assumed. If the harshness of the struggle was being alleviated, the state was the rectifying agency.

Spencer's view of the *volte-face* of Liberalism is understandable but inaccurate. Where he saw two stages, perfect orthodoxy until 1850, unmitigated heresy afterwards, the struggle between interventionism and individualism was

---

[1] Cited in A. Briggs, *Victorian People* (London, 1967), p. 134.

already evident in the 1830s, abated during the prosperous 1850s, and reasserted itself against the overweening confidence and materialism of the Great Exhibition era. The capitulation of the Liberal Party before this humanitarian onslaught, furthermore, was delayed by Gladstone until it was too late to save his party, or to forestall the Tory usurpation of the public conscience. The simplicity of Spencer's account illustrates the pitfalls of applying a sociological model to an historical problem. He saw only industrialism versus militancy, with the latter triumphant. He ought to have known better. In Gladstone, who was his friend, he failed to detect that the humanitarian and individualistic strands of Liberalism were so closely interwoven that they could coexist in the mind of one man, and still not find a peaceful reconciliation.

THE LIBERAL CRITIQUE OF SPENCERISM

Spencer's collectivist critics considered it inappropriate that his individualism should be founded in the theory of 'natural rights', a metaphysical assumption at odds with the physiological allusions elsewhere employed: 'When people speak of natural rights of liberty, property etc. they really mean, not rights which once existed, but rights which they believe ought to exist, and which would be produced by a condition of society and an ordering of the state such as they think desirable.'[1] Spencer, too, often presented his predilections in the form of precepts. He spoke of 'natural' laws as distinct from 'man-made' ones, yet these laws were no more than generalized hypothetical interpretations of natural processes, equally 'man-made' and bearing no greater moral validity.[2]

His scientific pretensions notwithstanding, Spencer was accused of being old-fashioned: 'In spite of the constant parade of biological illustration, it would appear that, in his political thinking, Mr. Spencer has not advanced beyond the arithmetical and mechanical conceptions of society.'[3] To Liberals who took their cue from German Idealism, the concept of society as a balancing of individual interests or rights seemed a quaint one, especially when it emanated from

[1]   D.G. Ritchie, *The Principles of State Interference* (London, 1902), p. 43.
[2]   H.S.'s usage of the term 'natural' is discussed below in Chap. 9, pp. 226–27.
[3]   D.G. Ritchie, op.cit., p. 22.

Spencer, whose organicism they were taking literally. The antithesis of one finite entity called 'Man' against another, 'the State' is a polemic abstraction, rather than an analysis of social relations: 'The individual, apart from all relations to a community, is a negation. You can say nothing about him, except that he is not another individual.'[1] Leonard Hobhouse agreed: 'The life of the individual would be utterly different if he could be separated from society. A great deal of him would not exist at all.'[2] John Hobson, reviewing the ideological 'crisis' of Liberalism, reaffirmed the contradiction between individualism and organicism as bases of a political creed:

> It is quite clear that the conception of society as a moral organism negates the old democratic idea of political equality based on the notion that every member of a political society had an inherent right to the same power as every other in determining the actions of society. The idea of natural individual rights as the basis of democracy disappears.[3]

Thomas Huxley, who styled himself 'individualist' out of regard for the maximum individual freedom consistent with the freedom of others, drew similar conclusions:

> It appears to me that the amount of freedom which incorporated society may fitly leave to its members is not a fixed quantity to be determined a priori by deduction from the fiction called 'natural rights'; but that it must be determined by, and vary with, circumstances. I conceive it to be demonstrable that the higher and more complex the organization of the social body, the more closely is the life of each member bound up with the life of the whole; and the larger becomes the category of acts which cease merely to be self-regarding, and which interfere with the freedom of others more or less seriously.[4]

Leonard Hobhouse saw 'in the organic conception of the relation between the individual and society' the starting-point of Thomas Hill Green's philosophy.[5] Green, exemplary spokes-

---

[1] Ibid., p. 11.
[2] L.T. Hobhouse, *Liberalism* (London, 1911), p. 126.
[3] J.A. Hobson, *The Crisis of Liberalism: new issues in Democracy* (London, 1909), p. 77. The problems of individualism versus social organicism are discussed below in Chap. 9, pp. 235–42.
[4] T.H. Huxley, 'The struggle for existence in human society', in *Collected Essays* (London, 1894), p. 125.
[5] L.T. Hobhouse, op.cit., p. 125.

man of Idealist Liberalism, rejected the natural rights thesis, not so much for its incompatibility with the social organism as for its reactionary implications for practical politics. The idea of individual rights not derived from society 'is seen in the inveterate irreverence of the individual to the state; in the assumption that he has rights against society irrespective of his fulfilment of any duties to society, that all "powers that be" are restraints on his rightful freedom, which he may rightly defy as far as he safely can.'[1] These assertions, emphatically promulgated in *The Man versus the State*, collectively comprise 'a reason for resisting all positive reforms, all reforms which involve an action of the state in the way of promoting conditions favourable to moral life.'[2]

'Problems of practical politics', wrote David Ritchie, 'may be discussed more profitably on the basis of the utilitarianism of Bentham or Mill, than on the basis of Mr. Spencer's incongruous mixture of "natural rights" and physiological metaphor.'[3] This is a revealing quotation. The refutations cited above indicate a consensus of opposition to the notion that liberty (of which Liberalism purported to be the political expression) could derive from individual rights extraneous to society. It affords little encouragement to Spencer's view of later liberalism as a departure from *laissez-faire* orthodoxy, but, on the contrary, supports the view that Idealist liberalism was the logical outgrowth of a mainstream of liberalism embracing Bentham, Mill, and Green, through which evolved a concept of freedom quite at odds with Spencer's, and which was unattainable without some recourse to the state. The 'collectivist' tendencies exhibited by Bentham and Green will be discussed presently. The critical stage in the development of 'positive' liberalism (as opposed to Spencerian 'negative' liberalism) was accomplished by John Stuart Mill.

Mill's *Principles of Political Economy* (1848) seemed to contain affirmation of the natural-rights theory of *laissez-faire*: 'There is a circle', he wrote, 'around every individual

---

[1] Cited in M. Richter, *The Politics of Conscience: T.H. Green and his age* (London, 1964), p. 232.
[2] Loc. cit.
[3] D.G. Ritchie, op.cit., p. 100.

human being which no government, be it that of one, of a few or of the many, ought to be permitted to enter.'[1] Mill, weaned on his father's philosophical radicalism, had rejected its narrow utilitarianism, and seemed to speak for a generation nurtured on individualism.

His most famous contribution to political thought, the brilliant essay *On Liberty* (1859) became the classic statement of the dilemma of individual freedom versus the requirements of society. Like all his writings, however, it defined problems and asked questions with unexampled clarity, but stipulated no dogmatic solutions: 'There is a limit to the legitimate extent of collective interference with individual independence and to find that limit, and maintain it against encroachment, is indispensable to a good condition of human affairs, as protection against political despotism.'[2] He concluded that 'To individuality should belong that part of life in which it is chiefly the individual that is interested; to society the part which chiefly interests society.'[3] Theoretically neat, this formula was curiously inconclusive when applied to the practice of government.

There is, implied in Mill's approach, a certain pragmatism in the application of principles to society; a hangover from utilitarianism. In *The Principles of Political Economy* he had written: '*Laissez-faire*, in short, should be the general practice; every departure from it, unless required by some great good, is a certain evil.'[4] In *Utilitarianism* (1861) he hinted that 'an existence made up of few and transitory pains, many and varied pleasures' might be approachable through reform: 'the present wretched education, and wretched social arrangements, are the only real hindrance to its being attainable by almost all.'[5] The implication is that social benefit, rather than dogma, should guide a liberal policy, and this allows for some breadth of interpretation.

Mill himself was led by an increasing commitment to practical reform into a position which he called 'socialism',

---

[1] J.S. Mill, *The Principles of Political Economy* (London, 1848), p. 947.
[2] J.S. Mill, *On Liberty* (London, 1965), p. 264.
[3] Ibid. p. 205.
[4] J.S. Mill, *The Principles of Political Economy*, p. 947.
[5] J.S. Mill, *Utilitarianism* (London, 1965), p. 264.

which, paying due attention to the need for freedom, saw the greater good in equality of opportunity:

While we repudiated with the greatest energy that tyranny of society over the individual which most socialistic schemes are supposed to involve, we yet looked forward to a time when society will no longer be divided into the idle and the industrious; when 'they who do not work shall not eat' will be applied not to paupers only, but impartially to all; when the division of the produce of labour, instead of depending as it now does, on the accident of birth, will be made by consent on an acknowledged principle of justice; and when it will no longer be, or be thought to be, impossible for human beings to exert themselves strenuously in procuring benefits which are not to be exclusively their own, but to be shared with the society they belong to. The social problem of the future we considered to be, how to unite the greatest individual liberty of action with a common ownership in the raw material of the globe, and an equal participation of all in the benefits of labour.[1]

Mill, whose influence in the worlds of practical politics and of ideas was enormous, thus steered the main course of liberalism away from the rigid individualism denoted by Spencer as orthodox, and prepared it for the stern challenge confronting it in the need to employ the state to create a society combining industrial prosperity, social justice, and some redistribution of wealth.

Henceforth, liberalism had less to do with crude 'liberty' and more with an approximation of 'greatest happiness'. Leonard Hobhouse wrote in 1911: 'By keeping to the conception of harmony as our clue we constantly define the rights of the individual in terms of the common good, and think of the common good in terms of the welfare of all individuals who constitute a society. Thus . . . we avoid the confusion of liberty with competition and see no virtue in the right of a man to get the better of others.'[2] The enemy of man is no longer the state, but other men: 'the function of state coercion is to override individual coercion.'[3] This is not to applaud state intervention for its own sake: its 'encroachment' must be justified in each instance to liberals whose primary concern will always be with individual autonomy. What has supervened is a new conception of that freedom. Pronouncing the death of 'the old *laissez-faire* liberalism' in

[1] J.S. Mill, *An Autobiography* (London, 1879), pp. 231-2.
[2] L.T. Hobhouse, op.cit., p. 212.
[3] Ibid., p. 146.

1909, John Hobson wrote: 'Though liberals must ever insist that each employment of the authority and functions of the state must justify itself as an enlargement of personal liberty, interfering with individuals in order to set free new and larger opportunities, there need remain in liberalism no relics of that positive hostility to public methods which crippled the old Radicalism.'[1] The 'crisis of Liberalism' was over reconciling these elements of a new, progressive policy, encompassing state intervention.

The two major sources of this challenge were the Radicalism of the *Fortnightly Review* group—whose elder statesman was John Stuart Mill himself and whose brightest recruit Joseph Chamberlain—and the Idealist followers of Thomas Hill Green. From the *Fortnightly* the most significant critique of Spencer was 'Administrative Nihilism', contributed by Thomas Huxley in 1871, significant in terms of its intellectual integrity, of Huxley's commitment to evolution, and of their deep mutual affection. Huxley made two principal points; that there is a 'no man's land' between Spencerian 'protection' and the artificial gratification of desires, in which governmental intervention is legitimate; and that the definition of 'freedom' suggests that the state may foster and extend it.

Following Adam Smith, Huxley described a sector of enterprise which is too expensive for effective private combination, affords no profit-incentive for investment, yet confers wide benefits on everyone: for example, the construction of roads and harbours. Spencer replied that the taxpayers are thereby mulcted, and the natural sequence of effort and gratification disrupted. Huxley rejoined that taxpayers both benefit by and acquiesce in such schemes. If government can stimulate commerce, widen the total exercise of the faculties and create happiness, then to argue that it should not becomes an irrational defence of an unrealistic principle.

Huxley, secondly, took Spencer's definition of freedom, and proposed that if freedom is the free exercise of the faculties, then government can positively create it. State education, for instance, extends the individual's capacity to gratify

[1] J.A. Hobson, op.cit., pp. 94–5.

himself; state medical care prolongs his opportunity to do so. These are examples of state 'philanthropy', the conferring of benefits, but even state regulations may widely extend freedom in this sense. Sanitary regulations are cited: 'If my next-door neighbour chooses to have his drains in such a state as to create a poisonous atmosphere, which I breathe at the risk of typhus or diptheria, he restricts my just freedom to live, just as if he went about with a pistol, threatening my life.'[1] Spencer had admitted 'that it comes within the proper sphere of government to repress nuisances,'[2] so that Huxley's example constituted an infringement of rights. The welfare of the threatened person, however, is not the absolute determinant of equity. Spencer invokes the law of equal freedom to determine a relative freedom between actor and injured. Thus 'the invalid is at liberty to buy medicine and advice from whomsoever he pleases; the unlicensed practitioner is at liberty to sell these to whomsoever will buy. On no pretext whatever can a barrier be set up between them, without the law of equal freedom being broken, and least of all may the government whose office it is to uphold the law, become a transgressor of it.'[3] The principle thus applied left no scope for a compromise with Huxley's latter-day utilitarianism.

Huxley likened the state to a physician. He agreed with Spencer that in three out of four cases diagnosis and prescription should be deferred until the symptoms have reached crisis, but in the fourth case, 'in which the symptoms are unmistakeable and the causes of disease distinctly known prompt remedy saves a life.'[4] It is in the nature of the remedy, however, that Spencer found fault. Social disease resulted from unnatural tampering with the functioning of the 'body politic', hence 'the course of treatment indicated . . . is the course which aims as far as possible to re-establish the normal functions—does not aim to readjust physiology in such a way as to adapt it to a pathological state.'[5] If free competition has been curtailed, and stagnation ensues, the

[1] T.H. Huxley, 'Administrative Nihilism' *Fortnightly Review*, Nov. 1871.
[2] *S. Stat.*, p. 406.
[3] *S. Stat.*, p. 425.
[4] T.H. Huxley, op.cit.
[5] H.S. to B. Webb, 2 Oct. 1886, in the Passfield Collection, II (I) ii.

answer is not to recast the principles of political economy, but to re-establish free competition. There is no way of circumventing Spencer's invocations of 'Nature'.

Huxley agreed with Spencer that happiness, in the social sense, means 'the attainment by every man of all the happiness he can enjoy without diminishing the happiness of his fellow-men'. He suggested, however, that the maintenance of happiness is the task of government, not only by restraining socially disruptive sentiments and impulses, but by promoting sociable ones. If attempts by government to accomplish this task had so far failed, this was not to discredit such attempts in principle: 'the fact proves, not that the idea which underlies them is worthless, but only that the science of politics is in a very rudimentary and imperfect state.'[1] If, properly instituted and capably run, the state may actively extend the scope of human gratification, not only by preventing individual constrictions on individual liberty, but by the actual creation of facilities.

Huxley's criticisms reflected a growing feeling among liberals that a new direction must be taken. The interventionist issue was constantly being raised by proposals of concrete policy; unlikely alliances were formed to promote public welfare through legislation. The Liberalism of A.J. Mundella, for example, incorporated the aspirations of the working class for free education and restricted hours of labour, although Mundella himself was a stocking manufacturer. He felt that state-aid would increase the self-reliance and moral stature of working men, and saw little constructive virtue in Spencer's view of the state: 'The function of the state is to protect human life, to protect children and to facilitate the administration of justice. If it is not the duty of the government to do anything but protect society against the thief, as Herbert Spencer maintains, what will be the result but anarchy plus the policeman?'[2] By 1880 disillusionment with the old formulas was widespread among liberals in journalism and politics.

---

[1] T.H. Huxley, op.cit.
[2] W.H.G. Armytage, *A.J. Mundella; the liberal background to the labour movement* (London, 1951), p. 115.

The turning-point of theoretical liberalism occurred in 1880 with the publication of *Liberal legislation and freedom of contract*, by Thomas Hill Green. Green's intellectual ancestry was a confluence of German idealism and Philosophic Radicalism; he viewed society as a moral institution, in which individuals may strive to improve themselves. The state may help them by removing all obstacles in the way of upward human progress, but this may entail positive governmental intervention. Ignorance is an obstacle; national education the means of removing it. Insobriety is an obstacle; temperance legislation can eradicate it. Disease is an obstacle; the state can and must reduce it. The end in view is always the self-determined advancement of the individual, but Green, unlike Spencer, observed injustice in the fact that some men were privileged to have a better chance of achievement than others. This egalitarian liberalism amounted, as Joseph Chamberlain observed, to 'helping people to help themselves'.

For Green the 'political obligation' to create happiness rested neither on natural law nor utility, but in 'a recognition of common good', a combination of Rousseau's 'General Will' and idealism. 'I am', he wrote, 'properly obliged to those actions and forbearances which are necessary to the general freedom; necessary if each is not to interfere with the realization of another's will. My DUTY is to be positively interested in my neighbour's well-being.'[1] In a sense, therefore, Green is not the continuator of Mill and Bentham; he prescribed, for a liberalism already torn between individualism and collectivism a synthesis of both, drawing for its authority on an alien philosophy. It was always the practical aspect of politics which excited Green; he was a reformer, interested in theory in so far as it constituted a doctrinaire barrier to reform. In G.H. Sabine's opinion 'Green's philosophy attempted to state a moral platform so broad that men of social good will could stand on it . . . Its purpose was to transform liberalism from the social philosophy of a single set of interests, seen from the point of view of a particular class into one which could claim to take account of all important interests seen from the point of view of the general

[1] M. Richter, op.cit., p. 248.

good of the national community.'[1] Significantly Green, like Spencer, saw an identity of interests between capital and labour. The 'Manchesterdom', of which Spencer was chief rationalizer, he regarded as divisive; an apology for the interests of capital against the rest.

Green's *Liberal legislation and freedom of contract* was in fact the transcript of a speech putting forward the case for liberal legislation. It did not propound the headlong collectivism feared by Spencer, but it did take a rational look at legislation already passed, seeking the principle behind it. In the 1870 Education Act, for example, Green saw 'a wholly new departure in English legislation,'[2] and a real breach of 'freedom of contract'. This necessitated an examination of the concept of liberty on which the principle of free contract itself was based. It is in the ensuing definition that the fine but crucial distinction is made between negative and positive freedom.

Semantically they are quite similar. The distinction lies in the direct application of 'social good' as an element in self-determination:

When we measure the progress of a society by its growth in freedom, we measure it by the increasing development and exercise of the whole of those powers of contributing to social good with which we believe the members of the society to be endowed; in short, by the greater power on the part of the citizens as a body to make the most and best of themselves . . . Thus the mere removal of compulsion, the mere enabling a man to do as he likes, is in itself no contribution to true freedom.[3]

Spencerian freedom, then, is 'a means to an end'; it enables men to pursue selfish objectives on the assumption that this will incidentally conduce to the social good. In Green's system, social good is inseparable from freedom; 'the liberation of the powers of all men equally for contributions to the common good.'[4]

Green's liberalism had a strongly moralistic flavour, upon which the sanction of state intervention is largely based.

[1] G.H. Sabine, *A History of Political Theory* (London, 1964), p. 737.
[2] T.H. Green, 'Liberal legislation and Freedom of Contract' in *The Works of T.H. Green* (London, 1906), iii. 369.
[3] Ibid., iii. 371.   [4] Ibid., iii. 372.

Green does not cease to be liberal; the state is to be kept at arm's length as far as is expedient. Neither can it, in Spencer's terms, 'create morality', but only 'maintain the conditions without which a free exercise of the human faculties is impossible.'[1] If private philanthropy could remove them so much the better, but their removal is an indispensable part of 'creating the conditions' in which morality can flourish. Private philanthropy has proved incapable of doing the job (despite Spencer's faith in it): 'Left to itself, or to the operation of casual benevolence, a degraded population perpetuates and increases itself.'[2] Strict individualism, therefore, is rejected in favour of the minimum of compulsion required to 'liberate' the faculties of all. It is worth noting that, on issues of pure morality, such as temperance, Green was prepared to use coercive legislation, but that it is justified as preserving the minimum condition of free agency; intemperance destroys freedom of the will (in Freudian terms freedom for the ego rather than for the id), and hence inhibits self-determination. Legislation merely removes another obstacle to freedom.

The bifurcation of liberal theory, therefore, hinges on the definition of 'freedom'. Spencer ignored the now commonplace distinction between 'freedom from' and 'freedom to'; assuming that the former, freedom from actual (specifically by the state) coercion, guaranteed the latter. His preoccupation with the external limitations of liberty neglects its more 'positive' requirements, and demands 'a statement of criteria relating to the value and purpose of liberty, the conditions and ways in which liberty is beneficially exercised, and the state of mind with which liberty is used.'[3] As S.I. Benn and W.L. Weinstein have shown, the simple distinction between 'freedom from coercion' and 'freedom of action' contains a partly concealed but crucial criterion, namely autonomy—the freedom to choose: 'a better way of characterizing conditions of unfreedom is that they restrict choice by making alternatives unavailable or ineligible.'[4] Freedom,

[1] Loc. cit.

[2] Ibid., iii. 376. For H.S.'s views see Chap. 6, pp. 150-1.

[3] W.L. Weinstein, 'The concept of liberty in nineteenth century English political thought', *Political Studies*, xiii (June, 1965), p. 146.

[4] S.I. Benn and W.L. Weinstein, 'Being free to act and being a free man', *Mind* Apr. 1971, p. 197.

then, is defined as 'the non-restriction of options, rather than as the absence of impediments.'[1]

This definition suggests serious inadequacies in Spencer's system, and damages his claim to the universality of his principles. Whether or not the curtailment of choice constitutes 'unfreedom' is a matter of interpretation; judgement is made according to 'normal standards and in normal circumstances'. Only the 'abnormal' restriction of his choice makes the individual 'unfree'. However, the definition of what is abnormal varies, both historically and with political conviction.

Benn and Weinstein take the case of the workman forced to accept subsistence wages by the state of the labour market. To an individualist liberal like Spencer the employer is acting normally; the restriction of the worker's choice is not his fault, but reflects current unemployment figures. The employer merely takes advantage of favourable conditions, in which the range of choices of both parties is predetermined. To a socialist, however, normality is defined in terms of the worker's need. The worker, forced to choose between exploitation and starvation, is unfree. Spencer's assessment of 'normal' standards and conditions has no intrinsic validity; it is a matter of political choice. The 'objective' condition, furthermore, i.e. the social experience to which any such decision must refer, is also variable. The inevitability of man's subjection to economic 'laws' (a corollary of Spencer's concept of freedom from the state) is no longer, since John Maynard Keynes, universally and uncritically accepted. Standards of normality, of the 'natural' limits to individual choice, are themselves liable to change. Accepting, then, that 'to abridge the possibility of choice is to abridge freedom',[2] and that no fixed criterion is available to control the definition, Spencer's 'negative' freedom appears monumentally inadequate.

The liberalism of Spencer's critics rested on a superior understanding of the complexities inherent in the concept of freedom. If Spencerian freedom from state interference did not meet the full requirements of liberty, neither did Spencerian freedom of contract. Free contract implies an absence

[1] Ibid., p. 201.   [2] Ibid., p. 197.

of duress exerted by one party over another, and can only take place between partners whose bargaining power is approximately equal, or at least not so unequal that the one can oblige the other to accept terms which, by 'ordinary' standards are regarded as exorbitant or unfair. In cases where social or other inequalities make for imbalance in contractual relations, those contracts cannot authentically be described as 'free'. Green's liberalism is partly based on recognition of this fact, and an attempt to redress the balance by legislation. When Green talks of 'positive' liberty he means the power to do something useful or morally uplifting. Ignorance, poverty, and disease are as clearly forms of restraint, in this context, as are formal political regulations.

There is, therefore, in Spencerian individualism a serious inconsistency: that he defined freedom as 'free exercise of the faculties', yet ignored the conditions of their exercise, such as approximate equality in power. Regardless of the intervention or non-intervention of the state, freedom without effective choice or actual facilities: freedom as a hypothetical concept (I am free to do something but have not the opportunity to do it) is empty. Later, 'collectivist' Liberalism was the expression in theory and practice of the realization that freedom from public coercion, associated with gross inequality of social power and opportunity, was for many no freedom at all, or a lower form of freedom for all.

To summarize, Liberal objections to Spencer's system centre on the following points:

(1) Spencer's individualism was partly based in the concept of 'natural rights'. He declared all rights to be theoretically of equal validity, yet treated some as 'more equal than others'. In evading the issue of the conflict of rights in society he normally gave priority to proprietorial rights. The idea of 'rights' in Spencer's conception of fundamental, inalienable rights accruing 'naturally' to every human being as the basis of a political theory was discounted by most later Liberals.

(2) In postulating a system of perfect competition, Spencer ignored the reality of competition, which is that the successful proceed to corner the market and forestall further threats to their supremacy. Later Liberals saw their task as that of

creating equality of opportunity by removing the entrenched privileges of the 'winners'. Nineteenth-century Liberalism from Mill to Hobhouse reflects the growing realization that Spencer's competitive freedom was a cruel myth. His negative concern with freedom from state compulsion was accordingly supplanted by a more positive emphasis on the freedom to use one's capacities, and with the employment of public resources to create conditions in which this was possible for everyone.

8

SPENCER'S THEORY OF SOCIAL EVOLUTION

'Evolution' is a word which defies simple definition. It com-
prehends all change, yet conveys not merely the actuality of
change, but implications of its direction. Evolution means
change for the better; each transformation contains a tiny
increment of improvement, culminating in the development
of 'higher' types. The difficulty inherent in such a concept is
the assumption of value which it entails, an assumption unsupported by empirical evidence. Evolution, a scientifically-
verifiable, 'value-free' process, is invested at the outset with
a moral purpose, and Spencer's account of it loses credibility
as a result.

This chapter begins by presenting a short account of
Spencer's social evolution. It then attempts to indicate stages
in the theory at which morality impinges, and the ensuing
difficulties arise, and to investigate the concordance indicated
by Spencer between social evolution and individualism in the
light of the political preferences of other social evolutionists.

PRINCIPLES OF SPENCERIAN EVOLUTION

In order to avoid undue repetition it is tempting to replace
the word 'evolution' at intervals with more or less appropriate synonyms: 'progress', 'development', 'growth',
'change', and so on. Spencerian evolution, however, has no
synonym: indeed it subsumes all verbal counterparts simultaneously. Evolution is an idea of almost frightening ramifications, all-pervasive continuity, boundless magnitude,
massive yet imperceptible power, ceaseless, restless, endless,
and relentless. Small wonder that humanist critics resented
the insignificance of the individual in this system. Evolution
is really a collection of ideas, moulded together in one
staggering concept of change and movement, comprising the
implications which Spencer envisaged whenever he used the
term himself.

Evolution is all-pervading and continual. Spencer's intuition of the ceaselessness and ubiquity of change preceded the complete definition of the theory: 'Every age, every nation, every climate exhibits a modified form of humanity; and in all times, and amongst all peoples, a greater or lesser amount of change is going on.'[1] Evolution, again, is endless. The processes of modification and adaptation cannot reach a final, static resolution. Spencer disowned Utopianism: the visionary description of some perfect state implying the cessation of change and the need for change, yet because of its hedonistic ethos, the theory of evolution was bound to a Utopian ideal, incorporating movement, which he rather paradoxically conceptualized as the 'moving equilibrium'.

Evolution, furthermore, is good. The idea of a determined, unimpeded upward growth was discarded by 1851 in favour of the more arduous process of alternating progress and regression, and of human effort rising above distressful circumstances. Evolution, however, is always invested with an aura of beneficence ('towards a greater and more unmixed good') and its imperatives superceded the Deity in Spencer's eyes as supreme moral arbiter. The definition of 'right' conduct as 'conduct tending to increase life' (in other words conduct tending to facilitate evolution) entails the assumption that the evolutionary consummation is devoutly to be wished.

Evolution embodies three distinct but interlocking concepts; it is a developmental process, a mechanism, and the motive force behind the mechanism. The motor of evolution is its last causal reduction, the Persistence of Force, which in turn reflects the inscrutable ultimate cause, the 'Unknowable'. The mechanism of evolution, by which this nameless impulse is converted into an evolutionary system, consists of natural selection, adaptation of species to their environment and the inheritance of acquired characteristics: the Darwinian-Lamarckian melange which the eclectic Spencer absorbed into his theory. The process of evolution described the metamorphosis undergone by all species subjected to the mechanism, including specialization of function, integration, and differentiation. It defines the stages through which the

[1] S. Stat., p. 46.

evolving social aggregate passes (i.e. from the militant to the industrial). The origins of this classification lie in eighteenth-century sociology (Spencer admired the work of Adam Ferguson in this respect) and is a common manifestation of nineteenth-century political theory. Henry Maine (status to contract), Walter Bagehot (the age of discussion) and Auguste Comte (the law of the three stages) shared Spencer's liking for compartmentalized progress.

In isolating the basic motive force of evolution, emanating from the Unknown Cause, Spencer began by defining the scope of the enquiry by the limits of human perception. No attempt to formulate the laws of existence is permissible which aspires to transcend this empirical basis: 'Philosophy, compelled to make those fundamental assumptions without which thought is impossible, has to justify them by showing their congruity with all other dicta of consciousness.'[1] Yet this does not necessitate a stultifying materialism: on the contrary, the ultimate causal agency is made the object of almost mystical reverence. To venture beyond the perceptory capacity of human beings is to indulge in metaphysical guesswork, and everything beyond these limits is abandoned as 'Unknowable'. Terms subsequently used to explain the dynamics of the universe, like 'matter', 'motion', and 'force' are merely symbols, 'signs of the Unalterable Reality underlying them all'. An ontological *caveat* is added, therefore, to every statement seeming to offer a concise causal explanation of the cosmic process: 'The explanation of that which is explicable does but bring out in greater clearness the inexplicableness of that which remains behind.'[2] The scientifically-minded philosopher can expect no solution to the problem of existence: 'In all directions his investigations eventually bring him face to face with the Unknowable, and he even more closely perceives it to be the Unknowable.'[3]

Each branch of science seeks out the widest generalizations of knowledge within its sphere, and establishes the most widely applicable laws governing it. Philosophy carries the process a stage further: its purpose is to subsume all the

[1] *F.P.*, p. 125.
[2] H.S., 'Progress: its law and cause', *Essays,* i. 60.
[3] Loc. cit.

truths of the sciences into a common synthesis: 'Knowledge of the lowest kind is *un-unified* knowledge, science is *partially-unified* knowledge, philosophy is *completely-unified* knowledge.'[1] The explanation of all phenomena in terms of a set of laws universally binding was the object pursued by Spencer throughout the gargantuan enterprise of the *Synthetic Philosophy*. It reveals in Spencer a curious duality; the last of the eighteenth-century Encyclopaedists masquerading as the prophet of nineteenth-century scientific progress.

The basic causal theory of evolution, therefore, purports to explain the cruder manifestations of the Unknowable. The ultimate reduction of all phenomena is expressed in terms of 'force'. Force is the ultimate philosophical deduction from the Unknown Cause. From it are deduced in turn the foundations of Spencer's philosophy.

Force is inconceivable, first of all, without the corollary of cause and effect, for force cannot derive from nothing, nor can it effect nothing. From this statement Spencer deduced the Persistence of Force, approximately the Conservation of Energy, though shrouded in agnostic qualifications: 'By the Persistence of Force we really mean the persistence of some Cause which transcends our knowledge and conception.'[2] The basic expression of evolution, then, is 'the transformation of Force under the modes of matter and motion'.

Cause and effect are similarly expressed: 'Supposing a given manifestation of force . . . be either preceded by or succeeded by some other manifestation it must, in all cases where the form and condition are the same, be preceded by or succeeded by such other manifestation.'[3] From this reactive cycle, Spencer derived the essential characteristic of all motion, which is *rhythm*. If Force is dissipated in action, it must be reconstituted as reaction, since it must persist. From these abstract hypotheses, Spencer deduced the fundamental law governing all phenomena, the 'Law of Evolution and Dissolution':

Evolution is an integration of matter and concomitant dissipation of motion; during which the matter passes from an indefinite, incoherent

---

[1] *F.P.*, p. 119.   [2] *F.P.*, p. 176.   [3] *F.P.*, p. 177.

homogeneity to a definite, coherent heterogeneity; and during which the retained motion undergoes a parallel transformation.[1]

Evolution moves organisms towards a condition in which their component units are diversified in function, yet integrated to the extent that the aggregate organism is perfectly functionally self-sufficient. At the same time each unit tends to become 'coherent'; in other words it evolves towards a state of individual perfection within the aggregate. Thus, unevolved organisms are simple, while evolved organisms are complex; unevolved organisms are composed of similar organs, haphazardly performing the same function, while evolved organisms exhibit a multiplicity of functionally-integrated but diversified organs.

Evolution proceeds through the equilibration of antagonistic forces, synthesized in the continuing struggle between evolution and dissolution, and reflected in the reconciliation of seeming opposites like increasing differentiation and functional unity. The balance is delicate, and destined inevitably to overturn when the evolving aggregate can no longer assimilate change through progressive adaptation:

When an aggregate has reached that equilibrium in which all changes end, it thereafter remains subject to all actions in its environment which . . . in course of time are sure, either slowly or suddenly, to give its parts such excess of motion as will cause disintegration.[2]

Evolution proceeds, therefore, in a rhythmic see-saw motion indicating the conflict between evolution and dissolution. It becomes clear, in the light of this precarious vision, why an almost obsessive emphasis on gradualism came to permeate Spencer's later political writings.

The foregoing formula is nothing more than a statement of the symbolic manifestation of Force. It fails to explain the causal nexus of progress: why natural evolution could have taken no other course. A deductive restatement was required to demonstrate that the Persistence of Force will manifest itself in a determined, predictable way. This reappraisal yielded the three laws under which evolution 'is presented under a rational character'.

[1] *F.P.*, p. 367.   [2] *F.P.*, p. 475.

The basic deductive law of evolution, the law of the Instability of the Homogeneous, states that homogeneity is a
condition of endemic instability, perpetually under attack
from unequal and conflicting forces which ultimately bring
about its dissolution, resulting in a progressively intensifying
heterogeneity. Secondly, the law of the Multiplication of
Effects states that every cause produces more than one
effect, and that evolution, consequently, perpetually tends
towards dissipation. This expresses, in terms of force, the
universal trend from homogeneity to heterogeneity. Thirdly,
the Law of Segregation lays down that unlike units of an
aggregate tend to separate and like units to cluster, resulting
in progressively sharpening structural differentiation. These
are the 'first principles'. The fourteen volumes of the
Synthetic Philosophy contain their application, in enormous
detail, to the natural world, which is held to include the
social existence of man.

SPENCERIAN SOCIAL EVOLUTION

The basic mechanism through which these laws are transmitted into organic, animal, and social evolution is natural
selection: 'Society advances where its fittest members are
allowed to assert their fitness with the least hindrance, and
where the least fitted are not artificially prevented from
dying out.'[1] If this injunction is observed, each generation
will contain a higher proportion of the 'fittest' and a smaller
of the 'unfit', a process of racial purification which continues
until unfitness is bred out altogether, and the superior inherit
the earth.

When the struggle for survival begins, Spencer asserted, 'all
start with equal advantages.' Competition for resources, however, yields an unequal distribution which reflects the uneven
incidence of natural ability: 'One part of the community is
industrious and prudent and accumulates property, the other
idle and improvident or, in some cases perhaps, unfortunate
. . . the children of the one class stand in the same relation to
those of the other that existed between their parents.'[2]

---

[1] *M.v.S.*, p. 81.
[2] H.S., 'Proper Sphere', 22 June 1842.

Equality, for Spencer, was competitive equality: 'Not the equality of men, but the equality of their claims to make the best of themselves within the limits mutually produced, has all along been my principle.'[1] Inferiority, therefore, entails distress, and distress is hereditary, for 'are we not told that the sins of the wicked shall be visited on the children to the third and fourth generation?'[2] Early Spencerian theory thus enrolled the Revd. Thomas Malthus, Jean-Baptiste Lamarck, and the Holy Bible in support of the contention that progress, via a form of natural selection, requires untrammelled competition.

Spencer's 'Essay on Population' (1852) explicitly criticized Malthus, but incorporated Malthusian pronouncements on the subject. The necessity of famine, pestilence, and war to preserve the balance between available resources and a population constantly threatening to outstrip them, is evaded by a physiological loophole. Spencer substituted his own 'general law of animal fertility' in terms of which all species tend towards a stabilization of their numbers: 'While any race continues to exist, the forces preservative of it and the forces destructive of it must perpetually tend towards equilibrium.'[3] The forces 'preservative of the race' are two: the ability of each member of the species to defend and sustain itself (individuation) and its ability to reproduce itself (reproduction), and Spencer's ingenious formula was that these faculties vary inversely with one another. The higher the development of the species, and, consequently, the greater the individual powers of defence and sustenance exhibited by its members, the lower falls its reproductive potential.

The human application of this principle assumes that current fertility is moving in excess of resources. The reduction of fertility, therefore, requires the development of a 'higher' type of human being, endowed with advanced physical, intellectual, and moral faculties. Excess of fertility initiates the development of this 'higher' type; pressure of population on resources creates competition, competition favours

[1] H.S. to W.H. Hudson, 7 June 1903, *L.L.* ii. 213.
[2] 'Proper Sphere', 27 July 1842.
[3] 'Theory of Population', p. 475.

the well-endowed and the ill-endowed are forced to the wall. The elimination of a proportion of the latter in each generation lowers the reproductive capacity of the constitutionally unfit, so that by the time numerical equilibrium is reached the race consists entirely of the perfected strain of highly-endowed humanity, each perfect couple producing, every generation, two perfect children.

The mainspring of the process is hardship: 'Difficulty in getting a aliving is alike the incentive to a higher education of children and to a more intense and long-continued application in adults.'[1] Families and races who do not respond to the stimulus of competition by increasing their productivity are destined for extinction. The social implication of natural selection, the necessity of suffering, survived the recasting of evolutionary theory to reappear in *Social Statics*:

Inconvenience, suffering and death, the penalties attached by nature to ignorance, as well as to incompetence—are also the means of remedying these . . . Partly by weeding out those of lowest development, and partly by subjecting those who remain to the never-ceasing discipline of experience, nature secures the growth of a race who shall both understand the conditions of existence, and be able to act up to them.[2]

In *The Study of Sociology* this conviction is reaffirmed: 'Mankind have eventually gone right after trying all possible ways of going wrong; the wrong-doings have been habitually checked by disaster, and pain and death.'[3]

Hardship is imperative because intellect is by itself incapable of moulding human nature: 'Only by repeatedly awakening the appropriate *emotions* can character be changed.'[4] The obvious implication is that the state should take no steps to mitigate hardship, since 'much suffering is curative, and prevention of it is prevention of a remedy.'[5] To banish pain is to 'favour the multiplication of those worst fitted for existence,'[6] and to contravene natural law, in which benefits are related to ability. In Spencer's vision the benign 'Mother Nature' is transformed into some stern mid-Victorian governess, ruthlessly shepherding her brood along the narrow, rocky path to felicity. The pathetic ruminant is

---

[1] H.S., 'Theory of Population', pp. 499–500.
[2] *S. Stat.*, pp. 412–3.   [3] *Stud. Soc.*, p. 307.   [4] *S. Stat.*, p. 385.
[5] *M.v.S.*, p. 34.   [6] *M.v.S.*, p. 83.

destroyed and consumed by the predator, the weak shouldered aside by the strong, the ill-endowed left to perish, all in the name of a 'larger, far-seeing benevolence'.

Even war, which Spencer detested, has in the appropriate historical context 'the effect of continually extirpating races which, for some reason or other, were least fitted to cope with the conditions of existence they were subject to.'[1] Warfare develops the cruder bodily powers, advances technology, causes the formation of larger social aggregates and promotes 'habits of subordination to social requirements'. At a given stage of civilization, however, war becomes self-defeating, exercises a regressive influence on social mores and systematically slaughters the flower of each generation. Competition then passes into a more enlightened arena: 'non-aggressive competition; maintenance of the implied limits and insurance of the benefits gained within the limits, being what we call justice.'[2] Even in the higher reaches of civilization, however, competition remains the 'law of life'.

The concept of adaptation appeared early in Spencer's writings, but only gradually became associated with natural selection in the idea that the 'superiority' ennobling certain individuals and species consists in their advanced ability to adapt themselves to the conditions of existence. In *Social Statics* the perfection of man is described as perfect adaptation to the social mode of life. This suggested a more sophisticated if less reassuring view of social progress: 'civilisation no longer appears to be a regular unfolding after a specific plan; but seems rather a development of man's latent capabilities under the action of favourable circumstances.'[3] 'The Development Hypothesis' (1853) categorically stated that 'any existing species—animal or vegetable—when placed under conditions different from the previous ones, *immediately begin to undergo certain changes fitting it for the new conditions.*'[4]

Adaptation, then, is a positive dynamic factor in social evolution:

---

[1] *Stud. Soc.*, p. 193.
[2] H.S., 'The Filiation of Ideas', *L.L.* ii. 364.
[3] *S. Stat.*, pp. 453–4.
[4] H.S., 'The Development Hypothesis', *Essays,* i. 3.

The social discipline which has already wrought great changes in men, must go on eventually to work out greater ones. The daily curbing of the lower nature and culture of the higher, which out of cannibals and devil-worshippers has evolved philanthropists, lovers of peace, and haters of superstition, may be expected to develop out of these, men as much superior to them as they are to their progenitors. The causes that have produced vast modifications are still in action; must continue in action as long as there exists any incongruity between men's desires and the requirements of the social state, and must eventually make them organically fit for the social state.[1]

This statement subsequently underwent significant qualifications and refinements. The implied perfection of adaptation is discarded; 'as fast as adaptation approaches completeness, it becomes slower and slower . . . the forces which produce change become less and less as the need for change diminishes; so that adaptation must ever remain incomplete.'[2] Complete adaptation would require a constancy of conditions which cannot persist in Nature. It follows, therefore, that adaptation depends on extra-social impulses:

Astronomic and geological changes must cause in the future, as they have done in the past, unceasing alterations in the climate and other characters of men's habitats; entailing slow migrations of races from regions which have become unfit to fitter regions. Along with such migrations must go modified habits of life, and of industrial arrangements. So that before adaptation to any one set of conditions has been approached, some other set of conditions will have to be met.[3]

In *The Principles of Sociology* adaptation is accorded still greater importance, for now superiority and inferiority are defined in terms of it. Environment is a mould, into which history forces each generation. The unfamiliar shape causes discomfort (again the necessity of suffering), so that 'where men's natures and their institutions are incongruous there exists a force tending to produce change.'[4] Some sections of the population are condemned to suffer for their inflexibility. Others, more resolute, more malleable or simply more fortunate, will thrive because of their ability to meet the new conditions. After 1860, therefore, adaptation of constitution to conditions succeeded pressure of population as the motive

[1] H.S., 'Manners and Fashions', *Essays*, iii. 30.
[2] *Aby* i. 361.   [3] Loc. cit.   [4] *Justice*, p. 148.

force of Spencerian social evolution, although in each case the immediate incentive is the avoidance of pain. What has changed is the source of the pain: 'the restlessness generated by pressure against the conditions of existence perpetually prompts the desire to try a new position.'[1]

The Principles of Sociology describes the operation of evolution in society. Society, like all 'organisms', develops according to the precepts of individuation, differentiation, and natural selection. Between each society and its environment (including the societies around it), and between individuals, societies, and races, a process of equilibration takes place. Until this is complete, conflict is endemic. Conflict generates fear, and fear stimulates the growth of sophisticated social systems. Fear of the living, of the man powerful enough to destroy you, is the basis of political power. Fear of his corpse, or of his dead ancestors, is the root of religion.

Conflict, institutionalized by political and religious power, produces militarism, a state of social aggression which moulds character, conduct, and social organization into fitness for war. Militarism, which demands corporate obedience from individuals, creates larger, more closely-knit social groupings. Social integration requires, however, that broader sections of the population are peacefully employed. Character, conduct, and social organization undergo the appropriate transformations, and there emerges a new type of society, geared to peace, in which coercion diminishes and individuality is fostered. Society becomes less hierarchically rigid; social mobility no longer threatens its cohesion. Sympathy and co-operation supplant fear. Only when war ceases can industrial society be permanently established. A final cautionary point: peaceful social cohesion depends upon the rate of its integration. The more completely evolved the society, the more gradual and slow has been its development.

Spencer, like Marx, prophesied the ultimate 'withering-away' of the state, leaving no trace but the self-regulation of free citizens: 'thus, as civilisation advances, does government decay.'[2] The balancing of sentiments guarantees against

---

[1] A.J. Nock, ed., *Herbert Spencer: The Man versus the State and other essays* (Caldwell, Idaho, 1965), p. 62.
[2] *S. Stat.*, p. 25.

premature change, for barbarism is associated with a concomitant reverence for power. Institutions must respect this
balance of moral forces, so that the amount of freedom at a
given time must *ipso facto* be the highest attainable.

In 'Progress: its law and cause' (1857) evolutionary terminology is first applied to social growth. Integration extends
the size of social units: differentiation and specialization of
function evolve a capitalist economic structure, the social
stratification consonant with it, and its various sub-cultures
of language, art, literature, music, law, and ethics. In *Political
Institutions* (1882) these evolutionary categories are applied
to political phenomena. Integration determines the formation
of the social mass, from small, initially nomadic aggregates to
nation-states. The process is conditioned by a variety of geo-
graphical and genetic factors, but the crucial determinant is
military capacity: 'Co-operation in war is the chief cause of
social integration.'[1] War requires internal regulation, social
immobility and solidarity within the social aggregate.

Integration entails differentiation: 'Whenever there is some
coherence and some permanence of relation among the parts,
there begin to arise political divisions.'[2] The subordination of
the female is institutionalized in permanent marital relations.
Class differences arise from the enslavement of other tribes.
The ownership of land, contested as soon as the tribe ceases
to be nomadic, accrues to the most warlike. Physical inequalities are thus compounded and perpetuated by the inheritance of property: 'Inequalities in the supplies and kinds
of food, clothing and shelter, tend to establish physical
differences; to the further advantage of the rulers and dis-
advantage of the ruled.'[3] A rudimentary class-structure is
established, therefore, the have-nots labouring to support the
haves. This is soon disrupted by the rise of a middle class
which, 'generating a wealth that is not connected with rank
. . . initiates a competing power.'[4] Its mission is to destroy
the old order and assert its own hegemony.

Social differentiation is mirrored in the diffusion of
political power, which, originally invested in the assembled

---

[1] *Pol. Inst.*, p. 286.   [2] *Pol. Inst.*, p. 308.
[3] *Pol. Inst.*, p. 309.   [4] *Pol. Inst.*, p. 310.

tribe, becomes divided between this assemblage and a nucleus of the wise and strong who effectively dictate policy. Primi tive political authority rests on the ability to fight and to appease spirits. The chief warrior and medicine men are initially the same person, and his supremacy gradually de- volves upon a single family in the tribe. The emergence of this dynasty is the germ of stable government; ancestor- worship is promoted, so that 'Rebellion . . . comes to be re- garded as alike both wicked and hopeless.'[1] The power of the king, however, is delegated as fast as it becomes too extensive to be wielded effectively by one man. The cluster of landed military leaders from which the king has arisen becomes in- corporated as a consultative body. The third estate, once the repository of political power, becomes a periodic representa- tive body, or parliament, destined to attain supremacy once war has ceased and peaceful industry (which it represents) prevails. Parallel agencies are quietly evolving. The king's household grows into 'an incorporated body of ministers having for its recognized function to execute the public will.'[2] The tributary authorities of provincial tribal chiefs proliferate into the organs of local government. Power, initially radiated from above, begins to percolate upward from below.

This pattern of integration, differentiation and specializa- tion of function is exhaustively applied to all subsidiary insti- tutions of social control. Spencer's favourite simile for the evolutionary process was that of a tree: law, religion, and custom are seen to ramify from a single root into patterns of endless complexity and sophistication. The evolution of ethics, which hypothetically proceeds according to the same laws, is important as describing the process whereby the in- creasing fitness of humanity for the 'social state' evolves out of barbarism.

In *Social Statics* the autonomous evolution of good con- duct is explained by the 'moral sense' implanted in all men. Spencer regarded conduct as basically instinctive. The function of the moral sense, therefore, is unconsciously to 'dictate rectitude in our transactions with one another'. Moral acts are thus as reflexive and irrational as any other. Morality

[1] *Pol. Inst.*, p. 364.   [2] *Pol. Inst.*, p. 450.

grows by a process of subliminal reinforcement: 'Every feeling is accompanied by a *sense* of the rightness of those actions which give it gratification.'[1] Ethical evolution, then, exemplifies the barely perceptible encroachment of the moral sense upon primitive barbarism. The obverse of the moral sense, meanwhile, is the sentiment of 'sympathy' (culled from Adam Smith's *Theory of the Moral Sentiments*) which convinces men not only that certain conduct is right, but also that the freedom which we claim as our own must be allowed to others equally. Adaptation is also involved in the process. The evanescence of evil is explained as a result of progressive adaptation of human character to the 'social state: Men living in this state suffer under numerous evils. By the hypothesis it follows that their characters are not completely adapted to such a state.'[2]

The Principles of Ethics relates the process more coherently. Ethical evolution tends towards the perfection of 'conduct'. Conduct is 'the adjustment of acts to ends', the ends being self-preservation and the continuation of the race, hence 'good' conduct is that which conduces to these ends, which 'fosters life in self and others'. A qualified hedonism helps men to distinguish 'good' from 'bad' conduct, by comparing their ultimate (as opposed to immediate) effects. The perfect man will be capable of 'effecting complete adjustment of acts to ends of every kind'; 'Complete life in a complete society is but another name for complete equilibrium between the co-ordinated activities of each social unit and those of the aggregate of units.'[3]

Justice describes the evolution of ethics as a development from pre-human to human state. Three rules govern 'good', species-enhancing conduct: that 'during immaturity, benefits received must be inversely proportioned to capacities possessed'; that 'after maturity is reached, benefits must vary directly as worth'; and that 'If the constitution of the species and its conditions of existence are such that sacrifices, partial or complete, of some of its individuals, so subserve the welfare of the species that its members are better maintained

---

[1] *S. Stat.*, pp. 37–8.   [2] *S. Stat.*, p. 77.   [3] *D. of E.*, p. 62.

than they would otherwise be, then there results a justification for such sacrifices.'[1] Justice remains at all evolutionary stages the same: 'each individual ought to be subject to the effects of his own nature and resulting conduct.'[2] Its only modification in the 'social state' is that the individual is restrained in his pursuit of gratification by the equitable claims of others.

Justice having been elucidated, Spencer traces the growth of its acceptance. The 'sentiment of justice' and the 'idea of justice' develop concurrently. The 'moral sense' as an inherent facet of the human psyche is replaced by the 'sentiment of justice', a developing perception of natural justice evolving out of less exalted impulses. It is compounded of a multiplicity of fears; fear of the retribution which anti-social conduct might bring, fear of penalties imposed by political authority and the superstitious fear of revengeful ghosts. The 'idea of justice', meanwhile, develops independently. It has a positive component in the recognition by each man of his own rights, and a negative aspect which recognizes the rights of others as of equal validity. The first relates justice to natural inequalities of ability. The second modifies this competitive ethic as recognizing the mutuality and equality of rights. The just conclusion incorporates both:

For as each of these opposite conceptions of justice is accepted as true in part, and then supplemented by the other, there results that conception of justice which arises in contemplating the laws of life as carried on in the social state. The equality concerns the mutually-limited spheres of action which must be maintained if associated men are to co-operate harmoniously. The inequality concerns the results which each may achieve by carrying on his actions within the applied limits.[3]

The evolution of justice, therefore, proceeds from aggression and counter-aggression, through retributive justice to reciprocal justice. It culminates in the spontaneous observance of the 'law of equal freedom' by all men equally.

Spencerian social evolution, then, anticipates a future in which continuing trends culminate in perfection. This inevitably raises the question of moral purpose in evolution; it

---

[1] *Justice*, p. 7.   [2] *Justice*, p. 8.   [3] *Justice*, pp. 42-3.

is essentially a teleological view of human development. The stages of the theory at which science and morality collide are the concepts of the Unknowable (the point at which morality enters the system) and of adaptation, in which an empirically-defined process is with great difficulty reconciled to the assertion of evolutionary perfectibility.

PROBLEMS OF SPENCERIAN EVOLUTION: THE UNKNOWABLE

The nineteenth century witnessed a head-on collision between theology and science occasioned by works like Charles Lyell's *The Principles of Geology* (1830) and Robert Chambers's *Vestiges of the Natural History of Creation* (1843). Science, deified by rationalists, confronted the Book of Genesis with the new orthodoxy of evolution. Many people, educated in theistic doctrines which their adult empiricism rejected, found the conflict difficult to resolve without the severance from the security of belief causing pain. Spencer, despite his claims to an early immunity to Christianity, was a conscious participant in the struggle; John Morley called him 'the head of the Agnostic School, on its philosophical and systematic side'.

Thomas Huxley coined the term 'agnosticism' to express the view that the existence of God could be no more scientifically disproved than proved. Spencer, incapable of such detachment, elevated agnosticism into a theistic concept. John Fiske, applauding Spencer's 'service to religion', claimed 'that the doctrine of evolution asserts, as the evident and deepest truth, that there exists a power to which no limit in time or space is conceivable, and that all the phenomena of the universe . . . are manifestations of this infinite and eternal power.'[1] The Persistence of Force embodies the rational perception that things *do* move and evolve, yet Spencer made it a manifestation of the inaccessible Ultimate Cause, incapable of scientific demonstration.

This has important implications for the theory of social evolution. Spencer deduced from the operation of evolution in fact the corollary that it ought to be allowed to operate in principle, thereby injecting a superfluous element of moralism

[1] J. Fiske, *Essays: literary and historical* (New York, 1902), ii. 235.

into social dynamics, for evolution will proceed regardless of moral sanction. Evolutionary determinism and moral exhortation, cited by Spencer in support of the same case, cancelled out, a contradiction which occasionally falsified his reasoning.[1] The quasi-religious sanction of the Unknowable strengthens the moral basis of evolutionary deductions.

The Unknowable undermines the evolutionary hypothesis because it is, by definition, unsubstantiated. Spencer could demonstrate empirically the operation of the evolutionary mechanism, and in the Persistence of Force had a strong ontological basis for his description of the universal traits of matter and motion, but rested the entire system on an imponderable cause. Like Henry Mansel, in the widely-read *The Limits of Religious Thought*, he seemed to conclude that although ultimate truths are not susceptible to reason, they are nevertheless essential to faith, in this case a faith in evolution. But faith is an intuitive commitment, and any proposition which depends upon it cannot be verified by science.

Spencer invented the Unknowable because it implanted into the theory of evolution the necessary element of purpose. He found his evidence intractable. Many events and processes did not fit the evolutionary scheme (and evolution must admit of no exception), unless it could be *assumed* that evolution has an ultimately beneficent destination. The goodness of evolution is Spencer's primary teleological assumption. If evolution is not towards 'a greater and more unmixed good', unthinkable consequences follow. Either men are doomed to eternal misery, or else they have a duty as rational beings to struggle against evolution, which would nullify Spencer's social conclusions. Regression and 're-barbarisation' cannot be dismissed as transient manifestations of rhythmic 'dissolution', but must be accepted as unalterable facts of the human condition. There can be no certainty of the ultimate perfection of man, in terms of current morality: 'We cannot be sure that evolution will always lead to what we should regard as the greatest perfection of any species.'[2] Spencer, whose evolution was inextricably associated with a firmly

---

[1] See, for example, J.A. Hobson's criticisms, above, Chap. 7, p. 179.
[2] D.G. Ritchie, *Darwinism and Politics* (London, 1903), p. 16.

hedonistic conception of ethics, could not afford such bland agnosticism. Spencerian social evolution, therefore, hinges on the unsupported assumption of benevolence in natural processes.

PROBLEMS OF SPENCERIAN EVOLUTION : ADAPTATION

The Lamarckian idea of progress as the transmission via inheritance of 'superior' acquired characteristics depends on the theory of adaptation to conditions. This concept is neither empirically demonstrated nor rigorously defined. It can be interpreted to mean either the adaptation of society to an unrealized perfection, or the more tangibly materialist process whereby individuals modify their characteristics in response to the immediate environment. Both readings entail difficulties.

Spencer's theory of adaptation attempts to reconcile environmental conditioning with the deterministic implications of heredity. In modern psychological theory heredity and environment are barely compatible; they complement each other as agencies influencing personality, intelligence, and so on, but are seen as intrinsically different in kind. The inheritance of acquired characteristics, in combining them, ignores the explosive nature of their combination. The retention of environmentalist elements in the theory, however, at least exonerates Spencer from the charge of racialism. He is accused of 'having crippled the explanatory power of cultural evolutionary theory by merging it and mixing it with racial determinism.'[1] As J.D.Y. Peel correctly points out, 'nurture' remains to qualify 'nature', even if perplexities ensue, so that the imputation of a theory of racial determinism is unfounded.

Pure environmentalism, on the other hand, held dangers for Spencer; to admit it would be to suggest that men, by manipulating the variable of social situation could mould character. The optimistic radicalism of his early days, however, was founded in a theory of malleability. His later pessimism reflected rather his growing preoccupation with the deterministic element of Lamarck; men will inherit certain

---

[1] M. Harris, *The Rise of Anthropological Theory* (London, 1969), p. 129.

characteristics which not only defy modification by socio-legislative means, but which positively mould society itself. This paradox bears heavily upon several aspects of Spencerian theory.

The adaptation of species to environment and the passing of resultant modifications to the next generation as acquired characteristics indicates slow, almost imperceptible change. An improvement in human nature sufficient to subserve up-ward societal evolution requires several generations of habitu-ation to an environment of peace and industry. The delay is essential, since political morality is an instinctual, emotive reaction rather than a reasoned process: 'It had become mani-fest to me that men are rational beings in but a very limited sense; that conduct results from desire, to the gratification of which reason serves but as a guide; and that hence political action will on the average be determined by the balance of desires, wherever this can show itself.'[1]

The primacy of human nature was acknowledged by Spencer long before the perfection of his evolutionary theory. In *Social Statics* he insists that 'Justice can only be well administered in proportion as men are just.' The Russian peasantry, for example, ought not to be encouraged to nurture expectations of legal reform, especially trial by jury, since 'they lack the substratum of honesty and truthfulness on which alone it can stand.' 'Character', the moral accom-plishment of associated men, is the final arbiter of the via-bility of institutions: 'let us never forget that institutions are *made* of men; that men are the struts, ties and bolts out of which they are framed; and that, dovetail and brace them together as we may, it is their nature which must finally determine whether the institutions can stand.'[2]

Adjustment of the political balance commensurate with the evolution of morality provides a continuous model of responsible social change consistent with social stability. As restraint recedes, so the faculty in men which prompts devo-tion to authority shrinks with it. There results a continuous contention of moral forces; the forces respectively of social discipline and of liberty, with the latter gradually, if inexor-ably, on the initiative, and in which 'the institutions of any

[1] *Aby* ii. 366.   [2] *S. Stat.*, pp. 288-9.

given age exhibit the compromise made by these contending moral forces at the signing of their last truce.'[1] The neat, mechanical precision of this model notwithstanding, the vital question of cause remains. Does institutional change precede and mould the character of citizens; or does the evolution of human nature render the appropriate institutional changes inevitable?

The indeterminate relation between institutions and character grows in importance throughout Spencer's writings. The emphasis is usually on the influence of character on institutions, rather than the reverse: 'The most carefully framed constitutions are worthless, unless they be embodiments of the popular character—governmental arrangements in advance of the time will inevitably lapse into congruity with the time.'[2] This undermining of premature reforms constituted an important factor in Spencer's pessimism: 'Year by year and day by day events convince me more that there is only a certain amount of liberty of which men having a given nature are capable, and if a larger amount of liberty is given to them they will quickly lose it by organising for themselves some other form of tyranny.'[3]

The political implications are, obviously, conservative; the retention of inequitable forms of political institutions to match the imperfection of men. Even in *Social Statics*, where the embers of radicalism still glow, it is regretfully concluded that 'men show themselves as yet, little else but barbarians in broadcloth. Hence we still require shackles; rulers to impose them; and power-worship to make these rulers obeyed.'[4] This conclusion is sweetened by the assumption that human nature naturally tends to perfection, but the twin retrogressions of militarism and over-legislation modified this view. In 1876 he wrote: 'Evolution is commonly conceived to imply in everything an intrinsic tendency to become something higher. This is an erroneous conception of it . . . Only occasionally does the new combination of factors produce a change constituting a step in social evolution.'[5] At

---

[1] *S. Stat.*, pp. 467-8.
[2] H.S., 'Railway Morals and Railway Policy', *Essays*, iii. 52.
[3] H.S. to A. Herbert, 22 Oct. 1890, *L.L.* i. 403.
[4] *S. Stat.*, p. 222.   [5] *P. Soc.*, i. 95.

this point adaptation becomes a conceptual liability, for Spencer never squarely addressed himself to the contradiction between adaptation to deteriorating conditions and the predetermination of human perfection, preferring to assume a harmonious concurrence of both.

The progressive unfolding of social evolution brings us up against the merry-go-round of character, institutions and environmental adaptation. Progress from the militant to the industrial type of society equips men for the purer system of government to be encountered there, yet such a transformation of political institutions is impossible without the precedent moral progress. Meanwhile, evolution must be gradual: the shackles of coercive government only grudgingly relinquished. There is involved here an obscurity of cause and effect:

There is, of course, a close connection between the sentiment of justice and the social type . . . as fast as voluntary co-operation which characterises the industrial type of society becomes more general than compulsory co-operation which characterises the militant type of society, individual activities become less restrained, and the sentiment which rejoices in the scope for them is encouraged.[1]

What is not clear is whether the sentiment precedes and determines the type, or vice versa.

Other sectors of evolution, meanwhile, are advancing simultaneously. The 'Religion of Amity' is slowly overhauling the 'Religion of Enmity'. This process cannot be an independent one, but must reflect social evolution and the concomitant balance of social forces. The incidence of brutality at a given moment is supposedly regulated by the evolution of 'social sentiments', but this psychological and moral evolution is elsewhere regarded as dependent upon the peace and security of industrial society. The only certainties are the permanence of evolution, in whatever causal sequence, and the inevitability of 'industrial society'.

The causal conundrum of adaptation obtrudes into three crucial sectors of Spencerian theory. The first is the evanescence of government, which can be explained in one of two ways. Either environment grows more civilized, and

---

[1] *Justice*, p. 33.

character adapts to it, or else enlightenment is fostered from above, through the establishment of civilized social institutions. The second is proscribed; 'There must be a despotism as stern as the people are savage.' The same savagery, however, militates against the development of 'favourable conditions.'

The second is the transition from international warfare to peaceful, economic competition. In the 'external' struggle, the fittest, strongest, most militant nations devour the weak. 'Strong' nations are those characterized by the maximum degree of individual subordination to the corporate requirements of the state. The ultimate state, however, is that in which coercion is minimal. If internal coercion results in military victories, however, its relaxation is dangerous, and it is unlikely to be relinquished. A nation which unilaterally abjures aggression and concentrates on peaceful production will be tempting and vulnerable to external attack. Only, therefore, if industrial 'progress' is closely associated with escalating military sophistication can the 'progressive' nation 'survive.'[1]

The same perplexity characterizes competition between individuals. If aggression brings success, why should the type of the successful man ever change? If war is the exigent state, men, having everything to gain by remaining warlike, have no incentive to develop a pacific strain, unless their 'Reason' prompts them to renounce the competitive mode of society (which would be to imply a renunciation of nature). Where 'superior' is defined as 'better adapted' and the social climate is one of barbarism, the 'best adapted' will be the most barbarous. In renouncing the proven methodology of survival the 'civilised' man invites his own destruction.

The reciprocity of adaptation, therefore, is a formidable stumbling-block. Character, shaped by inheritance, determines institutions. Institutions, the systematized face of environment, shape character. Spencer admits a mutuality of influence, but his ascription of determinacy shifts with context. Thus 're-barbarisation' demonstrates the influence of institutions on character: the pitfalls of parliamentary reform

---

[1] See also below, Chap. 10, pp. 251-2.

that of character on institutions. This interaction re-empha-
sizes the distinction between environmental adaptation and
hereditary determinism. A barbaric environment makes
people barbaric. Barbaric people create warlike institutions,
which compound their barbarity, which is then handed on to
posterity. The circle thus forged contains no avenue of escape
into civilization, unless civilization is somehow 'inevitable',
an assumption which implies a determinism which Spencer
was at pains to deny.

Politically, adaptation cogently rationalizes the perpetua-
tion of the *status quo*. The worship of authority, argued
Spencer, is still an indispensable aid to social cohesion and
the maintenance of order: 'It will be long before social
discipline has so far modified human character that reverence
for law . . . will serve in place of the reverence for the power
which enforces law.'[1] 'Worship of authority', however, is
precisely that characteristic which renders necessary the
continuation of authoritarian restraint. Adherence to this
formula would terminate political advance, which can only
then be achieved in one of two ways: by revolution, or by
the legislative installation of liberal institutions. Spencer
repudiated both equally unceremoniously.

An interesting recent invocation of this theory is to be
found in Roy Medvedev's *Let History Judge: an analysis of
Stalinism* (1972). Medvedev seeks to clarify the notion of
Russia's 'backwardness' as an explanation of the genesis of
Stalinism, quoting Spencer's dictum that 'no political
alchemy . . . can get golden conduct out of leaden instincts.'
While he maintains that 'no Marxist could agree with
Spencer's argument' he admits that 'the problem which
Spencer raised was not satisfactorily dealt with in Marxist
writings of the nineteenth century.'[2] The problem referred
to was that of tailoring 'advanced' institutions to a primitive
national character; or specifically, that of constructing
socialism in a society overwhelmingly dominated by the
culture of the *muzhik*, an unhelpful mixture of ignorance,

---

[1] *Stud. Soc.*, p. 174.
[2] R. Medvedev, *Let History Judge: an analysis of Stalinism* (London, 1972),
p. 431.

brutality, superstition, and inverted authoritarianism.

Medvedev steers an interesting middle course between Lenin and Spencer. The revolution did stimulate social change, but institutional change outran the inevitably slower transformation of culture. There thus developed a lag between economic and political change on the one hand, and social change on the other. From the tension thus generated 'many defects of the old society appeared in a new setting, often in a new form.'[1] He concludes that some struggle between atavism and progress was inevitable, but refuses to accept Spencer's determinism. The contradiction could, with foresight, have been overcome; the drift into bureaucratic oligarchy was not inevitable.[2] The problem remains of how it could have been avoided, and why it was not. Medvedev refers to safeguards and 'counterweights' which should have been adopted, but were not. Spencer would have riposted that this failure itself indicates the unfitness of the Russian people for a 'higher' stage of political development. If nothing else, the issue demonstrates the persistence of Spencer's influence in the unlikeliest places.

To summarize: the 'social state' to which humanity needs to adapt, 'requires that each individual shall have such desires as may be fully satisfied without entrenching on the ability of others to obtain like satisfaction'. It describes, as does the whole of *Social Statics*, a hypothetical, perfect condition. It does not describe Britain in the nineteenth century. Adaptation to the present can only consolidate imperfection. Adaptation to a mythical ideality is no adaptation at all. Yet 'the ultimate development of the ideal man is logically certain.'[3] The flaw lies in the premise. If life is brutal and men are brutish, they are well suited. 'Imperfection', therefore, must relate to abstract criteria, and the approach to perfection must either be assumed as determined, or artificially stimulated. Spencer denied both possibilities.

The core of the difficulty lies in the mechanical nature of the theory; the idea of an equilibrium between organ and environment is expressed in terms of physics, and predates

---

[1] R. Medvedev, op.cit., p. 552.
[2] Ibid., p. 554. [3] *S. Stat.*, p. 79.

the entrance of biology into Spencer's theory. In this sense adaptation, unlike natural selection, fits uneasily into the scheme of nature. The influences moulding humanity are biological (heredity) and socio-cultural (environment); the first transmits modifications attained by the second. While allowing for the upward evolution of the type, however, which is confirmed by biology, Spencer assumed that the balance between heredity and environment in this process would remain constant. This, in turn, is a mechanical assumption, positing an unchangeable physical relation. In fact, as M. Harris shows, 'the relationship between heredity and learned repertory has itself undergone an evolution, in which the modification of cultural forms becomes less and less dependent upon concomitant genetic changes.' As evolution advances, cultural conditioning, progressively independent of biology, becomes the medium through which men and society change. Men are not born with inherited ideas, and have evolved beyond the purely genetic transmission of characteristics: 'The acquisition of the bulk of one group's learned repertory by another need not require a single genetic innovation.'[1]

The political projection of this statement destroys the sanctity of *laissez-faire*. The moulding of society becomes a process of learning, and of applying lessons. Society moulds men in this way, but it can also be moulded by them. This implies the possibility of conscious social engineering, of change deliberately pursued, and 'artificial' in Spencer's catalogue of social behaviour. Social development, bereft of biology, becomes the prerogative of the legislator and the revolutionary: its direction the concern of the moral philosopher.

PROBLEMS OF SPENCERIAN EVOLUTION: 'NATURAL SELECTION' AND POLITICS

The point at which Spencer's thinking becomes a coherent whole is his invocation of evolution, and specifically of the survival of the fittest, in support of his individualism, the

---

[1] M. Harris, op.cit., p. 131.

negative theory of state. The assertion that state intervention infringes the 'natural laws' of eliminatory competition is Spencer's principal contribution to political theory.

Social evolution, however, did not necessarily entail any single political ideology. Spencer's most telling critics were those who shared his assumptions but rejected his conclusions. In the hands of theorists of other persuasions, social evolution became a weapon wielded with varying degrees of effect in support of various political standpoints already tenaciously held.

Objectively viewed, Spencer's descriptive account of human development through natural selection contains anomalies. It postulates a starting-line 'where all start with equal advantages' and goes on to justify inequalities of wealth and social status as the indices of 'virtue' (in the sense of evolutionary success). Spencer, having repudiated Rousseau's 'natural' equality as of right, and Hobbes's equality of competitive ability, was left with a definition of 'equal advantages' as mere equality of access to the fruits of the earth. If evolution is a continuum from inorganic to social modes, then men as the descendants of the beasts will be unequally endowed by inheritance. For this reason also the idea of an episodic starting-point to the race for survival is inconsistent.

Spencer assumed that in the second generation 'natural' inequalities will be compounded by the distribution of resources. Inherited superiority is denoted by inherited wealth. Spencer's political thought, however, is imbued with contempt for aristocracy; his hero is the self-made bourgeois entrepreneur whose rise confounds traditional property-relations. At some stage, inherited natural superiority and inherited wealth cease to coincide. The transference of inherited wealth into social power, furthermore, impedes the meritocratic mobility of 'industrial' society. Talent is excluded from lucrative and status-bearing careers; competitive equality is denied to the talented poor. Nothing could be more conducive to fostering the unworthy than allowing money or status to purchase or command advantage.

'Collectivist' liberalism identified aristocratic monopoly as the source of social injustice. John Hobson wrote 'These legal and economic privileges *which impede or cancel competition* are also recognized to be responsible for the degrading toil and poverty of the lower strata of our population, and the equally degrading idleness and luxury of the upper strata.' (my italics).[1] It is the Lamarckian strain in Spencer which confuses the issue. The inheritance of acquired characteristics in a materialist world ought to facilitate the identification of wealth with worth. Spencer vehemently denied their identity in reality, but was forced to assert it in theory.

The universality of competition in nature raised further difficulties. Spencer indicated two levels at which human struggle is carried on: between societies and between individuals within societies. Within societies, however, competition is waged not only between individuals, but between a variety of collectivities, including interest groups, racial minorities, and classes. 'External' struggle, too, ramifies into struggle between 'societies' and struggle between alliances of societies, reflecting alignments of economic, political, strategic, or ideological interest. The over-simplified classification of competition as 'internal' and 'external' raises the question of whether endemic hostility between members of a group does not detract from its efficiency as a competitive unit. Spencer sought to circumvent the problem by arguing that 'militant' societies enforce an artificial unity on their members, which dwindles with industrialization. He insisted, however, that competition would not disappear, but would merely be removed from the military to the economic sphere.

The perpetuity of competition implies two conditions inimical to the Spencerian notion of 'industrial' society. The competitive solidarity of a society can only be assured by permanent abeyance of the internal conflict. The co-ordination of social activity for military or economic struggle requires a strong state. Internal disharmonies can be exploited by external competitors. An international organization divided by national interests, a nation divided by class antagonisms, a class divided by sectional interests and a group by individual interests are not formidable antagonists.

J.D.Y. Peel, citing Spencer's distaste for colonial war and

---

[1] J.A. Hobson, *The Crisis of Liberalism; new issues in democracy* (London, 1909), p. 4.

preference for commercial over military conflict, contends that the logic of the Spencerian struggle is against nature, not between men: 'Evolutionary ethics does not mean for Spencer that behaviour appropriate and "natural" to savages and animals is also so for civilized men.'[1] Spencer's recipe for progress, however, contains competition as a permanent necessity; commercial struggle can eventuate in the annihilation of the losers as certainly as can war. A ceaseless internecine struggle, meanwhile, fought out in the factories and mines, on the farms and, infrequently, on the streets, accounts for more dead and ruined than the 'small wars' which Spencer castigated. In the age of altruism men might 'complete one another's lives', and even stoop to succour the 'unfortunate worthy', but progress was inseparable from some form of competitive striving. The ideal 'social state', in any case, is consigned to the unforeseeable future; it is Spencer's 'myth' in the Sorelian sense. Social evolution was about the grim realities of the Victorian present.

The persistence of competition contradicts the more pleasing predictions of social evolution, social harmony, peaceful industrialism, and altruism. The evolution of ethics does not, as Peel suggests, cancel out natural selection, but is continually disputed and retarded by it. To assert the continuity of struggle throughout the endless evolutionary process is to suppose its persistence beyond the point at which material and moral progress makes it unnecessary. Spencer identifies the source of competition as natural hardship, implying a Malthusian view of the relation between population and resources explicitly refuted in his 'Theory of Population'. Continued competition implies continued scarcity of resources. The alternatives, redistribution, or increased production are not entertained, even though the latter is the inevitable result of industrialization, and Spencer argued that the material condition of the people was spontaneously improving.[2]

Natural selection is prolonged, secondly, beyond ethical enlightenment. In the *Principles of Ethics* Spencer describes

---

[1] Peel, p. 152.   [2] See above, Chap. 5, p. 109 and Chap. 6, p. 142.

how evolution elevates altruism above egoism. Generation by generation the balance between Good and Evil in a given 'national character' is repeatedly readjusted in favour of the former, until the regime of peace, love, and co-operation is achieved. Socialism itself might be held to reflect an emergent altruism. In Spencer's view, social evolution effected a reconciliation between co-operation and competition. In modern political theory, however, these comprise the bases of two irreconcilable, polar ideologies; the society built on co-operation is the antithesis of the society framed in competition. The Spencerian synthesis is implausible; competitive strife threatens to be disfunctional to the perfect integration of industrial society, yet competition is retained as the indispensable spur to continued adaptation and evolutionary dynamism.

Spencer's case for the rationalization of individualism by natural selection rested on the absolute concomitance between them; not only did individualism guarantee the survival of the fittest, but natural selection could entail no alternative ideology. Spencer bound science to politics too closely for his own good, since the plausibility with which writers of other political persuasions embraced social evolution inevitably cast doubts on his own version. So profound was the impact of Darwinism on all walks of intellectual life that exponents of it in political terms are legion. Three examples will indicate the flexibility of its political interpretation: an anarchist, a conservative, and a socialist.

1. Peter Kropotkin

Peter Kropotkin stood Spencerian social evolution on its head, to give prominence to its ethical aspect. As society grows, there grows with it 'the consciousness of human solidarity': 'It is the unconscious recognition of the force that is borrowed by each man from the practice of mutual aid; of the close dependency of everyone's happiness on the happiness of all.'[1] Where Spencer sees in nature an unmitigated war of all against all, Kropotkin sees, at least within species, the trend to increasing co-operation: 'The vast

[1] P.A. Kropotkin, *Mutual Aid* (London, 1908), p. xiv.

majority of species . . . find in association the best arms for
the struggle of life . . . understood, of course, in its modest
Darwinian sense—not as a struggle for the sheer means of
existence, but as a struggle against all natural conditions unfavourable to the species.'[1] This restated the conflict
between 'internal' and 'external' competition, the first
vitiating the strength of the aggregate to prosecute the
second. Kropotkin viewed internal co-operation as the pre-
requisite of evolutionary survival: 'The animal species in
which individual struggle has been reduced to its narrowest
limits, and the practice of mutual aid has attained the
greatest development, are invariably the most numerous, the
most prosperous and the most open to future progress.'[2] This
applies with equal force to human societies. The victorious
nations will be those whose internal harmony is greatest. The
great impediment to co-operation, for Kropotkin, was 'the
iron rule of the state', hence his anarchism.

2. Benjamin Kidd

Oddly similar conclusions were reached by Benjamin Kidd,
whose *Social Evolution* (1894) made out an evolutionary
case for imperialism, the hegemony of the Anglo-Saxon race
and the cultivation of religion as a political coherent. Kidd,
like Kropotkin, was preoccupied with 'external' struggle, and
castigated Spencer for not diverting the working class from
class antagonism to constructive nationalist aggression. He
also accused him of a utilitarian identification of individual
with social interests, interests which, according to Kidd,
perpetually conflict.

The problem of politics is to subordinate private interests
to those of the state, thereby nullifying the pernicious influence of Reason, 'the most profoundly individualistic, anti-
social and anti-evolutionary of all human qualities.'[3] Human
rationality restricts the proper exercise of evolutionary forces
in society. Its antidote is religion. The 'efficiency of our
civilization' lies in the 'altruistic development that has been

---

[1] Ibid., p. 294.
[2] Ibid., op.cit., p. 293.
[3] B. Kidd, *Social Evolution* (London, 1894), p. 293.

slowly taking place' in it. The Anglo-Saxon race has Christianity, which lesser races have not. This theory, enthusiastically taken up by Kipling, explains imperialism in terms of
the moral superiority of the imperialist; it is the 'clear call of
duty or necessity', which provides its necessary moral force.[1]

Despite the polarity of their political beliefs, Kropotkin
and Kidd share a common criticism of Spencer: that in
attempting to reconcile 'internal' with 'external' struggle, he
confused them. The third writer shared Spencer's preoccupation with internal struggle, yet drew contradictory
inferences from it.

3. Enrico Ferri

Enrico Ferri, a prominent Italian Social-Democrat, saw in
socialism the only practical application of social evolution,
and identified class as the fundamental unit of intra-social
competition: 'What is the famous "class-struggle" which
Marx revealed as the positive key to human history, if not the
Darwinian law of "the struggle of life", transferred from
individuals to aggregates of individuals?'[2] The class struggle
is a noble vision, which 'renews in the history of men the
grand drama of the struggle of life among the species, instead of dedicating ourselves to the savage and insignificant
fight of one individual with another.'[3]

Ferri shared with many of Spencer's critics an admiration
amounting to reverence for their victim; he is 'our intellectual
father', 'the greatest living philosopher', and is incongruously
harnessed with Karl Marx as co-Messiah of 'scientific' as
opposed to 'Utopian' socialism: 'Marx and Spencer have
come to guide socialism from the "clouds of sentiment"
with the infallible compass of scientific thought.'[4] Ferri set
out to demolish the conservative and individualistic political
inferences from Spencerism drawn by Ernst Haeckel and the
conservative school of German evolutionists, thus dissociating
Spencer's scientific from his political pronouncements in a

[1] Ibid., p. 313.
[2] E. Ferri, *Socialism and positive science: Darwin, Spencer Marx* (London, 1906),
pp. 153–4.
[3] Ibid., p. 75.
[4] Ibid., p. 136.

manner which outraged him. An appendix to Ferri's *Socialism and Positive Science* (1894) notes Spencer's expression of astonishment 'at the audacity with which the use has been made of my name in defending socialism'. In reply Ferri made a telling point:

The personal opinion of Herbert Spencer is a different matter from the logical consequences of the scientific theories on universal evolution, which he has developed further and better than any other man, but of which he has not the official monopoly, nor the power to prohibit their free expression in the labour of other thinkers.[1]

Ferri rejected the socialism which assured all men, regardless of merit, of a certain standard of life. 'True' socialism exists to guarantee equal opportunity in the competition for the perquisites of existence. In language very reminiscent of Spencer's, he explains:

All men ought to be equal at the starting-point in the struggle for life; so that each may freely develop his own personality with equality of social conditions; whilst today a healthy and robust but poor child in competition with a feeble, but rich, child, goes to the wall.[2]

'Scientific' socialism should rectify this imbalance, allowing 'natural', not social superiority to assert itself. This 'struggle for life' is awkwardly juxtaposed with Ferri's notion of the struggle between classes just alluded to, which illustrates the dangers besetting those whose evolutionary convictions led them towards socialism. Ferri finds himself justifying individual competition in terms of the class-struggle which is supposed to transcend it. His vision of socialism commands little modern respect, but had some advocates in the late nineteenth century. It looked to the state for the creation and preservation of a free competitive environment (as did Spencer), but sanctioned 'the appropriation of communal revenues to the purpose of establishing greater equality among men.'[3] Spencer's evolution thus provided formidable ammunition for the opponents of his liberalism.

Social evolution, therefore, was sufficiently flexible a concept to enable writers of all viewpoints to impose congenial

[1] E. Ferri, op.cit., p. 153.
[2] Ibid., p. 13.
[3] Ibid., p. 133.

interpretations upon it. Spencer's evolutionary individualism was unique, but by no means the most persuasive of these. Its relative lack of conviction lay in its confusion of 'internal' and 'external' competition. Those who accepted the reality of 'external' competition (e.g. Peter Kropotkin and Benjamin Kidd) demanded harmony of interests and the cessation of internal struggle. Those who accepted 'internal' competition (e.g. Enrico Ferri and Thomas Huxley) demanded collective action by society, via the state, to make the outcome a fair reflection of 'natural' ability. The sheer variety of these conclusions throws doubt on the necessitarian character of the relation between Spencer's evolutionary and political theories. As in the case of his interpretation of Liberalism, his worst enemies, and most telling critics, were those who shared his assumptions but rejected his conclusions.

9

THE 'SOCIAL ORGANISM'

The concept of the 'social organism' is crucial to Herbert Spencer's theoretical system. The phrase 'social evolution' is only meaningful if biological, human, and social development are seen to constitute stages in one broad evolutionary continuum, subject to the same immutable laws and impelled by the same natural forces. Spencer's political dogmas, although derived from sources antecedent to the 'development hypothesis', were vindicated in his view as deductions from natural law. In order to validate these deductions he needed to demonstrate that social phenomena evolved, not only after the same pattern as pre-social phenomena, but out of them.

This proposal of a bio-social continuum not only attracted the antipathy of theists, but more significantly set Spencer apart from his fellow evolutionists. Charles Darwin, for instance, distinguished sharply between the operation of natural selection in human society and the mechanism of social 'progress'. While the former reflects the blind forces of competition and selection, the latter depends on a 'spirituality' which divides man from the lower species:

Important as the struggle for existence has been, and still is, yet as far as the higher part of man's nature is concerned, there are agencies more important. For the moral qualities are advanced, either directly or indirectly, much more through the effects of habit, of reasoning powers, instruction, religion etc., than through natural selection.[1]

The emergence of human consciousness constitutes a distinct break in the evolutionary process demanding for society new laws and a morality no longer dependent on the precepts of the survival of the fittest. Darwin drew a critical line between natural selection as description and as a guide to action. In Spencer's hands evolution became 'not merely a theory but

[1] Cited in D.G. Ritchie, *Darwinism and Politics* (London, 1903), p. 8.

a creed; not merely a conception by which to understand the universe, but a guide to direct us how to order our lives.'[1] Darwin demurred: 'I cannot see as plainly as others do, and as I should wish to do, evidence of design and beneficence on all sides of us. There seems to me too much misery in the world.'[2] Alfred Russell Wallace, similarly, attributed the development of human consciousness to 'some influx of the unseen world of the spirit', thus sharing what David Ritchie called 'a recognition of the difference introduced into natural evolution by the appearance of consciousness.'[3]

Ritchie argued that natural laws as generalized deductions *a posteriori* must be kept distinct from 'laws' in the prescriptive sense; such a law 'may tell us something convenient or something inconvenient; but of itself it is, like nature, absolutely non-moral.'[4] Spencer was apt to employ the term 'natural' for polemic effect, and without the grace of a definition. The dangers of so doing have been clearly indicated by A.O. Lovejoy:

'Nature' has, of course, been the chief and most pregnant word in the terminology of all the normative processes of thought in the West; and the multiplicity of its meanings has made it easy, and common, to slip more or less insensibly from one connotation to the other; and thus in the end to pass from one ethical or aesthetic standard to its very antithesis, while nominally professing the same principles.[5]

Amongst its multifarious definitions two are pertinent here: 'natural' meaning that which is pre- or extra-social (as employed, for instance, by Rousseau) and 'natural' having a teleological meaning (as in Hegel's usage) being that which tends to the full realization of human potential. Spencer preferred the latter; the idea of social evolution places society firmly in nature, as the medium through which human perfection is attained. Yet whatever social manifestations violated his view of progress were 'unnatural': strikes, for example. Beatrice Webb's rejoinder on this point is applicable to much of Spencer's rationalizing from 'nature': 'The plain

[1] D.G. Ritchie, op.cit., p. 2.
[2] F. Darwin, *Life and Letters of Charles Darwin* (London, 1887), ii. 312.
[3] D.G. Ritchie, op.cit., p. 29.
[4] Ibid., pp. 33–4.
[5] A.O. Lovejoy, *Essays in the History of Ideas* (Baltimore, 1948), p. 24.

truth is that to apply the antithesis of "natural" and "artificial" to social action is sheer nonsense. Anything that exists or happens to human nature in society . . . is equally "natural"; its very happening makes it so.'[1]

Spencer's most formidable critic on this point was Thomas Huxley, for whom civilization was the transcendence of natural evolution. Society, therefore,

differs from nature in having a definite moral object; whence it comes about that the course shaped by the ethical man—the member of society or citizen—necessarily runs counter to that which the non-ethical man—the primitive man or savage, or man as a member of the animal kingdom—tends to adopt. The latter fights out the struggle for existence to the bitter end, like any other animal; the former devotes his best energies to the object of setting limits to the struggle.[2]

Nature, according to Huxley, is a jungle; society is a garden. This contention was contemptuously dismissed by Spencer as 'a virtual going-back to the old theological notions, which put man and nature in antithesis.'[3]

Huxley's 'Evolution and Ethics' sought to wrestle society from the stark implications of its 'naturalness'. Reason constituted for him a qualitative departure from nature, hence evolutionary struggle and ethical adaptation are contrasting modes of development. Huxley admitted that 'for his successful progress through the savage state, man has been largely indebted to those qualities which he shares with the ape and the tiger', but these modes of struggle were now, 'by general consensus' deemed to be 'not reconcilable with sound ethical principles.'[4] Ethics provided instead a 'reasoned rule of life', an alternative to barbarism. Evolution, although it may describe the process whereby ethical norms become assimilated, was held to contain no rules of behaviour for civilized men.

Like Peter Kropotkin, Thomas Huxley saw incipient co-operation in nature; even wolves 'could not hunt in packs except for the real, though unexpressed understanding that they should not attack one another during the chase.'[5] His

---

[1] Webb, pp. 342-3.   [2] D.G. Ritchie, op.cit., p. 30.
[3] H.S. to J.A. Skilton, 29 June 1893, *L.L.* ii. 36.
[4] T.H. Huxley, 'Evolution and Ethics', *Collected Essays* (London, 1894), ix. 51-2.
[5] Ibid., ix. 56.

was a strictly phenomenological interpretation of ethics: 'The thief and the murderer follow nature, just as much as the philanthropist. Cosmic evolution may tell us how the good and evil tendencies of man may have come about, but in itself it is incompetent to furnish any better reason why what we call good is preferable to what we call evil than we had before.'[1] Ethical conduct, indeed, is part of the natural process; Huxley likens it to the governor of a steam-engine (a fine Victorian simile) which, though an intrinsic part of the mechanism, controls the scope of its operation and is indispensable to its efficiency.

Spencer's concept of 'evolutionary ethics' founders on the association of 'fittest' with 'best'. Key Spencerian phrases like the 'perfection' of man, natural 'superiority' and the 'highest type' confuse description with judgement. Huxley uncompromisingly prises them apart:

'Fittest' has a connotation of 'best', and about 'best' there hangs a moral flavour. In cosmic nature, however, what is fittest depends upon conditions . . . social progress means a checking of the cosmic process at every step and the substitution for it of another, which may be called the ethical process, the end of which is not the survival of those who happen to be the fittest in respect of the whole of the conditions which obtain, but of those who are ethically the best.[2]

Spencer, among others, used these concepts as value-judgements with which to classify his contemporaries, whereas 'the Darwinian law does not determine the survival of the best but only of the best adapted.'[3] In so doing, Spencer interjected a moral judgement, rooted in his perception of the present, into a process in which ethical evolution continues into the future, thus encompassing a dynamic worldview within the confines of a static morality.

The crucial criticism of Spencer's individualist–evolutionist scheme, then, is the distinction between the 'state of Art' and the 'state of Nature' drawn by Huxley; 'the characteristic feature of the latter is the intense and increasing competition of the struggle for existence. The characteristic of the former is the elimination of that struggle . . . by the removal of the

[1] Ibid., ix. 40.
[2] Ibid., ix. 81.
[3] E. Ferri, op.cit., p. 42.

condition which gives rise to it.'[1] Society is not a part of nature: 'The history of civilization details the steps by which men have succeeded in building up an artificial world within the cosmos.'[2] This body of criticism suggests the significance, for Spencer, of a convincing account of the organic structure of society.

SPENCER AND THE 'SOCIAL ORGANISM'

Writers and thinkers about society have always used analogies. The 'body politic', in particular, has a venerable pedigree in the works of Plato, Aristotle, Thomas Hobbes, Edmund Burke, and Auguste Comte. Its traditional rivals are the social 'machine' and the social 'contract', and it is interesting that the corporeal metaphor has always been associated with conservatism, as the 'theoretical foundation for advocating paternalistic or authoritarian government.'[3] Radical thinkers have tended to choose the machine, a dynamic balance of opposing forces, or the contract, a voluntary agreement of free men based in the mutual abdication of certain rights. Spencer, who numbered himself among progressive thinkers, adopted an analogy the subsequent applications of which led directly to Fascism, in Benito Mussolini's literally 'corporate' state.

Spencer admonished his precursors for using only superficial similiarities between the human body and society, and set out to divine greater truths from the comparison. His successors, however, made only moderate claims on it; even the 'organismic' school of social theorists, of which Spencer is considered the founder, and including the Germans Albert Schäffle and Paul von Lilienfeld, and Frenchmen Alfred Fouillé and René Worms, went no further than elaborate descriptive comparisons. It has since been pointed out that 'the more you labour the parallel, the more you determine the relation.'[4] This distinction between parallel and relation, vital to an understanding of the organic, or of any other

---

[1] T.H. Huxley, op.cit., ix. 13.
[2] Ibid., ix. 83.
[3] See W.H. Simon, 'Herbert Spencer and the Social Organism', *J.Hist. Ideas*, xxi, 1960.
[4] E. Barker, op.cit., p. 106.

analogy in political thinking, is one which Spencer never decisively recognized.

Where pre-Spencerians cited only vague similarities in order to convey social or political solidarity, the post-Spencerians drew many and close functional and structural comparisons in order to explain how social organizations worked. For Spencer, the rationale of social evolution depended substantially upon the degree of literalness with which it could be interpreted. A perplexing problem was set: is society an organism, or is it *like* an organism? If the former is true, organic evolution is applicable to social man without reservation. If not, there is no reason why men should defer to the merciless benevolence of natural selection.

Two complications emerged. First, Spencer's thoroughness in investigating the analogy led to the discovery not only of an impressive catalogue of similarities between an organism and society, but some important dissimilarities too. These are faithfully recorded, then dismissed as relatively inconsequential, yet they seriously undermine Spencer's case. Second, social evolution needs to be reconciled with the law of equal freedom, based on the liberty of the individual to exercise all his faculties freely. From the individual as master of his faculties to the individual as a unit of the social organism is a jarring conceptual step. In order to preserve the essence of individual free will, Spencer could not afford too literal an interpretation of the social organism.

The analogy winds a tortuous thread through Spencer's writings from first to last. It is presaged at first by vague allusions to 'natural law': 'We see nothing created but what is subject to the invariable laws given by the Almighty, and why should society be an exception'?[1] Recognition that nature and society observe the same rules led to the discernment of analogies between them. A striking affirmation of an organic relation between society and its components appears in 1853: 'The life and health of society are the life and health of one *creature*. One part cannot suffer without the rest being ultimately injured.'[2] In *Social Statics*, meanwhile, the assertion of social homogeneity had been expanded to

---

[1] 'Proper Sphere', 15 June 1844.
[2] H.S., letter on 'Transcendental Physiology', *Morning Chronicle*, Feb. 1853.

accommodate the detailed parallelisms which Spencer had since abstracted from it. Inverting the analogy he described an organic body as 'a commonwealth of monads, each of which unites with a number of others to perform some function needful for supporting itself and all the rest; and each of which absorbs its share of nutriment from the blood and has independent power of life, growth and reproduction.'[1] Grudging credit is accorded to the ancient philosophers who though scientifically ill-informed, made figurative references to the 'body politic', 'little suspecting how close the analogy, and how far it will bear carrying out.'[2]

Biology supplied similarities of function and process. An organism and a society pass through common evolutionary processes, 'the coalescence of like parts and separation of unlike ones' for instance, and evince the same tendency towards individuation and reproduction. Each social 'monad', while fending for himself, incidentally contributes to the vitality of the aggregate; each gains his sustenance from the circulating stock of commodities (blood) for which he competes with others, while combining with them to subserve the collective entity in which they subsist. The unit cells thus provide a perfect model of social welfare through individual competition: 'The analogy between an individual being and a human society, in which each man, whilst helping to subserve some public want, absorbs a portion of the circulating stock of commodities brought to his door, is palpable enough.'[3]

The question at issue was whether these projections were 'palpable' enough to sustain the weight of social evolution. At this stage it was still an extended metaphor, and the onus lay with Spencer to prove that an organism and society were not merely similar but that the life of both depends on the operation of the same universal causes.

This contention first appears in *Social Statics*, where societies and organisms are said to exhibit 'a coalescence of like parts and the separation of unlike ones'. Primitive

[1] *S. Stat.*, p. 493. [2] *S. Stat.*, p. 490.
[3] *S. Stat.*, p. 493.

societies, like rudimentary organisms, display 'a repetition of like elements' which subsequently proliferate in form and function. Human gregariousness is ascribed to instinctual impulses similar to the properties of organic cells: 'by virtue of this impulse individuals as units of the social mass tend to assume like relationships with the atoms of matter.' Spencer inferred from this an identity of motive force: 'When the nakedness of the essential relations in each permitted comparison of them, it became manifest that the fundamental analogy was determined by the operation of the same cause in each.'[1]

Spencer was, in 1851, ill-equipped to elaborate the analogy further. His grasp of the constituents of evolutionary theory was insufficiently consolidated. Nevertheless, four conspicuous instances of similarity between an organism and society were established. These were: first, the independent yet contributory relation between each cell and the aggregate; second, the dependence of each cell upon, and competition between them for a share of, the circulating blood-supply; third, observation of the same evolutionary process at work in each; and fourth, the determination of the properties of the aggregate by the properties of its units. Of these the third is essential, the others being figurative descriptions of social processes.

The full extent and limitation of the analogy are set out in 'The Social Organism' (1860). Its avowed purpose was to depart from the symbolic 'body politic' as employed by Plato and Hobbes ('these vague adumbrations of the truth') to a tangibly scientific concept, since 'in the absence of physiological science . . . it was impossible to discern real parallelisms.' Thus Plato, in a remarkably Freudian exercise, represented social order by the analagous subdivision of the human mind. Reason corresponds to government (superego), will to the military executive (ego) and passion to the unruly masses (id). Hobbes's use of the analogy was equally symbolic; his 'Leviathan' is portrayed as 'a vast human-shaped figure whose body and limbs are made up of a multitude of men' and, inappropriately, of manufactured rather than

---

[1] *Aby* ii. 434.

organic origin. Spencer set out to supersede such accounts by a clear exposition of 'the analogies which modern science discloses to us'.

Societies, he claimed, 'agree with individual organisms in four conspicuous peculiarities'. First, 'Commencing as small aggregations, they insensibly increase in mass'; second, 'at first so simple in structure as to be considered structureless . . . they assume, in the course of their growth, a continually increasing complexity of structure'; third, their parts acquire 'a mutual dependence which becomes progressively essential to existence'; and fourth, 'the life and development of society is independent of and far more prolonged than any of its component units, who are severally born, grow, reproduce and die while the body politic composed of them survives generation after generation increasing in mass, complexity of structure and functional activity.'[1]

There is insufficient evidence, however, to impute from these 'parallelisms' the operation of evolutionary causation in society. Emil Durkheim, for example, accepted all four propositions as being descriptive of social 'growth', but not the naturalist implications of them. Spencer had merely demonstrated that in certain particulars societies are like organisms. Undeterred, he launched gleefully into a mesh of proliferating allegory. As the embryo develops two distinct layers for the satisfaction of its needs, the mucous (ectoderm) to provide nutrition, and the serous (estroderm) to co-ordinate its actions, so the emergent society produces two distinct classes, the lower producing nourishment, the higher controlling the functions of both. The two-tier embryo, furthermore, gradually develops a third, or vascular layer, responsible for the distribution of commodities, just as society develops a middle class.

The life-blood of the developing organism acquires an unequivocally commercial character as 'the circulating mass of commodities in the body politic.'[2] The flow of both is stimulated by demand, limited by supply. Profit is the excess of nutrition over waste; over-exercise followed by inability to supply the deficiency results in slump. Railways

[1] 'S.O.', 270.
[2] Ibid., iii. 277.

become arteries, their branch-lines blood-vessels. The regulating structure of society becomes its nervous system, its cephalic ganglion (king) emerging from among the minor ganglia (aristocracy) to assert its (his) authority. Meanwhile the cerebral agency (parliament), co-ordinating stimuli from all parts of the organism, rises to challenge for supremacy. By this time Spencer seems transported by the potential ramifications of the analogy. He is half-way through explaining how telegraph-wires (nerves) accompany railway-lines (arteries) round the body (society) when he is abruptly brought to a halt 'because we have reached our limit'. Unfettered by journalistic exigencies, the analogy is pursued *ad absurdum* in vol. ii of *The Principles of Sociology*.

Telling differences between society and the organism are similarly listed, though Spencer dismissively finds in them 'little to conflict with the all-important analogies . . . such distinctions being scarcely greater than those which separate one half of the organic kingdom from another.'[1] The dissimilarities are these: first, society, unlike the individual organism, 'has no specific external form'; second, 'the living elements of a society do not form a continuous mass'; third, the units of an organism are fixed, whereas social units are mobile; and, fourth, disparities exist between the modes of sensory perception in each. This last point is an important one.

In society each individual is endowed with feeling, but the cells of an organism cannot 'feel' except through the aggregate, which registers sensations through an organization of specialized units. A society, furthermore, has no such specialized organ of perception. This distinction not only substantially contradicts the organic analogy, but is a vital concession to the nominalist theory of society, which Spencer denied. If society can 'feel' only through the perception of its units, then only through the perception of its units has it any existence. For Spencer, by contrast, society was a real entity, existing independently of the perception of its constituent members. Only if thus conceived can its development be considered subject to the immutable laws of nature. The absence, in society, of a collective consciousness thus neatly

[1] 'S.O.', 277.

incorporates three related problems; first, it sets up an insuperable barrier to literal acceptance of the 'social organism'; second, it confounds Spencer's realist view of society, and third, it raises the questionable status of the individual in evolutionary philosophy.

SPENCER, INDIVIDUALISM, AND THE 'SOCIAL ORGANISM'

The autonomy of the individual in Spencer's sytem fluctuates with context. The operation of natural forces in society postulates a necessitarian view of human conduct, with the individual at the mercy of forces beyond his control or comprehension. Spencer's ethical theory, however, is based on the maximum human freedom compatible with the equal freedom of others. Like Immanuel Kant, who originated the concept of equal freedom, Spencer took his ethical stand on the autonomy of the self-directed individual. This individualism is the antithesis of the organismic model of society, which presupposes the sacrifice of individual *autonomy* (not merely of self-interest) to the needs of society.

The reconciliation of apparent opposites—individualism and evolutionary determinism—is evident in Spencer's treatment of the individual as a component of the social organism. Two countervailing conceptions of the individual's role are offered; the first shows him powerless in the grip of evolutionary processes, the second identifies in him the demiurge of history. On the one hand, even that shaper of destinies the 'Great Man', is swept along in the current of evolution: 'men who seem the prime movers are merely the tools with which it works.'[1] Elsewhere the Great Man is accorded the role of catalyst, but the changes he sets in motion are inevitable and his identity a matter of indifference; if Alexander or Napoleon had not existed, we should have had to invent them. For the mass of mortality, however, impotence is clearly prescribed, and no individuality can break out of the predetermined cycle of events. Indeed, for Spencer, individuality found its highest expression in the acknowledgement of its own insignificance:

[1] *S. Stat.*, p. 473.

Nature's rules . . . have no exceptions . . . the so-called exceptions—
show either that the law eludes our perception or baffles our powers
of expression. Thus, rightly understood, the progress from deepest
ignorance to highest enlightenment, is a progress from entire uncon-
sciousness of law, to the conviction that law is inevitable.[1]

The requirements of his system of rights and the basic
individualism from which they sprang nevertheless dictated
that a prominent place be found in evolution for the individual impulse. Spencer drew from the individual perception of
men in society the conclusion that corporate needs should,
ideally, be subordinate to individual needs. While the
organism requires the total subjection of its cells, society can
make no such claims:

Since its living units do not and cannot lose individual consciousness,
and since the community as a whole has no corporate consciousness,
this is an everlasting reason why the welfare of citizens cannot rightly
be sacrificed to some supposed benefit of the state, and why, on the
other hand, the state is to be maintained solely for the benefit of
citizens.[2]

This affirmation of individuality is repeated, with equal
clarity, in *The Principles of Sociology*: 'The society exists
for the benefit of its members; not its members for the benefit of society . . . the claims of the body politic are nothing
in themselves, and become something only in so far as they
embody the claims of its competent individuals.'[3] The individual, therefore, has two dimensions in Spencerian theory;
he is a 'monad' of the organic society, which outlives him and
to whose subsistence his life is a subordinate consideration;
yet counterpoised to this bleakly homuncular figure is the
individual whose maximal freedom and self-determination is
the goal of this progress, and whose interests are considered
before those of society.

Spencer was fully aware of the embarrassingly necessitarian
implications of evolution. George Eliot noted that he was
'very sensitive on the point of being supposed to teach an
enervating fatalism.'[4] To forestall this imputation he insisted

---

[1] *S. Stat.*, p. 53.   [2] 'S.O.', 276–7.
[3] *P. Soc.*, i. 449–50.
[4] J. Cross, *George Eliot's life as related in her letters and journals* (London,
1885), iii. 256.

that individual human effort was the motor of social evolution: 'I have ever insisted that things will go well when each utters and endeavours to get accepted that which he thinks to be the truth, leaving the average opinion produced to work out such results as it may.'[1] He acknowledged that 'the difficulty lies in recognizing human actions as, under one aspect, voluntary, and under another, predetermined.'[2]

Within the framework of evolution individuals are cause and effect; their natures are determined by the inheritance of ancestral characteristics and the character of their environment, but the operation of their 'free will' itself constitutes the motive power of social evolution, even if the direction in which it moves is predetermined:

The error results from failing to see that the citizen has to regard himself at once subjectively and objectively—subjectively as possessing sympathetic sentiments (which are themselves the product of evolution), objectively as one among many social units having like sentiments by the combined operation of which certain social effects are produced.[3]

Evolution, furthermore, which heals all wounds and resolves all contradictions, will ultimately sweep away the cobwebs of perplexity. The highly evolved man will become reconciled to the limits of his contribution to progress:

Hereafter, the highest ambition of the beneficent will be to have a share—even though an utterly inappreciable and unknown share in the 'Making of Man' . . . While contemplating from the heights of thought, that far-off life of the race never to be enjoyed by them, but only by a remote posterity, they will feel a calm pleasure in the consciousness of having aided the advance towards it.[4]

Humble gratitude for an infinitesimal role in evolution will eventually replace the restless desire for instant amelioration which afflicted the nineteenth century: 'the man of higher type . . . has to see how comparatively little can be done, and yet to find it worthwhile to do that little; so uniting philanthropic energy with philosophical calm.'[5]

---

[1] H.S. to the Earl of Pembroke, 2 May 1883, *L.L.* i. 309.
[2] *M.v.S.*, p. 139.
[3] H.S., *Various Fragments* (London, 1900), p. 122.
[4] *P.Eth.* ii. 433.
[5] *Stud. Soc.*, p. 403.

Spencer's proposed reconciliation of evolutionary determinism and free will leaves the individual with little real autonomy; he is 'one of the myriad agencies through which works the Unknown Cause.'[1] Yet Spencer maintained that evolution culminates in the apotheosis of individuality, an outcome of little comfort to the present generation, firmly enmeshed in the coils of determinism. If human nature is predetermined, furthermore, then the 'free' exercise of individuality by the perfect man must be predetermined also. The genus of individuality allowed for in the 'social state' is very strictly conditional, not only on the unchecked operation of genetic and environmental influences, but also on the fulfilment of the requirements of that completely evolved society.

Spencer's claim is that civilization is distinguished by evidence of progress towards the fulfilment of individual needs; 'social organisation is to be considered high in proportion as it subserves individual welfare.'[2] Progress, furthermore, is the achievement of 'that constitution of man and society required for the complete manifestation of everyone's individuality.'[3] The culmination of other tendencies, however, realizes quite different aspects of the perfect society by which social functions become simultaneously more widely differentiated and more closely integrated; the perfectly evolved society is required to accommodate not only the apex of individuality but also the maximum of human interdependence. 'Civilisation', said Spencer, 'is evolving a state of things and a kind of character, in which two apparently conflicting requirements are reconciled.'[4] While individualism decrees that the perfect state shall guarantee to individuals unrestricted exercise of all their faculties, the complexities of an interdependent social system demand that they tailor their efforts to the requirements of highly-specialized social functions. The free-ranging liberty of the individual will clashes with the systematic functioning of an integrated society.

---

[1] *F.P.*, pp. 105–6.
[3] *S. Stat.*, p. 474.
[2] *P. Soc.*, i. 587–8.
[4] *S. Stat.*, p. 482.

The 'perfect individuality' is that which accords with this functional pattern. All obstacles to free will are removed, but the desires and needs of perfectly evolved human beings will be those which fit the pattern. Evolution indicates the evanescence of all impulses which do not conform to the perfected social organization. When all non-functional quirks have been extirpated, what is left?:

Just that kind of individuality will be acquired which finds in the most highly-organised community the fittest sphere for its manifestation . . . the ultimate man will be one whose private requirements coincide with public ones. He will be that manner of man who, in spontaneously fulfilling his own nature, incidentally performs the functions of a social unit.[1]

The zenith of individualism, then, is the absolute freedom to conform.

The problem of the scope of individual free decision arises whenever a systematic attempt is made to explain human behaviour. The tension between Historical Materialism and individual autonomy is equally problematic, but Karl Marx's solution carries more conviction: 'Men make their own history but . . . they do not make it under circumstances chosen by themselves, but under circumstances directly encountered, given and transmitted from the past.'[2] In Spencer's theory the evolutionary imperative ineluctably circumscribes individual autonomy.

Perfect individuation, furthermore, is incompatible with Spencer's model of organic evolution. The development of organisms is towards the integration of functions under the organ of cerebration, which grows increasingly to co-ordinate them in association with the nervous ganglia. On one hand, therefore, directive control becomes centralized as the threads of corporeal government are progressively picked up by the brain-centre. The triumph of individualism, however, posits the gradual evaporation of central authority over society. As morality develops, and self-discipline replaces social, the state with its repressive and deterrent functions is no longer necessary. Beatrice Webb noted this paradox in

[1] S. Stat., p. 483.
[2] K. Marx, The Eighteenth Brumaire of Louis Bonaparte (Moscow, 1972), p. 10.

Spencer's organic analogizing, a loophole through which the integration of organic functions under cerebral control could furnish justification for the kind of supervisory state which Spencer most feared: 'it is quite possible to argue that the government is a "naturally" differentiated organ (as he would express it) developed by the organism to gratify its own sensations. This might lead directly to a state-socialism.'[1]

Thomas Huxley agreed: 'The sovereign power of the body rules the individual components with a rod of iron':

If the resemblances between the body physiological and the body politic are any indication, not only of what the latter is, but what it ought to be, and what it is tending to become . . . the real force of the analogy is totally opposed to the negative view of state function.

Huxley preferred the idea of a 'social molecule', a biological projection of the social contract, and poured mild scorn on the individualistic rationale: 'Suppose that . . . each muscle were to maintain that the nervous system had no right to interfere with its contraction, except to prevent it from hindering the contraction of another muscle.'[2] In reply, Spencer, while maintaining an appearance of dignified consistency, virtually jettisoned the literal interpretation of the social organism. The correspondence between the phenomena of society and organism, he admitted, 'cannot, obviously, be analogies of a visible or sensible kind.'[3] He attempted to rescue the social organism by reviving the distinction between 'outer' and 'inner' organs, the former responsible for the relation of the body with the environment, the latter for nutrition and distribution. The function of the 'outer' organs, defence, attack, external relations, need to be controlled by the central cerebral authority, but the productive and distributive organs do not. Hence, whereas close state supervision is deemed essential for the legitimate functions of the state, the commercial organs function with spontaneous efficiency: 'When the members of the Ministry are following grouse or stalking deer, Liverpool imports, Manchester manufactures, London distributes, just as usual.'[4]

[1] Webb, p. 192.
[2] T.H. Huxley, 'Administrative Nihilism', *Fortnightly Review*, Nov. 1871.
[3] 'Specialised Administration', *Essays*, iii. 437.
[4] *Essays*, iii. 423.

Though superficially plausible, this distinction does not sustain detailed application; import and export, for example, are as much features of 'external' relations as are war and peace. 'Specialised Administration' marks the grave of Spencer's organic analogy. Society cannot be regarded as literally 'organic' in the sense that it is a natural outgrowth of presocial evolution, and to describe it as organic in any other sense is to dissipate the force of the analogy.

There are two plausible interpretations of the term which bear a significant relation to the theory of evolution: organism as a functional concept, and organism as a physiological one. The former relates to the interaction of the internal components of social and physical structures, and compares them. In this sense Spencer's analogy is minutely detailed but the definition is essentially mechanical. J.D.Y. Peel defines it as 'the systematic arrangement and co-ordination of specialised parts in a uniform whole', and goes on to explain that it is equally applicable to animals and to complex machines: 'both organism . . . and organisation . . . carry this general meaning.'[1] Functionally the organic analogy is easily reversible: what is a human body, after all, but an immensely sophisticated mechanism?

By contrast, the physiological definition of 'organic' is tightly specific. For an analogy to be credible, it requires a clear statement of the properties of each part, and a clear concurrence between them. The body is obviously a physical concept, but is society? On Spencer's own admission, obviously not: it is not physically integrated and it cannot feel. Because, therefore, socio-political forms have no continuous physical structure, they are not in the physiological sense 'organisms'. In insisting, however, that they are 'organic' Spencer narrowed his definition of the analogy down to the functional interpretation.

What, precisely, was Spencer trying to show? Briefly, that the relation between man (or animal) and his constituent cells is the equivalent of the relation between society and its constituent cells, which are men. This is almost an analogy of scale, and strongly suggests the continuity of all phenomena.

[1] Peel, p. 172.

Functionally, this can be shown to be almost the case. The purpose behind the comparison, however, exceeds that of elucidation. It is to extract generalizations, or 'laws', of the development and nature of societies from organic models. This purpose the functional interpretation of the analogy is inadequate to sustain. Spencer attempted to surmount this obstacle by varying his definition of 'organic' to suit the occasion. It is only meaningful where he expounds its functional nature in the language of mechanics rather than of ·biology. Elsewhere, however, he attempts to invoke the authority of its biological meaning, by reiterating it in unqualified form.

Semantic vagueness, therefore, conceals a large gap in Spencer's explanation of social development, and in his justification of evolutionary ethics, which a purely metaphorical comparison between the 'body politic' and the body physical, however elaborately drawn, is insufficient to close. It is worth noting that exponents of 'collectivist' Liberalism looked to the 'social organism' for the support of theories inimical to Spencer, and inferred from it that the 'natural rights' rationale of Liberalism was obsolete. John Hobson argued that 'True democracy is possible only when society, a true organism, becomes conscious of its intelligence and will.'[1] No one after Spencer attempted to reconcile the incompatibles of organicism and individualism.

[1] J.A. Hobson, op.cit., p. 87. See also above, Chap. 7, pp. 178-80.

10

'MILITANT' AND 'INDUSTRIAL' SOCIETY

Spencer categorized the second half of the nineteenth century as an age of social regression: a temporary hiatus in social evolution. His term covering this process, 're-barbarisation', is borrowed from the vocabulary of Cobdenite radicalism. The source of his alarm was the increasingly aggressive turn taken by British imperial policy during the 1880s and 1890s and its atavistic social repercussions. This preoccupation involved the theoretical distinction between the 'militant' and 'industrial' stages of social evolution. Early Victorian Britain, evincing an aura of prosperity, free trade and international goodwill, seemed to have reached the threshhold of the second stage; the Britain of the 1890s, jingoistic, militaristic, ingloriously scampering after colonies, seemed to be lapsing into its pristine barbarism. 'Re-barbarisation' afforded Spencer a practical application of his theories, and his perplexity highlights some of its difficulties, especially those entailed by the concept of 'stages' in social evolution.

Spencer's view of war underwent an intriguing transformation. In the unqualified idealism of his youth he condemned all war and advocated a unilateral renunciation of it by Britain, a 'bright and glorious example' which would soon be followed by other nations when they perceived its benefits. This out-and-out pacifism was modified in *Social Statics* in terms of the 'law of equal freedom'. By acquiescing in the spoliation of life and property, even his own, the conscientious objector is conniving at the deprivation of rights. While aggressive war is wrong, therefore, defensive war is a moral duty. Social evolution injected a certain equivocacy into this view, for whereas aggression in the modern context retards the growth of civilization, in a primitive society it might well advance it, through the extirpation of unfit races by better, 'more evolved' ones—another collision of evolution and ethics.

THE PHENOMENON OF 'RE-BARBARISATION'

The social regression which appalled Spencer mirrored a
psychological recidivism. War impedes the development of
the finer sentiments which alone can transform humanity
into an appropriate vessel for the enlightened social system.
Human nature eagerly and quickly re-adapts itself to the
congenital brutality of its former existence, and renders even
more remote the growth of civilized emotional responses.
Prolonged and total peace is essential to ameliorative adaptation: 'out of the lower stages of civilisation higher ones can
emerge, only as there diminishes this pursuit of international
revenge and re-revenge which the code we inherit from the
savage insists on.'[1] 'Re-barbarisation', then, is ethical evolution in reverse, and stimulated in Spencer a profound, almost
apocalyptic resignation:

At present there is an unusual resurgence of the passions of the brute
. . . men . . . pride themselves on approaching as nearly as they can to
the character of the bull-dog.[2] Did I but think that men were likely to
remain in the far future anything like what they are now, I should
contemplate with equanimity the sweeping away of the whole race.[3]

This regression indicates again Spencer's difficulties, previously alluded to,[4] with the causal relation between character and institutions. There is no apparent reason why a peaceful, prosperous society should suddenly embrace barbarism
without some institutional stimulus, yet such a stimulus must
itself originate in a defective national character. Although he
shrewdly isolates and stirringly denounces the various threads
of national sentiment and foreign policy which collectively
constitute the phenomenon, the blunt fact is that in terms of
evolutionary theory, 're-barbarisation' is very hard indeed
to explain.

Spencer isolates the initiating impulse in a ruling-class
culture 'which every day of the week holds up for admiration
those who in ancient times achieved the greatest feats of
battle, and only on Sundays repeats the injunction to put up

---

[1] Stud. Soc., p. 199.
[2] H.S. to M.D. Conway, 15 Aug. 1900, L.L. ii. 192.
[3] H.S. to W.S. Blunt, 10 Oct. 1898, L.L. ii. 192.
[4] This problem is discussed above, Chap. 8, pp. 209-16.

the sword.'[1] It is the expression of their militaristic ethos in colonial policy which provides for this bloodthirstiness a practical outlet. 'Among ourselves', complained Spencer, 'the administration of colonial affairs is such that native tribes who retaliate on Englishmen by whom they have been injured are punished, not only by their own savage principle of life for life, but on the improved, civilised principle of wholesale massacre for single murder.'

Spencer traces from the stimulus of war the awakening of dormant aggression and violence in society at large. War and religion become closely identified, a symbiotic process which results in the assimilation of military sentiments by spiritual organizations (the 'Salvation Army', the *War Cry*, 'Onward Christian Soldiers') and the evocation of religious observance for military purposes, exemplified by the singing of hymns by troops embarking for South Africa 'in a manner which substitutes for the spiritual enemy the human enemy.'[2] The manipulation of public antipathy towards specific enemies, real, potential, or imagined, rises to the surface in a multi plicity of institutions and situations, spreading the infection of militarism in all directions. 'The cultivation of animosity towards one imaginary object', furthermore, 'strengthening the sentiment of animosity at large, makes it easier to arouse animosity towards another imaginary object.'[3] Spencer's examples are occasionally a little far-fetched: the rise of Association Football, for instance, which 'approaches as nearly to a fight as the lack of weapons allows'. More perceptively, he noted the emergence of the O.T.C. network in Public Schools, and indeed, the anti-intellectual 'muscular Christianity' of the Public Schools themselves, upon which even Rudyard Kipling commented unfavourably.

The mobilization of violent mobs against 'Stop the War' campaigners, and the chanting of 'Remember Majuba' to troops departing for South Africa were cited by Spencer as instancing the escalating psychopathology of social aggression. Popular organs like the *Daily Mail* exploited and reinforced

---

[1] *M.v.S.*, pp. 134–5.
[2] H.S., *Facts and Comments*, p. 126.
[3] Ibid., p. 125.

a degenerate public taste. Its first editor, Kennedy Jones, when asked what sold a newspaper, declared: 'the first answer is war. War apart, a state funeral . . . next to a state funeral comes a first-class murder.'[1] Even the Great Exhibition of 1851 was commemorated in 1901 by a Naval and Military Exhibition, for Spencer a splendidly symbolic reversal of the pacific trend of the first half of the century, and further evidence of the 'recrudescence of barbaric ambitious ideas and sentiments, and an unceasing culture of blood-thirst'[2] which he saw on all sides.

A corresponding degree of coercive social discipline was being generated, for 'it is impossible to unite the blessings of equity at home with the commission of inequalities abroad.'[3] Education, in which 'great strides have been taken towards a regimental organisation for moulding children after an approved pattern,'[4] and Trade Unionism (the 'workers' army') illustrated the deterioration. A conquering people, he argued, enslave themselves by subordinating their legitimate claims to the national interest, by condoning the revival of military sentiments which corrode their culture, and by allowing their political institutions to harden in the military mould. The diversion of industrial resources and manpower to the wasteful production of armaments weakens the ability of a society to organize itself for peaceful industrial expansion. Spencer's attitude to war and colonization was authentically that of the Free-Trader; the expense incurred by both outweighs the gains achieved. Classical economics dictated that the maintenance of closed colonial markets raised the price of their products in the home market as a result of the artificially high prices of the commodities which they purchased from it: 'All profitable trade with colonies will come to us without the outlay of a penny for colonial administration—must flow to us naturally; and whatever trade will not flow to us naturally is not profitable.'[5]

Political institutions undergo a parallel degeneration: 'In

---

[1] Cited in E. Halevy, *Imperialism and the rise in labour* (London, 1926), p. 91.
[2] H.S., *Facts and Comments*, p. 133.
[3] *M.v.S.*, p. 135.
[4] H.S., *Facts and Comments*, p. 135.
[5] *S. Stat.*, pp. 396–7.

proportion as liberty is diminished in the societies over which it rules, it is diminished within its own organisation.'[1] Political power, even the framing of laws, gradually lapses into the hands of the executive, to whom, by virtue of their responsibility for the war effort, all rights are abdicated. Taxation becomes voracious; conscription claims the citizen's body as well as his wealth: 'as fast as our growing imperialism augments the amount of such compulsory service he is to that extent more and more a serf of the state.'[2] 'Re-barbarisation' thus finally entails upon the members of the community 'a state of complete slavery—a state which they will fully deserve.'[3] Spencer's analysis of imperialism was echoed by Joseph Schumpeter who, in criticizing Lenin's assertion that it constituted capitalism's 'highest stage', declared it to be inimical to capitalism: 'Imperialism . . . is atavistic in character . . . it is an element which stems from the living conditions, not of the present, but of the past.'[4]

THE CONCEPT OF STAGES IN SPENCERIAN SOCIAL EVOLUTION

Spencerian social evolution incorporates the concept of definite stages; progress is from the 'militant' to the 'industrial' type of society. The distinction is so sharp as to render questionable the principle of continuity which links them. Each is a perfect theoretical model (almost a Weberian 'ideal-type'), its characteristics deriving from the exigencies of the stage of civilization which it represents. Spencer rejected the suggestion that a society might exhibit characteristics of both types simultaneously, because the 'industrial' type is the 'perfect' state, and anything falling short of it is stigmatized as being semi-evolved.

The idea of recognizable stages in social development was not new. Adam Ferguson spoke of 'rude' and 'polished' nations[5], the former militaristic in character, the latter commercial. Adam Smith, Antoine Condorcet, and Harriet

---

[1] H.S., *Facts and Comments,* p. 114.
[2] Ibid., p. 120.
[3] Ibid., p. 141.
[4] Cited in B. Semmel, *Imperialism and social reform: English social and imperial thought 1895–1914* (London, 1960), p. 17.
[5] A. Ferguson, *Essay on the History of Civil Society* (Edinburgh, 1767), p. 124.

Martineau, among others, associated the advance from war to commerce as the dominant social activity with a refinement of mores.[1] Most provincial radicals identified 'tender-heartedness' with industry and peace,[2] while D.C. Rappoport writes of the assumption, held by most English political thinkers, that civil and military social systems were guided by 'mutually-exclusive spirits and principles of organisation.'[3]

Spencer envisaged an age of primeval tranquillity and virtue, like William Godwin's anarchist paradise: 'in these exceptional circumstances, unaggressive and for special reasons unaggressed on, there is so little deviation from the virtues of truthfulness, honesty, justice, and generosity, that nothing beyond an occasional expression of public opinion by informally-assembled elders is needed.'[4] War, however, demands a centralized authority whose scope becomes enlarged in proportion as warfare becomes habitual: 'The aggressiveness of the ruling power inside a society increases with its aggressiveness outside the society.'[5] The militant society, therefore, becomes distinguished by characteristics conducive to military efficiency.

It is identified as follows. All its productive forces are devoted to war; those who do not fight labour to support those who do. Individual rights are held in abeyance: 'the life, the actions and the possessions, of each individual must be held at the service of the society.'[6] The ruling agency is despotic, as befits a military government, and the minutiae of its directives are enforced at all levels by a squad of officials irrespective of individual requirements. The regime intervenes positively as well as negatively: 'it not only restrains, but it directs.' Social structure is rigidly hierarchical; there is little social mobility, and emphasis is placed on obedience, deference and order.

The character of men so regulated adapts accordingly. They display 'profound faith in the governing power, joined

---

[1] See S. Andreski, ed., introduction to H.S., *The Principles of Sociology* (London, 1969).
[2] Peel, p. 76. 5
[3] See D.C. Rappoport, 'Military and civil societies', *Pol. Stud.* xii, 1964.
[4] *M.v.S.*, p. 54.   [5] Loc.cit.
[6] *Pol. Inst.*, p. 691.

with a loyalty causing submission to it in all matters what-ever.'[1] Goodness is equated with bravery, strength, and the military virtues: 'They must have a patriotism that regards the triumph of their society as the supreme end of action', and 'the belief that official control is everywhere needful.'[2] The dominant ideology of such a society will constitute 'a political theory justifying their faith and their obedience.'[3] The militant type, therefore, is a regime which coerces the submissive and minutely regulates the acquiescent.

There is no way to the more congenial industrial type, but through the regimentation and violence of the militant stage. Consequently, 'During long stages of social evolution, there needs . . . a governmental power great in degree and wide in range, with a correlative faith in it and obedience to it.'[4] The industrial type of society grows slowly out of the peaceful, industrial habits of a more stable community, and favours the individual. It confers freedom and a self-regulating social conscience: the opportunity to choose and to fend for one-self: 'Being carried on by voluntary co-operation instead of by compulsory co-operation, industrial life as we know it habituates men to independent activities, leads them to en-force their own claims while respecting the claims of others.'[5]

The state, from being a totalitarian monster, becomes docile and negative in aspect, its sole function that of ad-ministering justice: 'to see that each citizen gains neither more nor less of benefit . . . than his activities normally bring; and there is thus excluded all public action involving any artificial distribution of benefits.'[6] In place of coercion there grow up habits of voluntary co-operation among individuals seeking to subserve their needs. Society becomes plastic, exhibiting an internal mobility which brings talent to the sur-face, rewards inventiveness and ingenuity. Individual characteristics, finally, develop in appropriate ways; there is less blind loyalty, more independence, individualism, and benevolence. Where militancy 'inevitably deadens the

---

[1] *M.v.S.*, p. 132.
[3] *M.v.S.*, p. 134.
[5] *Mv.S.*, p. 133.

[2] *Pol. Inst.*, p. 692.
[4] *Loc. cit.*
[6] *Pol. Inst.*, p. 728.

sympathies and generates a state of mind which prompts crimes of trespass', industrialism 'allowing the sympathies free play, if it does not directly exercise them, favours the growth of altruistic sentiments and the resulting virtues.'[1]

It is a tribute to Spencer's critical objectivity that, regarding this transition as inevitable, he voiced some personal reservations about it. Where less discriminating intellects regarded their century as the apotheosis of civilization, Spencer demurred. He rejected the Wesleyan 'Gospel of Work', speculating that this sanctification of effort would be left behind by evolution: 'The industrialism of modern life has so strongly associated the ideas of duty and labour, that a man has come to be regarded as the more praiseworthy the harder he toils . . . but the whole thing is a superstition. Life is not for work, but work is for life.'[2] The very distinction between work and life, however, was itself a product of industrialization. In pre-industrial societies social intercourse and labour were indistinguishable; the family, or living unit, was also the unit of production.[3]   Spencer prophetically identified technological advance with increasing leisure: 'the progress of mankind is, under one aspect, a means of liberating more and more life from mere toil and leaving more and more life available for relaxation.'[4]

Further misgivings were raised by the effect of advancing industrialization on the quality of life, a concern which Spencer unknowingly shared with the Fabians. Nineteenth-century progress seemed to him to have ignored the 'higher' needs of those subjected to it:

I detest that conception of social progress which presents as its aim, increase in population, growth of wealth, spread of commerce. In the politico-ethical ideal of human existence there is contemplated quantity only and not quality. Instead of an immense amount of life of low type I would far sooner see half the amount of life of a high type . . . Increase in the swarms of people whose existence is subordinated to material development is rather to be lamented than to be rejoiced over.[5]

[1] *Pol. Inst.*, p. 730.
[2] *Aby* i. 412.
[3] See E.P. Thompson, 'Time, work-discipline and industrial capitalism', *Past and Present*, xxxviii, 1967.
[4] *Aby* i. 412–13.
[5] H.S., *Facts and Comments*, pp. 4–5.

In Britain, productivity and technological advance were destroying beauty and erasing 'history': 'Where in some respects we may envy posterity, we may in one respect pity them. The disappearance of remnants and traces of earlier forms of life intrinsically as well as picturesque by association, will deprive them of much poetry which now relieves the prose of life.'[1]

This contrast between 'militant' and 'industrial' types of society is a rigid typological concept welded incongruously on to a model of continuous development. Spencer clearly uses this duality as a means of injecting value judgements into social evolution. 'Higher' institutions are those of which he approved; the transition from description to evaluation is imperceptibly subtle, but undeniable. Distinguishing, for instance, between the alimentary and regulatory systems of the 'social organism' (commerce and industry *vis-à-vis* the state), he celebrated the former as representing a 'higher' stage of development because it functioned independently of the conscious intervention of the brain. Historically, the idea of stages is ingenuous. The correlation of war with the rise of the state presupposes an era of primeval harmony, yet the very descent of man through natural selection implies endemic struggle. War has not always been a force for the political integration of states; while it has created some political units it has subdivided and dispersed others. Conversely, the 'new' nations of nineteenth-century Europe were unified by community of language, economic interest, and the mutual suspension of long-standing military rivalries. The super-powers of the twentieth century, furthermore, represent a conflation of both Spencerian categories in the so-called 'military-industrial complex'. The rise of Imperial Germany and the 're-barbarisation' of Britain in response should have indicated that the antagonism between war and industry is far from absolute, and that they could be mutually reinforcing.

The supreme difficulty lay in the supposed concomitance between 'industrial' society and individual freedom. That military societies are normally characterized by coercion is

[1] Ibid., p. 7.

beyond question; what is less obvious is that 'industrial' society can exist and compete without war (and hence its internal by-products), and that it entails a kind of freedom any more real than that offered by militarism.

It is an open question whether the escalation of military rivalries which Spencer deplored marked a reversion of evolutionary stages, or the inevitable collision of competing capitalist structures. Spencer predicted the continuation of international struggle through the medium of commercial competition, but this assumed that nations would not use force to secure compliance among their customers and suppliers, and respect among their competitors. The history of the nineteenth and twentieth centuries shows that the commercial mastery of even a free-trading world rests ultimately upon naval and military power. The modern industrial-capitalist state combines the immense technological sophistication, functional integration and economic profusion celebrated by Spencer with the barbarism, chauvinism, and unfreedom of the 'militant' stage.

Spencer predicted that industrialism would entail the growth of voluntary co-operation, the diminution of collective restraint and the diffusion throughout society of habits of freedom. Several elements of industrial organization and the social imperatives of a society so organized, however, militate against this outcome. The existence of corporate goals in any society necessitates some degree of individual 'sacrifice' of autonomy. Spencer's view of the natural harmony of interests in a free-enterprise market society has been almost totally discredited; more people now believe that 'the peace of civil society is impossible without a government endowed by authority to impose force and make law establishing subordination.'[1] This simple view, which ignores a whole range of alternatives, reflects a consensus of opinion that modern society has centrifugal tendencies only controllable by legitimized power.

It would seem that the more highly sophisticated and complex the society, the greater the degree of discipline, co-ordination and restriction of individual impulses are required

---

[1] D.C. Rappoport, op.cit., p. 196.

for its efficiency. To usurp an analogy from Spencer; the more highly developed a machine, the smaller and more numerous are its parts, the more highly differentiated and simple are their unit factions, and the less tolerance there is of deviation from those functions. Spencer, while predicting some dimunition of the 'quality of life', made no speculations about the quality of freedom, preferring to assume, like Andrew Ure, that 'when capital enlists science into her service, the refractory hand of labour will always be taught docility.'[1]

Spencer had no theory of alienation; hence he saw no contradiction between the buying and selling of labour-time and individual freedom. All social life imposes some constraints on the individual disposition of time, but industrialism greatly intensified them, though we now take its regime for granted. Factories demand the synchronization of labour; the labourer must regulate his timetable to the convenience of his employer. A whole culture of 'time-thrift' grows out of this arrangement.[2] Spencer's negative concept of rights omitted the freedom to organize one's working hours as one thinks fit, which industrialization negated.

The precise nature of the effects of technological innovation on social relations is not certain, but it is widely regarded as being a necessitarian one. Technology is now credited with built-in 'imperatives' producing in all situations conformities of social pattern which override cultural and ideological differences. Among predictions as to their nature (extrapolating from current experience) are trends which Spencer did not associate with industrial society: a stratified elitism based on the uneven distribution of expertise, the separation of functional groups into 'professional' affiliations, and a functionalist view of all social activity, including education, which, tailored to technical needs, produces 'a trained incapacity for dealing with human affairs.'[3] Moreover, the proponents of the theory of technological 'convergence' agree that the state will become increasingly

---

[1] Cited in R.K. Merton, *Social Theory and Social Structure* (New York, 1968), p. 619.
[2] See E.P. Thompson, op.cit.
[3] R.K. Merton, op.cit., p. 623.

dominant in advanced industrial countries. J.K. Galbraith has shown that the 'technostructure' of advanced capitalism has destroyed the old antithesis, so important to Spencer, between state regulation and entrepreneurial autonomy.[1] The state regulates and directs the flow of supply and demand and secures acquiescence by a variety of means in the prevailing political system.

Spencer's association of industrialization with enhanced freedom of choice is also dubious. Mass production and mass communication, while extending the availability and range of commodities, have generated new forms of encroachment on individual autonomy. Spencer could not have foreseen that needs could not only be satisfied by production, but also created by advertising, or that political behaviour in a democracy could be reduced to the manipulation of consumer-oriented images. The gap between the theory of freedom and the practice of disseminated conformity has been most forcefully suggested by Herbert Marcuse, whose notion of 'repressive tolerance' describes a state which creates false needs 'for the production and consumption of waste', mystifies the real nature of social power, monopolizes communications and discredits opposition by distortion and innuendo. Thus, 'confronted with the total character of advanced industrial society, critical theory is left without the rationale for transcending this society.'[2] This situation, in which men, having institutionalized their slavery, pronounce themselves totally free, is not unlike Spencer's vision of the 'perfect' humanity whose needs are coterminous with social requirements. It is not, however, consistent with his definition of freedom as 'free exercise of the faculties', some faculties, including the all-important critical faculty, having been blunted or excised.

Spencer's insertion of the idea of definitive stages into the scheme of continual social evolution was thus both inappropriate and highly problematic, and committed him to unfulfilled prognostications about the future of industrial societies. The postulated concomitance between industrialism

---

[1] J.K. Galbraith, *The New Industrial State* (London, 1967), p. 296.
[2] H. Marcuse, *One-Dimensional Man* (London, 1964), p. 12.

and individual freedom, in particular, is contradicted by the organizational 'imperatives' of the industrial system.

EPILOGUE

It was the great irony of Spencer's life that his scientific pronouncements were not only more widely received than his political ones, but were applied to politics independently of them. We have seen how the theory of natural selection yielded political conclusions, even including a cut-throat species of socialism, at extreme variance with his individualistic Liberalism [1] His 'social organicism' produced still more sinister offshoots, especially in Germany, where it contributed to a climate of political thinking favourable to Nazism. Spencer would have abhorred Fascism, yet in the idea of society as a coherent organism and in his popularization of the ethics of struggle, he contributed substantially to its rationale.

Spencer's struggle against imperialism, fired by lifelong Liberal principles, expresses this contradiction most forcibly, for it can be argued that his account of the operation of 'the survival of the fittest', applied internationally, helped to justify the very policies he attacked. Spencerism, for one writer, set forth 'a perfect rationalisation of the status quo of conquest.'[2] Elie Halévy demonstrates how, in Rudyard Kipling's *Jungle Book*, the young Mowgli is introduced to the 'truceless war' between species: 'Must this struggle, this war be condemned as evil? Not when it is the law of the world.'[3] The concomitance between the relation of predatory species to their ruminant victims and that between imperialist nations and their colonies was not lost on some evolutionary thinkers, notably Benjamin Kidd, Karl Person, and Walter Bagehot. Bagehot inferred from nature an ethical sanction for conquest: 'Conquest is the premium given by nature to those national characters which their national customs have made most fit to win in war, and in many most material respects these winning characters are also the best characters. The

---

[1] See above, Chap. 8, pp. 220–4.
[2] M. Harris, op.cit., p. 136.
[3] Cited in E. Halevy, op.cit., p. 21.

characters which do win in war are the characters I should wish to win in war.'[1] He defined the superiority of Englishmen to Australian aborigines thus: 'they can beat the Australians in war when they like, they can take from them anything they wish, and kill any of them they choose.'[2]

Spencer's influence in this respect was largely an involuntary one. His thought was rarely adopted as a totality, but was dismembered, and grafted piecemeal on to various antagonistic theories, some wildly improbable. This resulted from the fact that the political and scientific components of Spencerism were not compatible in the first place. Liberalism posits the harmonization of the interests of free individuals. Social evolution tends inexorably towards the hegemony of the centralized state, and perpetuates aggression. In this irreconcilable contradiction lies the major flaw of Spencerian social and political theory.

[1] W. Bagehot, *Physics and Politics* (London, 1869), p. 215.
[2] Ibid., p. 207.

BIBLIOGRAPHY

The following works were consulted and found useful in the preparation of the text:

A. MANUSCRIPT SOURCES

The Passfield Collection (British Library of Political and Economic Science).

The Huxley Collection (Imperial College, London).

The Spencer Papers, assord MSS. deposited at the Athenaeum by Spencer's Trustees, now transferred to the University of London Library.

B. PRINTED SOURCES

1. *Primary Sources* (Spencer's writings)

(a) *Books*

Social Statics: the conditions of human happiness specified, and the first of them developed (London, 1868).

Education: intellectual, moral and physical (London, 1864).

First Principles (London, 1900).

The Study of Sociology (London, 1880).

The Principles of Sociology (London, 1893): vol.i, Part 1, *The Data of Sociology*; Part 2, *The Inductions of Sociology*, Part 3, *Domestic Institutions*.

vol.ii, Part 4, *Ceremonial Institutions*; Part 5, *Political Institutions*.

vol.iii, Part 6, *Ecclesiastical Institutions*; Part 7, *Professional Institutions*; Part 8, *Industrial Institutions*.

Political Institutions (Part 5 of *The Principles of Sociology*). (London, 1882).

The Evolution of Society (The Principles of Sociology, edited, with an introduction, by R.C. Carneiro). (Calif., 1967).

The Principles of Sociology, edited, with an introduction, by S.L. Andreski (London, 1969).

The Principles of Ethics (London, 1891).

Justice (Part 4 of *The Principles of Ethics*) (London, 1907).

The Man versus the State (London 1950).

The Man versus the State, edited, with an introduction, by D.G. Macrae (London, 1970).

Various Fragments (London, 1897).

Facts and Comments (London, 1902).

Essays: scientific, political and speculative (London, 1891).

An Autobiography (London, 1904).

(b) *Essay.*

'The Proper Sphere of Government', *Nonconformist*, 15 June–14 Dec. 1842.

'A theory of Population deduced from the general law of animal fertility', *Westminster Review*, Apr. 1852.

'The Development Hypothesis', *Leader* Mar. 1852.

'Over-legislation', *Westminster Review*, July 1853.

'Manners and Fashions', *Westminster Review*, Apr. 1854.

'Railway Morals and Railway Policy', *Edinburgh Review*, Oct. 1854.

'Progress: its law and cause', *Westminster Review*, Apr. 1857.

'Representative Government: what is it good for?', *Westminster Review*, Oct. 1857.

'State tampering with money and banks', *Westminster Review*, Jan. 1858.

'The Morals of Trade', *Westminster Review*, Apr. 1859.

'The Social Organism', *Westminster Review*, Jan. 1860.

'Parliamentary Reform: its dangers and safeguards', *Westminster Review*, Apr. 1860.

'Prison Ethics', *British Quarterly Review*, July 1860.

'Reasons for dissenting from the philosophy of M. Comte', *Westminster Review*, Apr. 1864.

'The Collective Wisdom', *Reader*, 15 Apr. 1865.

'Political Fetishism', *Reader*, 10 June 1865.

'Specialised Administration', *Fortnightly Review*, Dec. 1870.

'The Americans: a conversation and a speech with an addition', *Contemporary Review*, Jan. 1883.

(c) *Letters and short articles*

'Reply to T.W.S.' (letter on Poor Laws), *Bath and West of England Magazine*, Mar. 1836.

'Address from the municipal electors of the Borough of Derby to the authorities of the town (on the imprisonment of Henry Vincent)', *Morning Chronicle*, 6 Sept. 1842.

'Effervescence; Rebecca and her daughters', *Nonconformist*, 28 June 1843.

'Mr. Hume and National Education' *Nonconformist*, 2 Aug. 1843.

'The Non-intrusion Riots' *Nonconformist*, 11 Oct. 1843.

Leading articles for *The Pilot* (Birmingham)
  'Railway Administration', 28 Sept. 1844.
  'A Political Paradox', 26 Oct. 1844.
  'A magisterial delinquency', 26 Oct. 1844.

'A political parable and its moral', 9 Nov. 1844.

'Honesty is the best policy', 16 Nov. 1844.

'The impolicy of dishonesty', 23 Nov. 1844.

'The great social law', 7 Dec. 1844.

'Justice before generosity', *Nonconformist*, 30 Dec. 1846.

'The Political Smashers', *Standard of Freedom*, 14 Oct. 1848.

'Tu quoque', *Standard of Freedom*, 11 Nov. 1848.

Letter on George Eliot's Education, *Standard* 26 Dec. 1880.

Letter on the Anti-aggression League, *Nonconformist and Independent*, 2 Mar. 1882.

'The Edinburgh Review and the Land Question', *St. James' Gazette*, 14 Feb. 1883.

'Herbert Spencer and the Comtists', *The Times*, 9 and 17 Sept. 1884.

Letter on the toast 'to the fraternity of the two nations', *Standard*, 14 Mar. 1892.

Correspondence on the Land Question, *Morning Chronicle*, 20 Aug.– 8 Sept. 1894.

Correspondence on the Land Question, *The Times*, 7–27 Nov. 1889.

Letter on 'Reasoned savagery, so-called', *Daily Telegraph*, 7 Feb. 1890.

Letter on the N.S.P.C.C., *Pall Mall Gazette*, 16 May 1891.

Letter on Re-barbarisation, *Morning Leader*, 5 Feb. 1900.

2. *Secondary Sources*

(a) *Books*

W.H.G. Armytage, *A.J. Mundella: the Liberal background to the Labour movement* (London, 1951).

W. Bagehot, *Physics and Politics* (London, 1869).

—— *The English Constitution* (London, 1867).

E. Barker, *Political Thought in England: 1848–1914* (London, 1942).

H.E. Barnes and H. Becker, *Social Thought from Lore to Science* (Washington D.C., 1952).

Mrs. Barnett, *Canon Barnett: his life, work and friends* (London, 1918).

M. Bowley, *Nassau Senior and the Classical Economists* (London, 1937).

A. Briggs, *The Age of Improvement* (London, 1959).

—— *Victorian People* (London, 1967).

C. Brinton, *English Political Thought in the Nineteenth Century* (New York, 1962).

J.W. Burrow, *Evolution and Society: a study in Victorian social theory* (Cambridge, 1966).

G. Combe, *The Constitution of Man* (Edinburgh, 1835).

J. Cross, *George Eliot's life as related in her letters and journals* (London, 1885).

F. Darwin, *The life and letters of Charles Darwin* (London, 1887).

A.V. Dicey, *Law and public opinion in England during the nineteenth century* (London, 1914).

D. Duncan, *The life and letters of Herbert Spencer* (New York, 1908).

E. Durkheim, *The division of labour in society* (New York, 1893).

R.C.K. Ensor, *Some reflections on Spencer's doctrine that progress is differentiation* (Oxford, 1946).

A. Ferguson, *Essay on the history of civil society* (Edinburgh, 1767).

E. Ferri, *Socialism and positive science; Darwin, Spencer, Marx*, trans. E.C. Harvey (London, 1906).

E. Finch, *The life of Wilfred Scawen Blunt* (London, 1905).

J. Fiske, *Essays: literary and historical* (New York, 1902).

R.S. Fitton and A.P. Wadsworth, *The Strutts and the Arkwrights* (Manchester, 1958).

W.M. Flinn, ed., *Edwin Chadwick's Report on the sanitary conditions of the labouring population of Great Britain* (Edinburgh, 1965).

J.K. Galbraith, *The New Industrial State* (London, 1967).

H. George, *Progress and poverty: an enquiry into the cause of industrial depressions and of increase of want with increase of wealth: the remedy* (London, 1893).

—— *Herbert Spencer: a perplexed philosopher; being an examination of Mr. Herbert Spencer's various utterances on the Land Question.* (London, 1893).

T.H. Green, *Liberal legislation or the freedom of contract* (1881) in *The Works of T.H. Green* (London, 1906), vol.iii.

G.S. Haight, *George Eliot: a biography* (Oxford, 1968).

E. Halevy, *Imperialism and the rise of Labour* (London, 1926).

M. Harris, *The rise of anthropological theory* (London, 1969).

F.W. Hirst, *The early life and letters of John Morley* (London, 1927).

L.T. Hobhouse, *Liberalism* (London, 1911).

S. Hobhouse, *Joseph Sturge: his life and work* (London, 1919).

J.A. Hobson, *The crisis of liberalism: new issues of democracy* (London 1909).

T. Hodgskin, *Labour defended against the claims of capital* (London, 1922).

R. Hofstadter, *Social Darwinism in American thought* (Boston, Mass., 1955).

W.E. Houghton, *The Victorian frame of mind* (New Haven, Conn., 1957).

W.H. Hudson, *Herbert Spencer* (London, 1916).

B.L. Hutchins and A. Harrison, *A History of factory legislation* (London, 1911).

B. Kidd, *Social Evolution* (London, 1894).

F.W. Knickerbocker, *Free minds: John Morley and his friends* (Cambridge, Mass., 1943).

P.A. Kropotkin, *Mutual Aid* (London, 1908).

H. Laski, *The Rise of European Liberalism* (London, 1935).

A.O. Lovejoy, *Essays in the History of Ideas* (Baltimore, Ohio, 1948).

S. Maccoby, *English Radicalism; 1832-5* (London, 1935).

C.B. MacPherson, *The political theory of possessive individualism* (Oxford, 1970).

D. MacPherson, *Herbert Spencer; the man and his work* (London, 1900).

H. Marcuse, *One-dimensional Man* (London, 1964).

R.B. McCallum, *The Liberal Party from Grey to Asquith* (London, 1963).

R. Medvedev, *Let History Judge: an analysis of Stalinism* (London, 1972).

R.K. Merton, *Social Theory and Social Structure* (New York, 1968).

A. Miall, *The life of Edward Miall* (London, 1884).

J.S. Mill, *The principles of Political Economy* (London, 1848).

—— *On Liberty / Utilitarianism* (ed. M. Warnock) (London, 1962).

—— *An Autobiography* (London, 1879).

J. Morley, *Life of Ricard Cobden* (London, 1920).

—— *Recollections* (London, 1917).

A. Peckover, *The Life of Joseph Sturge* (London, 1890).

J.D.Y. Peel, *Herbert Spencer: the evolution of a Sociologist* (London, 1971).

H. Perkin, *The origins of modern English society* (London, 1969).

J.M. Prest, *The Industrial Revolution in Coventry* (Oxford, 1960).

J. Priestley, *An essay on the first principle of government: The nature of political, civic and religious liberty* (London, 1768).

D. Read, *The English Provinces c 1760-1960: a study in influence* (London, 1964).

—— *Cobden and Bright: a Victorian political partnership* (London, 1967).

H. Richard, *Memoirs of Joseph Sturge* (London, 1864).

M. Richter, *The politics of conscience; T.H. Green and his age* (London 1964).

D.G. Ritchie, *The principles of state interference* (London, 1902).

—— *Darwinism and politics* (London, 1903).

L. Robbins, *The Theory of Economic Policy in English Classical Political Economy* (London, 1952).

J. Royce, *Herbert Spencer: an estimate and review* (New York, 1904).

J. Rumney, *Herbert Spencer's sociology* (London, 1934).

G.H. Sabine, *A history of political theory* (London, 1964).

B. Semmel, *Imperialism and social reform: English social imperial thought, 1895-1914* (London, 1960).

—— *The Governor Eyre Controversy* (London, 1962).

A. Smith, *The Wealth of Nations* (London, 1904).

J. Sturge, *Reconciliation between the middle and labouring classes* (Birmingham, 1842).

G.M. Trevelyan, *Life of John Bright* (London, 1913).

262 BIBLIOGRAPHY

'Two', *Home life with Herbert Spencer* (Bristol, 1906).
A.R. Wallace, *My life; a record of events and opinions* (London, 1905).
B. Webb, *My Apprenticeship* (London, 1926).
M. Weber, *The Protestant ethic and the spirit of capitalism*, ed. R.H. Tawney (London, 1968).
R. Williams, *Culture and Society* (London, 1963).

(b) *Articles*

J.B. Brebner, 'Laisser-faire and state intervention in the nineteenth century', *Journal of Economic History* (Supplement), viii (1948).
J. Chapman, Review of *Social Statics, Leader* (15 Mar. 1851).
H.M. Druckner, 'Just analogies?; the place of analogies in political thinking', *Political Studies*, vol.xviii (Dec. 1970).
K. Eisen, 'Herbert Spencer and the spectre of Comte', *Journal of British Studies* (Nov. 1967).
E.M. Elliott, 'The Political Economy of English Dissent', in R.M. Hartwell, ed., *The Industrial Revolution* (Oxford, 1970).
K. Fielden, 'Samuel Smiles and self-help', *Victorian Studies*, xii (1968).
G. Gordon, 'The London *Economist* and the high tide of *laissez-faire*', *Journal of Political Economy*, lxiii (1955).
W.H. Hudson, 'Herbert Spencer; a character-study', *Fortnightly Review* (1904).
T.H. Huxley, 'Administrative Nihilism', *Fortnightly Review* (Nov. 1871).
—— 'The struggle for existence in human society' (1888), in *Collected Essays*, vol.ix (London, 1894).
—— 'Evolution and Ethics' in *Collected Essays*, vol.ix. (London, 1894).
G.I.T. Machin, 'The Maynooth Grant; the Dissenters and Disestablishment', *English Historical Review*, no.322 (Jan. 1967).
M.P. Mack, 'The Fabians and Utilitarianism', *Journal of the History of Ideas*, xvi (1955).
R.M. MacLeod, 'The X Club; a social network of science in late-Victorian England', *Notes and records of the Royal Society*, xxiv (1970).
H. Parriss, 'The nineteenth century revolution in government; a reappraisal re-appraised', *Historical Journal*, iii (1966).
J.D.Y. Peel, 'Spencer and the neo-evolutionists', *Sociology* (May, 1968).
D.C. Rappoport, 'Military and civil societies', *Political Studies*, xii (1964).
D. Roberts, 'J. Bentham and the Victorian Administrative State', *Victorian Studies*, ii (1958–9).
W.H. Simon, 'Herbert Spencer and the social organism', *Journal of the History of Ideas*, xxi (1960).
W. Stark, 'Herbert Spencer's three sociologies', *American Sociological Reveiw*, xxvi (1961).
E.P. Thompson, 'Time, work-discipline and industrial capitalism', *Past and Present*, xxxviii (1967).
W.L. Weinstein, 'The concept of liberty in nineteenth century political thought', *Political Studies*, xiii (June 1965).

W.L. Weinstein and S.I. Benn, 'Being free to act and being a free man',
  Mind (Apr. 1971).
R.M. Young, 'Malthus and the evolutionists', *Past and Present*, xliii
  (1969).

INDEX